PHILOSOPHICAL

# FROM PLATO TO POSTMODERNISM

*by*

## GREG JOHNSON

**Counter-Currents Publishing Ltd.**
San Francisco
2019

Copyright © 2019 by Greg Johnson
All rights reserved

Cover image:
Luc Olivier Merson, *Rest on the Flight into Egypt*, 1879
Museum of Fine Arts Boston

Cover design by
Kevin I. Slaughter

Published in the United States by
COUNTER-CURRENTS PUBLISHING LTD.
P.O. Box 22638
San Francisco, CA 94122
USA
http://www.counter-currents.com/

Hardcover ISBN: 978-1-64264-134-9
Paperback ISBN: 978-1-64264-135-6
E-book ISBN: 978-1-64264-136-3

# Contents

Preface ❖ iii

1. Introduction to Plato's *Republic* ❖ 1
2. The Myths of Plato ❖ 25
3. Introduction to Aristotle's *Politics* ❖ 42
4. Our Marx, Only Better: Vico & the New Right ❖ 68
5. Rousseau as Conservative: The Theodicy of Civilization ❖ 83
6. Notes on Philosophical Dialectic ❖ 97
7. Why Read Hegel? Notes on the "End of History" ❖ 116
8. A Hole in Being: Notes on Negativity ❖ 129
9. Notes on Nihilism ❖ 133
10. Yeats' Pagan Second Coming ❖ 142
11. A Leveling Wind: Reading Camus' *The Stranger* ❖ 147
12. Alexandre Kojève & the End of History ❖ 152
13. Postmodernism, Hedonism, & Death ❖ 169
14. The Beginning & the End of History ❖ 173
15. A Little Death: Hegelian Reflections on Piercing & Tattoos ❖ 178
16. Postmodernism vs. Identity ❖ 181
17. Why We Meet as We Do: Thoughts on Liberal Education ❖ 193

Index ❖ 201

About the Author ❖ 212

# PREFACE

A title like *From Plato to Postmodernism* is usually a sign that a book has a unity problem. What unifies this collection of lectures and essays, over and above the fact that I wrote them? An anthology is not a treatise, which should be an organic unity in which all parts contribute to the functioning of the whole. But a good anthology can't just be a heap of *disjecta membra*. The parts at least have to *resemble* one another. The parts may not all harmonize with one another, but at least they should not *clash* with one another. An anthology is more of a bundle, in which the distinct parts become stronger by being bound together, and I guess this Preface is the string.

Let's begin with the distinctions. These essays and lectures cover a period of more than twenty years. The earliest pieces are lectures presented in Atlanta to The Humanities Forum, The Invisible College, and The Atlanta Philosophical Society circa 1995 to 2000. The lectures on Plato and Kojève are edited transcripts of extemporaneous lectures. I have tried to eliminate wordy constructions and repetitions, but they still retain qualities of the spoken word. Chapters 7 through 10, plus chapter 17 — on Hegel, nihilism, Yeats, and liberal education — are texts from the same period written for oral delivery. The chapters on Aristotle, Rousseau, and philosophical dialectic also come from this time, but they were written as academic essays and can be slow going.

The rest of the texts date from 2011 to 2017. The chapter on Vico is an edited transcript of an extemporaneous lecture given at The London Forum in 2014. "Postmodernism vs. Identity" is a written text, parts of which were presented to an identitarian dinner gathering in Budapest and at The Scandza Forum in Oslo in the summer of 2017. The remaining texts — on Camus' *The Stranger* and chapters 13 to 15, which are extracts from my mammoth Trevor Lynch essay on *Pulp Fiction* — were written for online publication at *Counter-Currents*.

These texts have a number of things in common.

First, they are unified by the premise that the true "first philosophy" is not the study of nature (the first things we notice) or "being" (what is first in itself) but the study of human nature. First philosophy is what Plato called "erotics," the exploration of the nature of the soul and what perfects or corrupts it. The method of philosophy is dialectic, which is a process of articulating what we always-already know because we humans are both the subject and object of philosophical inquiry.

Second, a proper understanding of the human soul leads to the rejection of liberalism and nihilism, which arise from false and reductive understandings of man.

Third, politics and culture have irrational foundations, thus philosophy needs to find a way to rationally understand politics and culture without subverting and destroying them.

There are other, subtler unities that I will leave to the careful reader to ferret out.

The thinkers I discuss most in this volume are Plato and Hegel. The thinker who most influenced my reading of Plato is Leo Strauss, although I make it clear where I accept and depart from his approach in the chapters on Plato and Rousseau. The thinker most influenced my reading of Hegel is Alexandre Kojève. But sometimes the thinkers you discuss the most are not the thinkers you *use* the most. In this volume, the thinkers I use the most are Vico and Nietzsche.

The issue on which these essays diverge the widest is the status of belief in topics like God, providence, and the immortality of the soul. Plato and Rousseau offer pragmatic arguments for such beliefs, whereas Camus offers pragmatic arguments against them. I am genuinely undecided, which may mean that pragmatic considerations are not enough to decide such matters.

A couple of caveats. First, the lectures on Plato, Vico, and Kojève are extemporaneous. In such lectures, unless there is a footnote to a particular source, the words I attribute to other writers are paraphrases, not verbatim quotes. Second, because this is a collection of essays and lectures rather than a treatise, you don't have to read it in any particular order. But *don't* begin with the chapters on Vico and philosophical dialectic.

The Vico lecture is the weakest piece here, but I include it simply because I want to encourage more people on the New Right to read Vico, and I don't want to delay circulating that message by waiting to write something more definitive on him. The chapter on philosophical dialectic is deep and useful but dense and technical. I fear that some readers who start there would never go on to the rest of the book.

Although the title and the arrangement of the texts run *From Plato to Postmodernism*, the intellectual journey of my readers moves in the opposite direction. They begin amidst the dregs of postmodernity. My goal is to lead them back towards Plato.

Because these texts were written over many years, in many different contexts, there are a lot of people to thank.

First, I wish to thank everyone connected to The Humanities Forum, The Invisible College, and The Atlanta Philosophical Society. I can't thank everyone by name, but I wish to at least allude to J.V.P., who got the whole thing going, as well as J.T., M.S., J.&B., Vera and Michael, and Sally for hosting many gatherings.

Second, I wish to thank the organizers of The London Forum, The Scandza Forum, and a dinner gathering in Budapest, where two of these texts were presented, as well as the many readers, writers, and donors who make *Counter-Currents* possible.

Finally, I wish to thank Kevin Slaughter for his work on the cover; V.S. for his transcriptions; Collin Cleary for his careful editing; James O'Meara and Alex Graham for their help with the index; and F. Roger Devlin and James O'Meara for their kind words of praise.

This book is dedicated to Josh Buckley, because of a fateful conversation about Kojève.

Budapest<br>
June 8, 2019

# Introduction to Plato's *Republic*[*]

Plato's *Republic* is one of the greatest philosophical works. If you were to make a small list of the most influential books in all of history, clearly the *Republic* would have to be near the top. It's one of those books that contains an account of everything, like the Bible, like Dante's *Inferno*. It's a book about the whole, and it has had an absolutely enormous influence ever since it was written, particularly in the West, although now that Western civilization has effectively been globalized, it has a global reach and a global influence. Given the enormous influence of this book, we all should read it. To have read the *Republic* is a cornerstone for being a well-educated person.

But what is the *Republic* about? Many people think that's obvious. The *Republic* of Plato is a book of political philosophy. Its title in Greek is *Politeia* and is translated as "republic." That sounds like politics. If you open the *Republic* you will find all kinds of discussions of political issues.

The dialogue begins with the question "What is justice?," which occupies the first book and really all the rest of the *Republic* as well. When you get into the second book, the topic becomes the founding of cities. Socrates and his companions talk about the nature of culture, the founding of civilization, and the unfolding of civilization towards some kind of completion. As it turns out, the complete and best form of civilization is described as a city that has three classes. There's a working class, a warrior class (the soldiers and policemen, called guardians), and then a

---

[*] This is a transcript by V.S. of a lecture on Plato's *Republic* from January of 2000, which was presented in Atlanta to my adult education organization The Invisible College. Originally, the lecture was supposed to be the final lecture in a course on Plato's *Timaeus* and *Critias*, but I ran out of things to say on those dialogues and decided to devote the last session to what is in effect an advertisement for my next class, a ten-week overview of the *Republic*.

ruling class, who are philosophers, of all things.

The education of guardians and of philosopher-rulers is laid out in great detail in the *Republic*. There is also an extensive discussion of the marital and family relationships that exist amongst the ruling class. There is no such thing as the private family or private property among the rulers. Children are raised by the state in common. Property is held in common. Sexual pairing is determined by lottery, so that personal preferences don't enter into it. No one knows their own children or their own parents, because that would create conflicting loyalties. When people know their own offspring and parents, this provides them with objects of loyalty over and above the state, and the ruling class is to be bred to have no conflicting loyalties that would get in the way of their allegiance to the public good.

As it turns out, though, we discover that one simply can't leave to chance who ends up running societies. Every society has to have some mechanism by which we can assure that the *best* people rule. The mechanism by which the best come to rule in the *Republic* has two forms.

One is an educational mechanism by which the brightest minds are promoted, and it doesn't matter from what class they come. Even the children of the working classes, if they are extremely bright, can be promoted. And the children of the upper classes, if they're very stupid, can be easily demoted and gotten out of the way.

But before education there comes a breeding program, a eugenics program, which is run in secret by the rulers. And although the warriors, the guardians, think that their matings are being determined by random chance, by lottery, actually the lottery is rigged in such a way that scientific breeding takes place to improve the overall quality of the herd, of the stock. The aim is that eventually the ruling class would be as distinct from the working class as well-bred Dobermans are from mutts that you find in the pound.

Sounds like a lot about politics.

Then when you get to books VIII and IX of the *Republic* you find that the reasons why this ideal sort of state would break down are laid out, and it has to do with the impossibility of calculating what they call the "nuptial number." Commentators can make no sense of it, which may be the whole point. Could Socrates have anticipated the idea that a planned society will always founder on the "calculation problem"? Namely that central planning requires that we collect and take into account more data than is humanly possible. Therefore, such an ideal state inevitably degenerates.

What follows is a description of cities into which the ideal state would degenerate. Five cities are discussed. There is one best city plus four degenerate ones. The best city degenerates, necessarily, into a regime called *timarchy* or *timocracy*, which is a city ruled not by philosophers but by warriors who are concerned primarily with honor. This regime degenerates into *oligarchy*, where the rich rule, which is still better than what comes after it, the *democratic* regime where the many rule. Finally, there is *tyranny*, the very worst regime, which comes about as a necessary consequence of the internal forces of democracy. With tyranny, one hits rock bottom, and the only place you can go from there is up. So, the hope is that history will begin to cycle back through. This, again, sounds like an extremely interesting political teaching.

Book X of the *Republic*, the final book, begins with a discussion of philosophy and poetry. This theme is discussed earlier on in *Republic* II, but it is revisited with a vengeance when Socrates argues that for the good of the city poets will have to be expelled. His critique is specifically of what you might call art for art's sake, a particular take on poetry that claims that poetry is somehow an autonomous, self-justifying end-in-itself, and that the poets don't need to look to any higher authority to guide their activities. The only authority they look to is their own inspiration.

Plato thinks that this is a terrible idea, because it places poetry above philosophy, whereas on Plato's account everything should be subordinated to philosophy. All the arts need to be subordinated to philosophy because philosophy pursues wisdom, and if you don't have wisdom then you can't use any art rightly or properly. Wisdom is what bends all the arts towards the good or orients them towards the good.

When poetry insists that it can stand on its own and be autonomous, it is really saying that it doesn't have to be good, or that it sets its own standards of the good. Plato thinks that this is very bad for a society, and so he thinks that poetry has to become not autonomous but what we can call ministrative. Poetry has to be subordinated to philosophy and used to edify people morally.

Any poet who doesn't wish to write morally edifying poetry under the guidance of philosopher-censors will have to leave the city. This means that the Tupac Shakurs would have to leave the city. The Beatles would have to leave the city. Dante wouldn't have to leave the city because, of course, he's all into edification.[1]

The end of the *Republic* is somewhat disconcerting. It ends with a strange myth about the afterlife. In this myth, people have the potential to choose the kind of life that they would like lead in their next incarnation. The dialogue concludes on this oddly apolitical note. But I want to argue that actually the whole purpose of the *Republic* is to lead up to this issue of choosing one's life, of what kind of life is most choiceworthy.

The theme of choosing your life appears throughout the *Republic*. It appears in Book I, Book II, Book VII, Book IX, and Book X. There are different ways of formulating the choice of lives. It's

---

[1] A student asked about the relationship of Plato's critique of poetry to the defense of poetry in Boris Pasternak's *Dr. Zhivago* and the film based upon it. This is my answer:

What the Communists objected to is any notion of private life or values. Poetry seems to be such a private thing. Zhivago is writing love poems about Lara. But poetry can exist even if it is private in some sense. I don't think the idea of privacy would be bothersome to Plato, but the idea of purely entertaining poetry, or poetry for its own sake, or poetry that is actually lurid, prurient, corrupting—justifying itself by saying the artist doesn't have to bend before any higher standards: This is the kind of stuff that Plato wants to rid the city of.

But, of course, there were poets writing Red poetry. "My love is a tractor tilling the soil. My love is smoke from the factory oil." That kind of poetry. The best kind of love story was between a worker and a peasant. Those were always the best. Those are the most socially approved. The hammer and sickle love stories.

the choice between the private life and the public life, the philosophical and the political life, the life of justice versus the life of injustice, the contemplation of reality versus the manipulation of appearances.

The manipulation of appearances is the life of sophistry, whereas the contemplation of reality is the life of philosophy. The sophists were teachers of rhetoric. They basically taught one to massage and manipulate the truth, and facsimiles of the truth, in order to persuade people to do one's bidding. Sophists manipulate appearances, whereas philosophers contemplate reality, then act on the basis of reality.

There is the choice between the authentic and the inauthentic life. A choice between knowing one's self versus knowing others, pleasing one's self versus pleasing others. It's the life of Odysseus versus the life of Achilles. That's one way in which it is posed. And there's the life of Socrates versus the life of Thrasymachus. Thrasymachus is a sophist who appears in the first book of the *Republic*. All of these are different ways in which this choice of lives is posed.

There is a Homeric subtext to the entire *Republic*. Specifically, it has to do with the *Odyssey*. In the *Odyssey*, Odysseus slaughters some animals, pours their blood into a trench, and has a mystical descent into the underworld. The Greek word for this descent is *katabasis*. Odysseus goes down to the underworld, and he sees the shades of many dead people.

One of the dead men he sees is Achilles. Remember that Achilles was given a choice of lives. He was given the choice between a long, anonymous private life and a short, glorious public life, and he took the short, glorious public life. Achilles was the paradigmatic Greek public man. He spent his entire life oriented towards public deeds: conquest and competition and the pursuit of honor and power.

Yet when he died and went down into the underworld, he came to regret his choice. Achilles tells Odysseus that he would rather break sod for a peasant on the surface of the Earth than be king among the dead. This is a repudiation of the political life for the lowliest of private lives.

This is very important for understanding the *Republic*, because the *Republic* itself is a *katabasis*, a descent into the underworld. The first word of the *Republic* is *kataben*, "I went down." And the lesson of the *Republic* is the same lesson learned by Achilles: that the public life of striving for honor is not worth choosing.

The *Republic* is a literary work by Plato, but it's based on actual events that took place in the life of Socrates. Plato had a brother named Glaucon, and when he was coming of age, Glaucon went to the public assembly where the citizens of Athens were deliberating on some matter, and he tried to get up before the crowd and harangue them. He was obviously bent on leading a public life. He wanted to be a politician. Why?

Because in Ancient Greece the political life was how one pursued glory. Public men would vie for positions of responsibility in the city-state, and once they had attained these positions of responsibility, they would strive to acquit themselves well and to be acclaimed and receive honor and glory from their fellow men. Of course, they tried to gain as much power and wealth as they possibly could. Often times their careers would be cut short by death, often violent death, at the hands of rivals who were struggling after the same things.

Plato's family was very concerned with Glaucon because he seemed to be excessively hubristic, excessively arrogant, and this was not a good strategy for long-term survival. Glaucon had all the qualities of the most infamous associate of Socrates, namely Alcibiades, who in his pursuit of glory ended up being a traitor to Athens and eventually was assassinated when he was relatively young. It was very clear that the family of Plato and Glaucon did not want their son following the same path. So, according to Xenophon, in his book *Memorabilia*, they asked Socrates to talk to Glaucon and to talk him out of this obsession with politics.

Glaucon is the central character, the central interlocutor, of the *Republic*, aside from Socrates himself. If you read the *Republic* carefully, the entire argument is constructed around the education of Glaucon, and its aim is to lead him away from the political life, the public life, to the private life or the philosophical life.

So the *Republic* is about what is the best life for a human being. It's not about politics. Those who say it is about politics are guilty of a superficial reading. There's a lot about politics in it. But it's not *fundamentally* about politics.

The *Republic* is fundamentally about the question "What is the best life for a human being?" Only two choices are really considered: the life of philosophy and the life of politics. The life of making money is not considered at all. In ancient Greece, it was never considered an option for a gentleman to go into business or the crafts. The only truly respectable life was politics.

But Socrates and Plato made philosophy a respectable alternative to the political life for the Athenians. What we find here is Socrates actually pleading the case for the philosophical life as the best way of life for a human being.

In order to make that argument, Socrates and Plato have to argue about the nature of justice. The initial question in the *Republic* is "What is justice?" The Greek word for justice, *dikaiosune*, has two meanings. Aristotle discusses this in his *Nicomachean Ethics*. The first sense of justice is simply what you would call political justice, which has to do with treating other people properly, fair dealing with others. It's an interpersonal relationship. Justice is governing your interpersonal relationships morally.

But there's a broader sense of justice that isn't an interpersonal kind of justice but, if you will, an intrapersonal kind of justice. Justice is a kind of relationship that you have not with other people but with yourself. A good English translation of this sense of justice is *righteousness*.

What is righteousness? Righteousness, ultimately, refers to all-around virtue. Virtue is understood as primarily a matter of the proper ordering of the soul. So, it's an inner state. It's a kind of relationship, but not a relationship between you and others but between one part of you and other parts of you within your soul. In the *Republic* Plato gradually transforms the topic of justice from the political sense of justice to this broader comprehensive spiritual sense of justice: righteousness. He exploits the ambiguity of the Greek word for justice.

The challenge that Socrates has in the *Republic* is to argue that the life of the philosopher is better than the life of the politician.

To do this, he argues the hardest possible case. The challenge is to show that a just man, a person who is just in his soul, a man of good character, is better off than an unjust man, a man of bad character, even if the just man is not recognized for his justice but instead is punished for it, and the unjust man is not recognized as unjust but instead is rewarded for his injustice.

What Socrates has to argue is that justice is intrinsically valuable such that you'd want to be just, even if you didn't get any rewards for being just, and even if all the proper rewards for being just were distributed to those who were unjust.

My favorite example of such an inversion is the treatment of Bill Clinton and Ken Starr, who investigated the Monica Lewinsky scandal. Starr is, by all accounts, a just and decent man. Yet he's been smeared mercilessly as an evil man, and people have treated him as such. Whereas very few people really believe that Bill Clinton is a good man—aside from maybe Bill Clinton himself, in his state of utter delusion. No one *believes* that Clinton is a good man. Yet during the whole impeachment crisis, a substantial number of citizens treated him like he was a decent man. He got all the rewards of being a decent man, even though he wasn't. Whereas the most decent person in the whole sordid scandal was treated the worst.

Now Linda Tripp is being prosecuted as a criminal. There's another example. One of the few people in this whole sordid mess who behaved morally and prudently, and she's being prosecuted as a criminal. Monica, the person who suborned perjury, is not being prosecuted as a criminal. Instead, she's being given an advertising contract from a diet company and being paid $10,000 for each . . . What is it? A ton or a pound? . . . that she loses. I guess it's a pound.

You see these kinds of shocking inversions all the time. What Plato wants to argue in the *Republic* is that Ken Starr is better off, and would be better off, even if they hung him up and gouged out his eyes—than Bill Clinton, even though he will be treated with all the respect and dignity due the President or former President of the United States for the rest of his life. Ken Starr would still be better off than Clinton, even though all just rewards have been sent to the wrong guy.

The question is who is really better off? Plato wants to argue that the just man is better off even if he receives no rewards for his justice, even if he's punished as if he were a scoundrel, whereas the unjust man is still not to be envied even though he's never punished for his injustice, even though he might be rewarded as if he were just.

The life of the just man is choiceworthy regardless of any extrinsic rewards or punishments that accrue to it, just as the life of the unjust man is not choiceworthy regardless of what extrinsic punishments or rewards accrue to it. Now, that means that Plato has to argue that being just is *intrinsically* as opposed to *instrumentally* good and that being unjust is intrinsically as opposed to instrumentally bad.

An intrinsic good is *good in and of itself,* whereas an instrumental good is only *good for some purpose beyond itself.* Many people will argue, for instance, that honesty is the best policy, which means that honesty is instrumentally good. It's useful as a matter of policy to be honest. But some people would argue that it's not just the best policy, it's just the best, period. There's something intrinsically good about it. Plato wants to argue that virtue is intrinsically good. Another way of putting it is that virtue is its own reward.

How does Plato argue this?

First, we must establish that virtue and vice are things that inhere inside the human being. Where do you find them? Virtue and vice dwell in the human soul. Socrates says that we have to understand the structure of the soul. We have to understand the soul's nature and its parts and how the parts function together harmoniously to produce health or disharmoniously to produce illness. Once we understand this, we will understand what virtue is, because virtue is the health of the soul, and vice is the sickness of the soul.

The trouble is that the soul is intangible, invisible. If it has size at all, it's very small. So, how do you see something that is very small, or something that can't be seen at all, for that matter? You need something analogous to it that is large and visible. What is offered as the large, visible analogue of the soul — the soul writ large — is society. So, the political theme enters merely as an analogy for the soul. The structure of the city is treated as analogous to the structure of the soul, and by exploring the large visible structure of the city, we can throw light on the intangible, invisible structure of the soul. This is how the political enters into the *Republic*.

There is a long discussion of the nature of a city. By the end of Book IV, a solution is proposed to the question that is raised in Book I which is whether justice is intrinsically good or bad and what justice is. So, by the end of Book IV, the question of the *Republic* is answered.

But then we get a long digression, and this digression occupies Books V, VI, and VII. In V, VI, and VII, we get the most astonishing political proposals of the *Republic*. Namely, that wives and children should be held in common, the abolition of private property, and the rule of the philosopher-king. Here we encounter the most famous part of the *Republic*, namely the Parable of the Cave, and the images of the divided line and the sun which are used to lay out Plato's metaphysical scheme. And all of this is a vast digression from the main argument of the *Republic*.

Then we have a strange segue at the beginning of Book VIII back into the political with what I can only describe as a mathematical farce, the nuptial number, which is the argument that the political regime that has been described merely to illustrate the structure of the soul cannot actually exist, and if it did exist it would degenerate into the four known forms of political regimes that they saw around them which are timarchy, oligarchy, democracy, and tyranny.

Then what happens in Books VIII and IX is a very careful, detailed description of the different types of souls that are characteristic of the citizens of these four degenerate regimes. In turns out that just as there is a strict analogy between the best city and the best soul, there is a strict analogy between degenerate cities and degenerate souls. Degenerate cities give rise to degenerate souls that are corrupt in the exact same way as the city, just as degenerate souls give rise to appropriate cities. There's a kind of circular causation at work here. Oligarchy raises up oligarchical men, and oligarchical men demand more oligarchy.

The leading factor, though, is the soul. Timarchy degenerates into oligarchy when the souls of the rulers degenerate into oligarchical souls. So, the driving force of history is really human character, the human soul, and when people's characters begin to change, the kinds of regimes that they live in will change, too. Thus, we find a whole philosophy of history and culture in these two books. At the core of this philosophy of history and culture are the different transformations that the human soul can undergo.

Then, at the end of Book IX, finally, Socrates brings us back to the question of what life do we choose. At this point, Glaucon is willing to choose the life of philosophy rather than the political life. In effect, the argument of the *Republic* is completed.

Then we have Book X, which is almost an appendix where you have side-by-side an attack on autonomous poetry, poetry for poetry's sake, and a myth that is an example of poetry with an edifying aim. So, there's something interesting about that last book. It attacks poetry, and it is poetry. After attacking poetry and arguing for the banishment of the poets, Plato then gives a poetic work, the Myth of Er, as a model of what poetry will be like in a perfected society. The *Republic* is just loaded with myths—myths and parables and stories. It not only contains myths, but it also theorizes about the importance of myth—why one would tell such tales.

Plato did write a dialogue called *Laws*, where he lays out more of his real political philosophy. It doesn't really bear much resemblance to what you find in his *Republic*. The reason for that is, again, that the *Republic* isn't really about politics. It's about the soul. We have to read this as an exercise in what Plato in the *Phaedrus* calls *psychagogy*. Psychagogy just means the art of leading souls.

All of Plato's dialogues are psychagogical because you have Socrates working with a particular human being who has a particular kind of character and particular psychological or spiritual needs. Socrates is trying to craft the speeches he gives and tailor them to the soul of the person he is speaking to in order to lead that person in the direction of health or virtue, which boil down to the same thing when you're talking about the soul. Leading the soul to health is the same as leading it to virtue. This means that there are all kinds of hyperbolic and bizarre stories and proposals put forward in the *Republic*, but these things have to be read in terms of the underlying psychagogical project.

I think it will be clearer if I talk a bit about the structure of the soul that Plato discusses in the *Republic*. Plato claims that the soul has three parts. The parts of the soul are *reason, spirit,* and *desire*. Now, for Plato, these parts of the soul all have their appropriate "loves," if you will, or needs. The soul is directed towards particular things in the world. It loves or needs the things that satisfy it. Reason has a particular love. Reason loves the truth. Spiritedness loves honor. And desire loves the necessities of life.

The basic structure of the soul is that it has three parts. But all of these parts are directed towards particular things needed for its satisfaction. Plato calls this directedness of the different parts of the soul towards their specific satisfactions *love* or *eros*. So, he speaks of the different parts of the soul having different loves. Love of victory or of honor, which characterize spirit. Love of gain or the necessities of life or money, which characterize desire. Love of the truth or love of wisdom, which are characteristic of the rational soul.

The different parts of the soul can relate to one another in essentially political ways, by which I mean in terms of *ruler* and *ruled*. Plato believes that human beings have a certain amount of freedom. Our basic freedom is to establish one part of our soul as the ruler over the others. We have a certain choice of the character that we have, the kind of life that we'll lead. We make that choice by understanding the parts of the soul, then choosing which part will rule. There are three basic types of men for Plato: men ruled by reason, spirit, or desire.

What we get in the *Republic* is an extraordinarily exaggerated image of a soul ruled by reason, namely the philosopher-king, and also of a city, namely what is called the *Kallipolis* or ideal city, the "city in speech," the republic in the *Republic*, which is ruled by reason, too. At the core of the *Republic*, then, is the image of the philosopher as a superlatively rational human being and of the ideal utopian city as the kind of city where reason in the form of philosopher-kings rules over other human beings.

There are all kinds of things that go wrong, though, when you establish the absolute dominance of reason in society. Plato illustrates these problems in the *Republic* by proposing things like the community of wives and children and the philosopher-king—or what he treats as an extraordinarily paradoxical, preposterous claim, namely the equality of the sexes, specifically the equality of the sexes among the guardians. Basically, he is talking about women in the military.

Why does Plato make these proposals? Well, one of the reasons is precisely to show the limitations of reason in ruling the soul and in ruling the city. Because he shows the extraordinary deformations of spiritual and political life that take place if they are ruled entirely by reason. But on the other hand, he's very much concerned to implant within Glaucon this idea of being entirely ruled by reason.

By the end of Book IX, Socrates has convinced Glaucon that the kind of city ruled by philosophers could never come into existence. But Glaucon is just as much convinced that the kind of *soul* in which reason rules can and should come into existence and that he should strive to make himself as rational a human being as he possibly can be.

Why does Socrates do this? Is it because Socrates thinks that the healthiest soul is the kind of rational soul he presents in the *Republic*? The kind of rationality Socrates praises is oddly bloodless and mathematical. Why does he try to implant this kind of ideal into Glaucon's mind if he gives reasons along the way that this might not be the healthiest thing?

This brings us to the psychagogical intent of the *Republic*. To understand this, we have to take a detour through Aristotle who gives us an explanation of how this kind of education works. In his *Nicomachean Ethics*, Aristotle talks about how every virtue is a mean between two extremes, two vices. One is a vice of excess and the other is a vice of defect. You thought that you only had one vice to worry about. But actually with every virtue there are two vices to be avoided, which is why Aristotle said being virtuous is hard. You go a little too far, and you're in one vice. You fall short, and you're in another.

Let's concretize this with an example. Consider the virtue of courage. The vice of excess associated with courage is *foolhardiness*, which is a kind of excess courage, whereas the vice of defect is *cowardice*. The foolhardy man has too much fighting spirit. The cowardly man has too little. Courage is the mean. Practical reason is the ability to discern the mean. Thus discretion really is the better part of valor. Indeed, discretion is the better part of all virtues, because it allows you to hit the mean.

Aristotle gives a couple bits of helpful advice for becoming more virtuous, and one bit of advice is absolutely fundamental for understanding Greek philosophy: If you tend towards the vice of excess, the way to get to the mean of virtue is to aim for the opposite vice of defect.

Say a stick is bent, and you want to straighten it. How do you straighten a bent stick? You dampen it, then apply pressure to bend it back to the opposite extreme, and it ends up becoming straight. Or if you're aiming at a target, you aim a little above the bull's eye, because you know that gravity will then bring your arrow down to the point that you want to reach. This is the rule of thumb that Aristotle gives for moral education.

In the *Republic*, reasonableness and spiritedness are related to one another as vice of excess and vice of defect. Glaucon is characterized by an excess of spiritedness, and the way for him to correct his excess of spiritedness is to aim for the opposite extreme, which would be an excess of rationality.

I hate to use examples like this because people will think of me as a vulgarian, but let's talk about *Star Trek*.

Consider Mr. Spock and Dr. McCoy. Mr. Spock represents an excess of rationality, whereas Dr. McCoy has an excess of what you might call spiritedness. He's emotional. He gets angry a lot. "Spock, you and your Vulcan logic!" and "These people are butchers!" One of the manifestations of spiritedness is a propensity to anger. Dr. McCoy really is excessively spirited. He's always getting out of hand. Spock is a typical Vulcan, and I guess McCoy is supposed to be typically Scots-Irish.

Now, Dr. McCoy really needs to moderate his anger. He needs to become less spirited, less irascible in the same way that Glaucon needs to be less spirited and less irascible.

So, how could McCoy aim to be a more moderately spirited person? He could imitate Mr. Spock. You would never recommend anybody imitate Mr. Spock if you thought he would actually *become* Mr. Spock, because Mr. Spock is not an ideal person to be either. But if a person's temperament is diametrically opposed to Spock, and the proper state is somewhere between him and Mr. Spock, then by aiming at Mr. Spock, you would end up getting to the mean which is the proper state.

Of course, if you have the two extremes of under-acting and over-acting, then you'd have Leonard Nimoy aim for William Shatner, and somebody would be a happy medium in between. The Captain would be more of a happy medium between McCoy and Spock. In fact, he functions that way in many of the episodes. *Star Trek* will now seem much richer to you, I hope. Plato has become impoverished, but *Star Trek* has become enriched through this analogy.

Socrates is trying to implant within Glaucon the desire to be more Spock-like. Not because he thinks that Glaucon can become Spock-like, or because it is a good thing to be Spock-like, but because he thinks that Glaucon needs to aim at that in order to get himself closer to what he really should be, which is an absent and unspecified middle position.

This unspecified position, which is never explicitly discussed in the *Republic*, is actually Plato's model of the healthy soul, and, by analogy, it's his model of the best city. This brings us to one of the most extraordinary characteristics of Plato: the way Plato teaches.

Plato writes in his Seventh Letter that he never set forth his own philosophy in any of his writings. That's a pretty extraordinary statement for one of our greatest philosophers to make. But the question is: If Plato never wrote down his philosophy, then why in the world are we reading these dialogues?

Well, he never wrote it down, but you can infer his philosophy from the dialogues not just by reading what he *says*, but also by looking at what he *does*. The dialogues are not doctrines or compendia of doctrines, but they are psychagogical or spiritual dramas.

If you read the dialogues as compendia of positions, you find that Plato seems like a rather extravagant and goofy fellow. Plato believes in communism and in eugenics and in censorship, and things like that. How disreputable. "Thank God we've progressed beyond Plato!" Plato becomes an odd sort of footnote, essentially irrelevant to the modern consciousness, because we are all so sure that we've progressed beyond him, and he's a sort of intellectual pygmy compared to anybody who lives today who happens to be in tune with our superior culture. So, any second-rate mind who's in tune with our modern culture can feel superior to Plato. Frankly, I find this sort of attitude irritating. But you get this with college undergraduates, who patronizingly suggest, "Well, wasn't Plato just a product of his time?"

Well, yes, but nothing important about anybody is really a product of his time. If Plato were merely a product of his time no one should read him. And insofar as Plato was a product of his time, he fails to be a philosopher, because what is essential about the philosophical ambition is precisely to become untimely, to transcend one's time and place and make statements that are true universally.

Plato's dialogues, if read as spiritual or psychagogical exercises, can lead us to an understanding of Plato's views *if* we can follow where he's leading our souls. Because the *effect* of the Platonic dialogues, the state of mind the dialogues lead us to, is Plato's real philosophy.

There are four dimensions of Plato's dialogues that must be taken into account to understand Plato's teaching: the *words*, the *events*, the *characters*, and the spiritual *effect*. We don't fully know Plato's philosophy by treating the dialogues as mere compendia of arguments and myths. The dialogues are also stories, with characters and events, which the reader must also take into account. Moreover, as the dialogues unfold, the arguments and stories within them have an *effect* on the characters. The dialogues don't just change the participants' thinking. They also reorient their souls. And when the reader grasps the spiritual transformation taking place within the characters in the dialogue, that brings about spiritual changes in the reader as well.

The meaning of Plato's dialogues cannot be grasped through any of these elements taken in isolation. The meaning is, rather, the *total effect* of all these aspects of the dialogues on the soul of the reader. Once you put this total effect into words, you have arrived at Plato's teaching.

So, what would be the best soul for Plato? The best soul for Plato isn't a soul simply ruled by reason, spirit, or desire. The best soul is ruled by a kind of fusion of rationality and spiritedness. What does that mean?

Spiritedness for Plato is directed towards values or ideals. But in the simplest forms, spiritedness is directed towards values. There are many things that humans can value. Our ability to value is extremely fluid and polymorphous. But the first thing that anybody seems to value is one's self.

A spirited attachment to the self is not, however, what one would call an instinct for self-preservation. Why is that? Such an instinct would be a desire. Desire is the prompting to maintain life, to gain the necessities of life. You could talk about a life instinct, but spiritedness isn't a life instinct. A spirited attachment to the self is not an attachment to one's physical existence. It's an attachment to the *idea* of the self. Spirit is an attachment to ideal values, unreal, non-concrete ideal values.

What is the idea of the self? It's one's self-image. When one forms an attachment to one's self-image one can call that one's sense of honor, one's self-esteem. But along with this notion of self-esteem comes the concept of honor.

The clearest example of this is when someone treats you in a way that doesn't fundamentally accord with your image of yourself. What happens when somebody does that to you? If you think well of yourself, and somebody cuts you off in traffic or barges in front of you at a movie theater or pushes you aside with his overladen basket in the grocery store, what's the reaction that you have? Anger. You feel dishonored, disrespected, and you get angry. So, anger is always connected with the spirited part of the soul. It gets angry over ideals that are not properly respected, including the ideal of one's self.

The trouble with spiritedness is that it's a somewhat *undiscerning* capacity to value. So, for instance, even murderers and psychopaths have a certain attachment to themselves, a certain fondness for their selves that goes over and above their self-preservation instincts. You also form spirited attachments to things that are close to you like your family and your friends.

What we call *sentimental* attachments are spirited attachments because they are affixed to things that are intimately connected with and almost definitive of one's identity. So, there's a broadened sphere of the self. One gets upset when somebody attacks a member of one's family. If somebody disrespects your sister, you get angry over that. If somebody says "Your momma wears army boots," you might want to knife them.

But sadly some families are just packs of wolves. Some people would be better off being raised by wolves than by their own parents. And yet people still form attachments to them. Or attachments to one's hometown. Or one's native tongue. Or one's homeland. Spiritedness forms attachments that are somewhat undiscriminating as to the true and proper things that one really *ought* to value.

When writers like Adam Smith talk about moral sentiments, they are really referring to is this part of the soul. Let's not treat it as *mere* sentiment, though, because there are some sentiments that are good. When you talk about sentimental attachments you are talking about attachments to things that are familiar and old. These things are very much caught up with your sense of self, your personal history. But sentimentality can easily take on a negative, dark quality because is often connected to a false sense of innocence, including one's own innocence.

But, on the other hand, the last thing you want is a human being who is not fundamentally oriented towards values—values over and above creature comforts and self-preservation. Human beings can be turned into very mean animals by devoting themselves to creature comforts and self-preservation. People can be enslaved by their desires.

The lack of values is nihilism. The rule of pure reason in the soul is in danger of becoming nihilistic. A concern simply with facts, with the logical, with the mathematical, with the rigorous, leads to scientists who say, "This is just a morally neutral activity. We're just hired brains, and we'll work for anybody. We're not concerned with ethics. We're concerned with simply getting to the facts." This morally cowardly or nihilistic attitude has been transformed into a kind of moralistic mission, a high calling and purpose, a kind of religion of science.

The possibility of a Mr. Spock strikes me as deeply disturbing. Since pure reason—reason understood as a mere calculative faculty—doesn't give rise to values, but people still have to act, the Mr. Spocks end up being ruled, oftentimes, by their basest desires. There's an alliance between amoral, scientific rationalism and hedonism.

Here, again, I will lapse into *Star Trek*. Just think of Mr. Spock. What makes Mr. Spock tick? It's kind of hard to understand what motivates him. Being in a ship that explores the cosmos and collects facts is the perfect place for a Vulcan. But every seven years Mr. Spock goes insane and runs amok when his desires take over. He oscillates between a distracted scientific rationalism and an unhinged hedonism.

Another example of this from pop culture is an episode of *The X-Files* that I call "The Robot Cockroaches from Outer Space" episode, because I forget the episode's real name.[2] In one scene a sexy female entomologist, a bug scientist, is talking to Fox Mulder in a darkened lab at night. She says, "I admire insects. They don't have any pretensions. They just eat and sleep and breed, and that's it." At that point, you expect the two of them to tear one another's clothes off. Because that's what it's leading up to.

Here again we have a scientific mind that sees values as essentially subjective and arbitrary and thus unworthy of any respect, teamed up with a kind of hedonism that thinks that animals are superior because they lack morality and self-consciousness. Human beings have this strange tendency to erect systems of values that tamp down on purely physical impulses like sex. Cockroaches don't write love sonnets or commit suicide over broken hearts. They just reproduce and die in a sort

---

[2] I hate *The X-Files* because of the combination of cynicism and credulity that it tries to spread through our culture. It's also boring and farcical. The characters never grow. After seven years of seeing aliens and all manner of vampires, Scully just couldn't be the same sceptic that she was at the beginning.

of blissful unconsciousness. Wouldn't we all be better off if we were that way?

We live in a culture where there's a tag-team routine between pure science, which sees through values and creates an atmosphere of cynicism, and a carnivalesque, hedonistic popular culture that's all too happy to have all these pretenses torn away, because after all these things get in the way of our satisfaction.

There's something deeply disturbing about a mind that's ruled by pure reason, because pure reason needs to be ruled itself. It needs to be ruled by an orientation towards what is good. Nothing we excogitate is unconditionally good. There are all sorts of ideas and inventions that maybe shouldn't exist, if we think in terms of oughts, of what is good. The activity of reasoning itself needs to be governed by an orientation towards the good, towards values.

The Platonic view is something like this: The mind that is ruled by an orientation towards ideals, bereft of reason, could be swept up by irrational enthusiasm. But at least it's idealistic. At least it's open to the good, however mistaken it might be about it. Whereas the mind that is exclusively rational without a value orientation is capable of seeing through the difference between truth and falsehood, but it has no values to guide its activities. So one needs a kind of fusion of value orientation with rationality. One needs, in short, *knowledge* of the *good*. One needs an orientation of the rational soul towards the good and by the good.

The whole reproductive regime of the *Republic* is a picture of a world where human attachment is annihilated except for attachment to the city. It's an inhuman and unrecognizable world, based on the rule of a pure functional rationality that insists that human beings have one aim, which is to perform their function in society, and everything that competes with that aim has to be eliminated in the name of mechanical perfection. Thus natural human love of one's own, our preferences for things other than society as a whole—our families, our friends—must be uprooted. It's a kind of engineering mentality. There's something insane about that. Especially when you apply it to human beings.

The proposal about sexual equality is made in total abstraction from the body. We're talking about putting women in the military, and the first thing that Socrates proposes is that physical differences are absolutely irrelevant. Only mental faculties should be taken into account. What a preposterous notion! We're talking about soldiers and the police. Why would one abstract away from the body? Well, if one has a kind of autistic bloodless logicality, these aren't differences that make any difference.

Then there's the discussion of wives and children in common and community of property: the communist proposals. Again, these illustrate the impropriety of abstracting away from natural human partiality. Such partialities are just part of human nature. They could be good or bad, but they can't be gone. All of these weird proposals are there precisely to illustrate the limits of a kind of bloodless rationality in ruling over of life.

These proposals are not Plato's actual policy prescriptions, and he knows they are problematic if taken as such. They are instead offered as psychagogical exercises to help Glaucon. However, I wish to argue that reading the *Republic* as a psychagogical exercise still points to Plato's true model of the best regime.

You find this claim in Socrates: To know what's good is to do it. If you know what is right, and if there are no forces preventing you from acting on it, then you do it. Virtue is a kind of knowledge of the good. With virtue, it's possible to bring knowing—rationality—together with the good. It's possible to educate our sentiments, to educate our spiritedness, to imbue it with the capacity to distinguish between truth and falsehood in the realm of values. This is at the core of what Platonic philosophy is about.

The best kind of soul, therefore, is a soul that is primarily oriented towards values, but is purified by and educated by reason in such a way that it becomes discriminating between true and false values. It represents a kind of fusion of rationality and spiritedness.

But the ruling principle seems to be spiritedness. Spiritedness is the final ruling factor for the simple fact that reason has to be ruled by values. Yet, at the same time, your value orientation needs to be informed by reason, to be educated by reason, to be made subtle by reason, and to have its illusions purged away.

Now, let's ask what kind of city would be analogous to that ordering of the soul. It would be a city ruled by spirited types, but these spirited types would be liberally educated. They would be educated by philosophers to be discerning about issues of truth and falsehood. It would be a city ruled by gentlemen, gentlemen who go to school and get liberal educations from philosophers.

Now let's stand back and look at the whole drama of the *Republic*: That is exactly what we see. We see an ambitious young gentleman being educated by an older philosopher. The best kind of regime is not the rule of philosophers, nor the rule of mere spirited barbarians, but the rule of spirited men who are educated by philosophers.

The concept of spiritedness, *thumos*, first appears and is developed in Books II, III and IV. *Thumos* is located in the chest. In the *Timaeus*, Plato associates the three parts of the soul with three parts of the body. There's reason which is in the head, spiritedness which is located in the chest where the heart and lungs are, and desire which is located in the belly.

Why is *thumos* associated with the chest? Because when you get angry your heart beats. When you hear stirring music, like a national anthem, you feel it in your chest. So, there's actually a physiological meaningfulness to locating this capacity to value in the heart and lungs.

It turns out that whenever Glaucon is described he is characterized as being spirited. Glaucon is described as erotic, musical, and spirited, and when these topics come up, Glaucon is the one who discusses them.

The musical dimension of Glaucon is what makes him susceptible to liberal education, because as it turns out music refers to all the liberal arts, all of the things having to do with the muses. So, the best regime is a society where you have gentlemen who are educated in the liberal arts by the philosophers, but the philosophers don't rule.

Alfarabi was a Medieval Arabic philosopher. This is Leo Strauss on Alfarabi's commentary on Plato:

We may say that Alfarabi's Plato eventually replaces the philosopher-king who rules openly in the virtuous city by the secret kingship of the philosopher, who being a perfect man precisely because he is an investigator, lives privately as a member of an imperfect society which he tries to humanize within the limits of the possible.[3]

The philosopher is a person who strives for spiritual perfection in the midst of a society that he doesn't expect to become perfect, but he seeks to humanize that society as much as possible. How? Ultimately, by educating its rulers.

The *Republic* tries to make clear that the analogy between the city and the soul is extremely useful, but that it ultimately breaks down when you talk about philosophy, because there can be no city that's analogous to the philosophical soul. There's a kind of incommensurability of the interests of philosophy and the city. There's never going to be a complete harmony between the interests of philosophy and the interests of society.

Why is that? There are two important reasons.

First, for Plato, every society is ultimately partial, parochial. Even the best societies are going to have an *Us* or *Them* quality to them, whereas philosophy can't be limited by those kinds of considerations. Philosophy is cosmopolitan.

Second, every society needs to make some opinions authoritative. Every society has to have basic, unquestioned presuppositions that the average functioning citizen simply believes in if the society is going to work. But philosophy can't have any unquestioned presuppositions. You can't let certain things go undiscussed. So, the interests of political stability are always going to be inimical to the interests of philosophical investigation.

One of the things that the *Republic* tries to teach is precisely this disanalogy, the fact that there will never be a society analogous to the soul of the philosopher, and that philosophers will

---

[3] Leo Strauss, Introduction to *Persecution and the Art of Writing* (Chicago: University of Chicago Press, 1952), p. 17; cf. "Farabi's Plato," *Louis Ginzberg Jubilee Volume* (New York: American Academy for Jewish Research, 1945), p. 384.

always, therefore, have to live in imperfect cities. But if you look at what Socrates does in the *Republic*, he's trying to improve that imperfect city by educating the minds of its ruling class.

*Counter-Currents*, May 12 & 16, 2014

# THE MYTHS OF PLATO*

Plato's dialogues are filled with myths. Virtually every Platonic dialogue has a little narrative in it, usually a real gem of a narrative that takes up themes and images from Greek myths and weaves them into a new kind of story. It's very interesting to contemplate what these myths mean and to ask oneself "What is the relationship of myth to philosophy?" "What is the possible role of myth in philosophy?"

The Greek word *muthos* just means story or narrative. If you want to use that concept very broadly, then everything about the Platonic dialogues is mythic, because all of the dialogues are stories. There's one event and then another event and another event, and they are all narrated or acted out in front of us. However, within the dialogues are more specifically fictional stories — the myths of Plato. The question that intrigues me is "Why does Plato write myths, and what possible good are myths in the pursuit of wisdom, which is what philosophy is all about?"

Isn't philosophy in some sense an emancipation from myth? If you look at the history of thought, you find that every known culture has a set of myths, and these myths are always about gods, heroes, demi-gods, life after death in one form or another, and the "men of old," the ancient men, especially the first men. Every culture has myths about these five topics: gods, demi-gods, heroes, ancient man, and the after-life. Not every culture has a myth about the origin of the cosmos. The term for a creation myth is a *cosmogony*.

Myth is primitive in some sense. Myth is always associated with the earliest origins of a culture. And philosophy, whatever it is, isn't primitive. Philosophy always comes later, after myth, usually — if it comes at all — many thousands of years after the origins of a civilization. And the origin of philosophy always

---

* This is a heavily edited transcript by V.S. of the first part of the opening lecture of a course on Plato's *Timaeus* and *Critias* from Autumn, 1999, given to the Invisible College in Atlanta. The second part of the lecture dealt specifically with the *Timaeus* and *Critias*.

involves a gesture of emancipating the mind from opinion. Opinion just means any views accepted from others. The most authoritative opinions are those passed down from generation to generation, including myths. This is true of all three independent philosophical traditions: Indian, Chinese, and Western, which really means the Greek and post-Greek. Philosophies all deal with such topics as man's nature, the nature of the cosmos, our place in the cosmos (our status, the human condition), and the good life. But myths deal with the very same topics, only in a very different way.

Every myth takes the form of a story. They are always narratives involving concrete events and usually concrete characters. Sometimes these characters are gods or demi-gods. Other times they are personifications of phenomena. For instance, here's an example of an old Latin myth that Heidegger recounts in *Being and Time*:

> Care was walking along the river. [Here we have personification of a force: Care.] She bends down and scoops up some mud, and she forms it into a creature. She calls upon Jupiter to breathe life into it, and then she decides to name it. But, of course, this creates a problem, because the Earth has donated the stuff that it's made out of, the mud, and Jupiter has donated the principle of life, soul. Although she has manufactured it, she doesn't have complete claim over the thing, and so the three forces, Jupiter, the Earth, and Care begin arguing about what to name it. What do we name this new creature? They settle the dispute this way: Earth, because it gave its substance will receive its substance back when it is dead. Zeus, or Jupiter, who gave it its soul will receive the soul back after it's dead. And Care, because it manufactured this creature, will possess it throughout its entire life. They decided to name the creature *Homo*, man, from *humus*, earth.

So, this is a myth about the origin of man, and it is specifically a myth about the fact that care possesses us throughout our lives. What does that mean? We're always worrying about something. We are always concerned about things. This myth is an attempt to give us some reason, some account, some explanation for why human life is always beset by worries and cares.

Every myth has a narrative structure, concrete, specific events, and concrete characters. Yet, every myth tries to deal with something of universal significance. The most universally significant things are, again, man's nature, the cosmos, our place in the cosmos, and what the good life is.

These are the topics that philosophy deals with as well. It would seem, therefore, that philosophy and myth are going to be quarreling with one another eventually, because both are attempts, using different methods, to try to answer the same basic kinds of questions.[1]

When philosophy encounters myth it applies a new kind of critical intellect to it. Primitive peoples exist entirely in the atmosphere of myth and tend to have rather uncritical minds. Some of them believe the literal truth of myths. Yet, it's clear that for the most part myths can't be literally true. They involve violations of easily known laws of causality. What does it mean to say that Care is a person? Why is Care female? None of these things can literally be true. Many myths are clearly relative to time and place, and they undergo all kinds of transformations, sometimes for the most obvious pragmatic reasons.

For instance, there's a beautiful book by a French author named Paul Veyne called *Did the Greeks Believe Their Myths?* That question makes sense because the Greeks were rather cavalier about changing their myths. But why would they change something they regarded as sacred or holy? Sometimes they changed myths for political purposes. For instance, if Athens came to dominate another Greek city-state, they might legitimize this new state of affairs by rewriting the founding myths of the newly dependent society. Now, this seems terribly cynical, and the

---

[1] A parable is just a particular kind of story that has a meaning to it or a moral to it, like a fable. Aesop's fables are parables. Sometimes parables have all the hallmarks of myth. There will be talking animals or forces of nature personified, etc. So there's generally not that much difference between a myth and a parable.

question then becomes how can people really believe myths if they treat them in such a cynical way? It is an important question.

The Greeks believed their myths, but they didn't believe they were literally true, if they could transform them for completely pragmatic purposes. But clearly they did have some sort of claim on people's credence. People were very powerfully motivated by these myths. People understood themselves and their place in the world in terms of these myths. Myths answered the most fundamental questions any human being can raise. The Greeks certainly spent lavish amounts of time and energy building temples, worshipping at them, and holding festivals in honor of these gods. So, clearly they believed them in some sense. Myths had the power to command people's actions. Yet, they didn't seem to believe they were literally true. So there has to be some other kind of truth here.

Myths are clearly not believed to be literally true once you start looking at them with a critical mind. They're filled with contradictions and thus cannot be literally true. And if you compare mythic traditions, they are so radically different in many ways that all of them can't be true. We're applying certain basic principles of logic. Contradictions can't exist in reality, so contradictory stories can't be true. Or we are applying a correspondence theory of truth, which says that a story is true if, and only if, it mirrors the way the world really works. Myths can't be true in that sense.

Philosophy inaugurates a kind of critical attitude towards myth, and it is philosophy's attempt to emancipate itself from myth that leads to a conflict between philosophy and myth. They are dealing with the same issues. Philosophy, however, deals with these issues in a much more rigorous and intellectually lucid way. Philosophy tries generally to speak in terms of abstractions, not in terms of concrete stories. Philosophical treatises generally don't take the form of stories. Open any academic journal of philosophy. None of the articles begin, "Once upon a time . . ." Philosophy attempts to become timeless, to emancipate itself from the relativity of any particular culture and historical epoch. Philosophy attempts to speak to all men. This is why mathematics has always been such a tempting model for philosophers, because has a greater universality than any natural languages, which are tinged with history and custom and relativity to time and place.

It seems like philosophy is the last place that you would expect to see myths popping up. But then we reach Plato, who is the first philosopher in the Western tradition whose complete works have survived. I would argue that Aristophanes' *Clouds* is a philosophical work, but most other people wouldn't put him in the canon, so Plato is first. Plato is the first philosophical thinker in the Western canon from whom any single complete work survives. And, as it turns out, all of his works have survived.[2] And yet all of his works, except for his letters, are myths.

---

[2] From the very beginning of the tradition, it has been claimed that there were 35 Platonic dialogues, and 35 dialogues have come down to us, plus a collection of letters. We know that Plato destroyed his early poetic works, but all of his philosophical works have survived.

We don't have any of the works that Aristotle published in his lifetime. Aristotle wrote dialogues just like Plato did. Apparently, they were somewhat different than the Platonic dialogues, because actually they were more like the *Timaeus*, which consists of a little bit of dialogue and then a big long speech. There was none of the Socratic question and answer. They were more like debates rather than dialogues. They were not conversational. Apparently, Cicero modeled his dialogues on Aristotle's. His tend to contain long speeches by people with different, opposing viewpoints. But Aristotle did write dialogues, and those are the only things he published, and every single Aristotelian dialogue has been lost. Only fragments embodied as quotations in the texts of other authors have survived.

All of the writings we have of Aristotle's were works that he never intended for publication and that came to light long after his death. Actually, 80 B.C. is the date when most of these seem to have come to light. The Roman dictator Sulla found these texts in Asia Minor and brought them back. It was during that period that they were edited and widely disseminated.

There are all kinds of questions about which of these works are really Aristotle's. Many works have been excluded or included, and it has been fertile ground for classicists who love to make arguments about authenticity, sometimes on the craziest and most spurious of

They are narratives. They are dialogues, which are narratives. And within these dialogues are little narratives as well.

The dialogues are plays of a sort, which means that they are myths in a very broad sense, because the word *muthos* in Greek just means a narrative or a story. Then there's the more specific sense of *muthos*, i.e., stories filled with talking animals and personified forces of natures: stories about gods, demi-gods, heroes, the netherworld, the first men, the creation of the cosmos, and so forth. Those kinds of myths are also found within the Platonic dialogues. But they are clearly not just reports on accepted Greek myths. They take up elements of Greek myths, and also foreign myths, and weave them together to create something entirely different.

So, what's going on here? Why did Plato regard myth as necessary for philosophy?

One of the most important texts in Plato's corpus for the question about myth is the *Phaedrus*. The *Phaedrus* is very beautiful. It's Plato's most poetic dialogue, and it contains a number of myths that are really wonderful. At the beginning, it has a little reflection on the nature of myth. Socrates and Phaedrus are outside the walls of Athens, and they find a shaded, sylvan spot near a stream, and Phaedrus asks Socrates if this is the particular place where Boreas bore off a certain young girl—Boreas being a

---

grounds. It doesn't really matter from the point of view of a person who is just interested in wisdom whether Aristotle wrote these or not.

There's a joke that I find very amusing. A classicist rushes into his classroom all excited and announces the most momentous discovery: that Homer was not the author of the *Iliad* and the *Odyssey*, but instead it was a different Greek with the same name.

Of course, it's absurd, because the only thing we know about Homer is that he was named Homer and he wrote the *Iliad* and the *Odyssey*. But the same thing goes for disputing the authenticity of one text or another. If you're a classicist, it is always tempting, or if you've got an ax to grind, and you don't like what this text says, you can always say, "Well, that's not the authentic work." But if you're just interested in pursuing wisdom, it doesn't matter who wrote these things, really. You can say that they were all written by Homer for all the good that it does you. It makes no difference at all.

wind god. Socrates said, "No, that's further down the stream, actually." Then they get talking about myths because, of course, Phaedrus is a product of the sophists. He's educated by them and associates with them. The sophists were, in a sense, an outgrowth of the earliest Greek philosophers, who were known as natural philosophers. Greek natural philosophy really is the beginning of Greek philosophy, and it is the most radically uncompromising in its critique of the mythic self-consciousness. Again, philosophy always begins with an attempt to emancipate thought from myth and opinion. How do you do that? You go back to nature and try to use nature as your guide.

The early Greek natural philosophers were extremely critical of myth. They viewed it as their most serious rival. One of the ways they tried to eliminate their rival was to show that myth was just a primitive form of science and that they were going to replace it with a less primitive form of science, namely natural philosophy, which used reason to explain things in terms of mechanical causes and forces. So they would take up the Greek myths and give them allegorical interpretations as mere fanciful accounts of natural phenomena. They would demythologize the myths, in other words. This demythologizing activity was very popular.

Socrates says that he can appreciate the labors of the demythologizers. They have a huge task on their hands, because they have to do more than explain how some little girl disappeared: If not by the wind god, maybe she was blown over the rock and drowned in the stream below. Maybe that's the natural explanation. But beyond that, they have to deal with the Pegasuses and the Chimeras, the multi-headed Typhon, all the strange monsters of myth, and explain those in naturalistic terms, too.

But Socrates says, "I have no time for this because I'm still trying to know myself. I want to know if I'm a multi-headed Typhonic monster or something altogether more gentle and noble in nature." And the word "gentle" is *atuphos*, the opposite of Typhon. Typhon is the monster from which we get the word *typhoon*, this extravagant, many-headed force of nature.

It's a beautiful little speech. Socrates is indicating that he doesn't have time to demythologize the world because he's more interested in himself than he is in nature. So, what Socratic philosophy represents is a turn from a kind of philosophy that is centered on science and nature—natural philosophy—towards a philosophy that centers itself on man. It's a humanistic turn. The central questions it deals with are questions of man's nature, our place in the world, and what is the good life. Socrates, concerned as he is with the nature of man, finds these myths very useful, and that's why he says he's more interested in finding out if he's a Typhonic, many-headed beast or something of a gentle nature.

By using myths to understand different ways of being human, Socrates is showing the relevance of myth to his humanistic conception of philosophy. Myth is a tool for self-understanding. Scientists have no need for myth. They think they can replace it. But humanists who are trying to understand themselves start having to grapple with the darkness of the soul. It is very dark and hard to understand. And once you start grappling with it, you find that these stories and these images—these wild beasts and so forth—from myth are extremely helpful for understanding our souls. This is the purpose of Platonic mythologizing. So the first argument I want to make is that Plato writes myths because he is a humanist interested in self-knowledge. He's starting with himself and trying to understand his place in the whole. In order to do that, he finds myth is a very helpful thing. Why is myth helpful when you're trying to know yourself?

That brings us to a second topic: Science always understands the universal. There is no such thing as a scientific understanding of a particular thing. If you go to a scientist, say an anthropologist, and say, "Help me to understand myself." The anthropologist can say, "Well, you're a *Homo sapiens sapiens*." And he can tell you of our evolution and our primitive ancestors. But if you say, "No, I want to know about *me*!" He's going to say, "I'm sorry. I don't know anything about *you*! I don't know anything about you as an individual."

And we might send him on to other natural scientists. You can go to somebody who studies anatomy, and he can talk about the general anatomical nature of your body, but, again, you might say, "No, I want to know about *my* body!" And he might say, "Well, I don't know! Go look in the mirror!"

Science doesn't have any understanding of individuality or particularity, for a very good reason: It doesn't have to. It's really interested in understanding general natures. It speaks to the universal. It speaks in terms of species and generalities.

So how do we talk about the individual? What kind of language is necessary to talk about individuals? Plato doesn't think that scientific talk about universals is sufficient for grasping the nature of what's particular or individual. And yet, he's not just interested in the human condition in general. He's also interested in knowledge of the self, of the individual in particular. This is why he needs a different way of speaking than the scientist.

Scientists talk in terms of generalities whereas Plato always talks about individuals and particulars. How do you do that? You tell stories—narratives—and you use language poetically. What is poetic language? Well, all language consists of universal terms, universal categories: trees, plants, flowers. You can talk about a man being tall or short. All of these are general terms. How is it, then, that one can talk about something concrete and particular in general terms?

One uses language poetically. Poets take language and use it to evoke something completely concrete and particular. They tell stories, which is another way of dealing with the concrete and particular. So, Plato writes dialogues that narrate concrete events and give us signs about the nature of the individual characters in them. He couldn't do this if he were writing treatises.

Today's academic philosophy not only dispenses with narratives and characters, it also has no style. Today's journal articles are written to efface the individuality of the writer. Every journal article could be written by pretty much the same person. This is part of the scientific model of academic philosophizing. It is not about you. It's just about the facts. There's nothing creative or artistic about it, and for good reason. No scientist writes about himself when he writes reports. He's talking about nature. If you follow that scientific model, then there is no need to talk about the self.

Plato believes, though, that man is the center of philosophy— and not just man in general, but the many types of men—and not just human types but unique human individuals. Therefore, he has to tell stories that narrate concrete events and give us insight into the characters of particular human beings. So he writes poetically. So he writes myths. Thus the second reason for Platonic myths is simply that the language of myth is the only kind of language that can capture concrete particularity.

There is a third reason Plato uses myths.

The early Greek philosophers had some rather remarkable ambitions. Their assumption was that one could use reason to completely replace opinion, custom, myth—all the pre-scientific, pre-rational ways of understanding the self and the world. Their assumption was, in short, that reason can be autonomous, meaning that it can stand on its own as the sole foundation for thought and action, and it didn't require supplementation by any other external power. And if reason can stand on its own, then each individual can stand on his own by leading a rational life. Reason emancipates us from opinion and tradition, from all kinds of nonsense that's been handed down to us from the past that we accept on trust. Ideas that we accept on the basis of reason are our own. We're no longer living on borrowed ideas.

This conception of philosophy is ultimately based on experience of nature. The early Greek philosophers would observe natural phenomena and then generalize on that basis to draw conclusions. If reason couldn't speak about some things, the Greek natural philosophers were happy to say, "Well, we will just remain silent." And really, if your primary concern is just understanding the cosmos as a scientist, it doesn't matter if you can't talk about the netherworld or demi-gods or heroes. It's not interesting.

Plato and Socrates, however, were primarily concerned with moral philosophy, i.e., with self-knowledge and self-cultivation. It is, of course, possible to give a rational, scientific account of the nature of the soul and what makes it healthy and sick. But what if the care of the soul requires that we speak of other things of which we have no experience, like the first and last things: the origins of the world and the soul and its ultimate destiny? If purely rational philosophy does not allow us to speak of such things, Socrates and Plato thought "so much the worse for philosophy." The limits of natural philosophy and the imperative of the care of the soul license us to look elsewhere, to discourses that have something to say about things that lie outside our experience. In short, we can look back to myth.

However, as philosophers we can't just return to myth in a completely credulous and irresponsible way. We can't forget all that we have learned about reason, intellectual responsibility, clarity and coherence, and so forth. So, there's no going home, in a sense of returning to a completely naïve pre-philosophical state of mind. That's a perennial temptation for people, though. Many people become reflective and intellectual, and it just makes them feel alienated and unhappy. They look around and they see simple, doltish, unquestioning people, and they envy them. "If life could only be that simple!" "Ignorance is bliss." "If only I could be that ignorant again!" Well, there's no going back to that state of ignorance.

However, it is still possible to return to myth with a more critical eye. This is what Plato does. Plato's main critical tool for evaluating myths is his knowledge of the soul: its structure, its function, its healthy order, and its many possible derangements. For Plato, the return to myth is only permissible as a tool of self-knowledge and self-cultivation. Myth has to make us better people. It has to be edifying, not corrupting. This leads to two principles for evaluating myths.

The first and primary principle is that the gods have to be good. Indeed, the whole cosmos has to be good. Now, this pretty much blows away all of Greek myth, which is filled with awful gods.

The second principle is the idea that the afterlife has to be just. The Greeks believed that when we died most of us would just go down to Hades and fade away into nothingness over a very long period of time. The good and the bad alike were thrown together into this great pit. The very, very bad were subjected to certain torments, and the very, very good could become demi-gods. But most of us were treated as all of the same cloth and just tossed into the pit.

Now, this is a ghastly and unjust view of the cosmos, and so at the end of the *Gorgias*, Socrates lays out what is probably his earliest myth about the afterlife. Basically, there are three different categories. There are the Isles of the Blessed, where the good people go, like heaven. All of the bad people go to Tartarus, but there are two kinds of bad people. One kind, the smallest one, are the incorrigibly rotten, and the incorrigibly rotten are simply tormented for all eternity as an example to others, as a deterrent to others. However, the majority of bad people are curably bad, and, therefore, they undergo a kind of purgation in the afterlife. It's a kind of purgatory, and it is hoped that after sufficient chastisement they can eventually go on to the Isles of the Blessed.

This is pretty much Dante's view in the *Divine Comedy*. There's heaven, hell, and purgatory, and all three of those are necessary in order to validate the goodness of the cosmos. Why do we need to believe in heaven, hell, and purgatory to begin with? Because justice doesn't seem to be very well enforced in this life. There are all kinds of scoundrels who prosper, and all kinds of good people who are ground underfoot. If justice is going to triumph, then that means it's going to triumph in the long run. But people die, so there's got to be a run longer than just this life, and so you have to look forward to the next life.[3]

---

[3] Was Socrates influenced by ancient Egyptian myths? I think that's a really interesting issue. I have thought about this a lot, and my view is this: The Egyptians clearly had a scheme of the afterlife that's much more in keeping with the kinds of stories that Socrates tells than the kinds of stories that the other Greeks told. The most commonly painted scene in the Book of the Dead is the weighing of the heart in the afterlife, and if the heart is found wanting, there is a hideous monster waiting near the scales to devour the soul. If the heart is found honest, then it is suitably rewarded. There's a sense that the afterlife is run by stricter rules of justice than this imperfect world, which is very different from the Greek afterlife. The Greeks had a quite bleak and unjust view of the afterlife. It's like some huge, Kafkaesque bureaucracy where everything's arbitrary and completely insane. So, Socrates is much more Egyptian if you will.

Another thing is this: Socrates swears oaths by "the dog, the Egyptians' god," in various places. In the *Gorgias* explicitly he identifies it as the Egyptians' god. Now, the trouble is that the Egyptians didn't treat any dogs as gods, although they did have a jackal-headed god, Anubis, and there were other jackal-headed gods, too. And he does

This is a kind of pragmatic or moral argument for believing in the goodness of the gods and the cosmic order. Socrates is very undogmatic about his conceptions of the afterlife, and, in fact, they change from dialogue to dialogue. In this, it's very clear that Socrates and Plato agree with the basic Greek pragmatism about myth exemplified by their willingness to change their myths from circumstance to circumstance. But they have a higher kind of pragmatism. It's not just political expediency, but the care of the soul that licenses this kind of attitude.

Thus Socrates and Plato take up the inherited body of Greek myth and transform it dramatically. They transform it into morally salutary stories, stories that are good for the care of the soul. Then, depending on the types of souls that they are dealing with — the characters they are talking with in the dialogue — they will change the stories to fit the particular audiences.

The question that one immediately has to raise is: Isn't this sort of cynical? Aren't they just lying? Aren't they just deceiving people? If one holds to a very simple correspondence model of truth, yes, it's deception. If truth is simply "telling it as it is," then clearly they're lying. But I don't believe that Plato holds this model of truth.

If one argues that we have to make statements about things that we don't know anything about for sure, then we really can't have a correspondence model of truth. If you're going to talk about the afterlife, the only way you have of determining the truth or falsehood of your views — the only way of testing it — is to die. That means that on this side, we need other criteria besides the correspondence model of truth.

So, what is that model? It's basically a pragmatic model. The goal is very much the *this-worldly* care of the soul. This licenses a

---

tell Egyptian tales in a number of places. So, it's very clear that Plato and Socrates had a certain respect for the Egyptians. How much they really knew about them is another question. The Atlantis myth was transmitted via the Egyptians. But I think that Socrates is just as willing to be critical and also somewhat cavalier about the transformation of Egyptian stories because, again, although they are better than Greek myths, they are still lacking. The story of Horus and Set and Osiris is just as horrifying as any story of the Greek gods.

somewhat cavalier attitude towards inherited myths, so there's a lot of censorship that goes on, a lot of purgation of the myths of bad elements, and a willingness to change them from context to context, dialogue to dialogue, person to person. But the goal is always the same, namely the care of the soul.

In the *Phaedo*, Socrates, on the day of his death, tells a myth about the underworld that is rather different from the stories you get in the *Republic* or the *Gorgias*. I just want to give you the beginning and the end of the story. I don't want to go through all the descriptions of all the underworld sewers and lakes and streams. Socrates says, "It is right to think then, gentlemen, that if the soul is immortal it requires our care." It's a hypothetical statement.

> If it is immortal it requires our care not only for the time we call our life but for the sake of all time and that one is in terrible danger if one does not give it that care. If death were an escape for everything, it would be a great boon for the wicked to get rid of the body and their wickedness together with their soul, but now that the soul appears to be immortal there is no escape from evil or salvation for it except for becoming as good and wise as possible for the soul goes to the underworld possessing nothing but its education and upbringing which are said to bring the greatest benefit or harm to the dead right at the beginning of the journey yonder [namely at the judgment that you face as soon as you go yonder].[4]

In the *Gorgias*, Socrates uses this phrase "education and upbringing." Polus says, "What, Socrates, are you going to say that even the Great King [namely the Persian emperor, the most powerful man in the world] might not be happy?" He says, "I can't say anything unless I know about his education and upbringing." Polus says, "Why? Does happiness depend entirely on these?" And Socrates says, "Yes. Entirely on these: education and upbringing."

Now, in the *Phaedo*, Socrates tells this long story about the

---

[4] Plato, *Phaedo*, trans. G.M.A. Grube (Indianapolis: Hackett, 1977).

underworld and the various lakes and rivers and punishments of the wicked, what happens to father-beaters and things like that. Then he ends as follows, and it is very telling.

> No sensible man would insist that these things are as I have described them, but I think it is fitting for a man to risk the belief, for the belief is a noble one, that this or something like this is true about our souls and their dwelling places since the soul is evidently immortal and a man should repeat this to himself as if it were an incantation, which is why I've been prolonging my tale. [The word there is *muthon*, tale, myth.] That is the reason that a man should be of good cheer about his own soul if during life he has ignored the pleasures of the body and its ornamentation as of no concern to him and doing him more harm than good but has seriously concerned himself with the pleasures of learning and adorned his soul not with alien but with its own ornaments, namely moderation, righteousness, courage, freedom and truth and in that state awaits his journey to the underworld.

This is very telling. "No sensible man would insist that these things are as I have described them." Well, he's a sensible man, and he recognizes that myths aren't literally true, and they're very easily destroyed if you treat them as literally true. Any sophist or natural philosopher can pick all kinds of holes in them. They can say, "How can there be a first or a second or a third day of Creation because there wouldn't be any days before the Earth is created." You can start picking holes in these stories if you start treating them literally. "No sensible man would insist that these things are as I have described them, but I think it is fitting for a man to risk the belief . . ."

In English, when we put forward a guess, we say "I venture that . . ." "I venture that the soul is immortal." There's a sense of risk here. Why is there a sense of risk? Because we don't know for sure, and therefore there's always going to be a chance that you're wrong. But he says it's worth risking belief that something like this is true. Why? Because it's necessary to risk this belief if one is going to do the best one can in caring for one's soul in this life. So, there's a kind of pragmatism here, a concern with self-cultivation that licenses one to take certain leaps of faith, or risks of belief, even when one recognizes that one can't know for sure that some things are true. But one can risk believing that something *like* this is true, which is a recognition that it's probably not 100% accurate and never could be. It would be foolish to expect that. So, this is the Platonic attitude. It's very pragmatic about standards of truth, and it's very concerned with self-cultivation and self-improvement.

The question is: Does Plato believe it too? Plato has this notion of noble lies. In the *Republic*, he's constantly saying that the guardian class in the republic should be brought up believing certain things that are false. For instance, mating is determined by a lottery when actually it's determined by a eugenics program that the elite are running. So, it's clear that the elite don't believe certain stories that they tell people who are lower on the rung. Is Plato a cynic about these stories of the afterlife or not?

My sense is that no, he's not. These aren't stories that he's telling *other people* because he thinks it will make them better people. These are the kinds of stories that he told *himself*.

Now, many commentators want to say that myths about providence and the afterlife are just noble lies that Plato is telling because he wants to help poor schmucks who can't face the meaninglessness of life to delude themselves into thinking there's a divine plan and that the world is just and nonsense like that. I think that's mistaking Plato for Nietzsche, and that's a big mistake to make. In fact, it's far harder to believe that Plato was as cynical as someone like Nietzsche about the order of the cosmos. It's far harder to believe that, than it is to believe that he could believe these stories.

The arguments that many people make to the effect that Plato couldn't have believed his myths are premised on the assumption that no serious person, no real philosopher, could hold these views. But the history of philosophy is replete with examples of very serious philosophers who have held views just like this. Now, I guess one could say they couldn't have been serious either, if you really want to stick with this view.

If you look at the history of philosophy you find that people like Pascal or Kant or Rousseau or William James have all held similar positions. James' essay "The Will to Believe" is the most clear and lucid account, I think, of this basic position in the history of thought. But I think Plato is really the first pragmatist in James' sense, the first person who argues that we should risk believing things about matters that we don't know, if we find that the moral necessities of life—the necessities of self-cultivation—demand that we form beliefs about things that we cannot know.

Just to sum up: There are three basic reasons for why the Platonic dialogues are myths and contain myths. They are myths in the broad sense and they contain myths in the more specific sense.

The first reason is the images of myths are useful for self-understanding.

Second, the language of myth—the use of narrative and poetic language to evoke concrete particularity—is useful if one regards the goal of philosophy as self-understanding and self-actualization.

Third, myth is necessary to philosophy once philosophy recognizes, on the one hand, the limits of reason in dealing with ultimate things and, on the other hand, the absolute moral necessity of having some views or beliefs about the ultimate things. If you must have some beliefs about ultimate things, you need to go to myths. But an intellectually responsible turn to myth subjects them to the good. The gods and the afterlife must be good, if belief in them is to make us good. Thus Socrates and Plato both take up the inherited myths of Greece and other cultures and transform them in dramatic ways.

*Counter-Currents*, October 23, 2010

# INTRODUCTION TO ARISTOTLE'S *POLITICS*\*

## PART I: THE AIM & ELEMENTS OF POLITICS

### 1. THE NECESSITY OF POLITICS

Aristotle is famous for holding that man is by nature a political animal. But what does this mean? Aristotle explains that,

> even when human beings are not in need of each other's help, they have no less desire to live together, though it is also true that the common advantage draws them into union insofar as noble living is something they each partake of. So this above all is the end, whether for everyone in common or for each singly. (*Politics* 3.6, 1278b19–22)[1]

Here Aristotle contrasts two different needs of the human soul that give rise to different forms of community, one pre-political and the other political.

The first need is material. On this account, men form communities to secure the necessities of life. Because few are capable of fulfilling all their needs alone, material self-interest forces them to co-operate, each developing his particular talents and

---

\* Revised from an earlier version published in *Liberty and Democracy*, edited by Tibor R. Machan, with the permission of the publisher, Hoover Institution Press. Copyright © 2002 by the Board of Trustees of the Leland Stanford Junior University.

[1] All quotes from Aristotle are from *The Politics of Aristotle*, trans. and ed. Peter L. Phillips Simpson (Chapel Hill: University of North Carolina Press, 1997). Simpson's edition has two unique features. First, *The Politics* is introduced by a translation of *Nicomachean Ethics* 10.9. Second, Simpson moves books 7 and 8 of *The Politics*, positioning them between the traditional books 3 and 4. I retain the traditional ordering, indicating Simpson's renumbering parenthetically. Unless otherwise noted, all quotes are from *The Politics*. Quotes from the *Nicomachean Ethics* will be indicated as such.

trading his products with others. The classical example of such a community is the "city of pigs" in the second book of Plato's *Republic*.

The second need is spiritual. Even in the absence of material need, human beings will form communities because only through community can man satisfy his spiritual need to live nobly, i.e., to achieve *eudaimonia*, happiness or well-being, which Aristotle defines as a life of unimpeded virtuous activity.

Aristotle holds that the forms of association that arise from material needs are *pre-political*. These include the family, the master-slave relationship, the village, the market, and alliances for mutual defense. With the exception of the master-slave relationship, the pre-political realm could be organized on purely libertarian, capitalist principles. Individual rights and private property could allow individuals to associate and disassociate freely by means of persuasion and trade, according to their own determination of their interests.

But in *Politics* 3.9, Aristotle denies that the realm of material needs, whether organized on libertarian or non-libertarian lines, could ever fully satisfy man's spiritual need for happiness: "It is not the case . . . that people come together for the sake of life alone, but rather for the sake of living well" (1280a31), and "the political community must be set down as existing for the sake of noble deeds and not merely for living together" (1281a2). Aristotle's clearest repudiation of any minimalistic form of liberalism is the following passage:

> Nor do people come together for the sake of an alliance to prevent themselves from being wronged by anyone, nor again for purposes of mutual exchange and mutual utility. Otherwise the Etruscans and Carthaginians and all those who have treaties with each other would be citizens of one city. . . . [But they are not] concerned about what each other's character should be, not even with the aim of preventing anyone subject to the agreements from becoming unjust or acquiring a single depraved habit. They are concerned only that they should not do any wrong to each other. But all those who are concerned about a good state

of law concentrate their attention on political virtue and vice, from which it is manifest that the city truly and not verbally so called must make virtue its care. (1280a34–b7)

Aristotle does not disdain mutual exchange and mutual protection. But he thinks that the state must do more. It must concern itself with the character of the citizen; it must encourage virtue and discourage vice.

But why does Aristotle think that the pursuit of virtue is political at all, much less the defining characteristic of the political? Why does he reject the liberal principle that whether and how men pursue virtue is ultimately a private matter? The ultimate anthropological foundation of Aristotelian political science is man's neoteny. Many animals can fend for themselves as soon as they are born. But man is born radically immature and incapable of living on his own. We need many years of care and education. Nature does not give us the ability to survive, much less flourish. But she gives us the ability to acquire the ability. Skills are acquired abilities to live. Virtue is the acquired ability to live well. The best way to acquire virtue is not through trial and error, but through education, which allows us to benefit from the trials and avoid the errors of others. Fortune permitting, if we act virtuously, we will live well.

Liberals often claim that freedom of choice is a necessary condition of virtue. We can receive no moral credit for a virtue that is not freely chosen but is instead forced upon us. Aristotle, however, holds that force is a necessary condition of virtue. Aristotle may have defined man as the rational animal, but unlike the sophists of his day he did not think that rational persuasion is sufficient to instill virtue:

> . . . if reasoned words were sufficient by themselves to make us decent, they would, to follow a remark of Theognis, justly carry off many and great rewards, and the thing to do would be to provide them. But, as it is, words seem to have the strength to incite and urge on those of the young who are generous and to get a well-bred character and one truly in love with the noble to be possessed by

virtue; but they appear incapable of inciting the many toward becoming gentlemen. For the many naturally obey the rule of fear, not of shame, and shun what is base not because it is ugly but because it is punished. Living by passion as they do, they pursue their own pleasures and whatever will bring these pleasures about . . . ; but of the noble and truly pleasant they do not even have the notion, since they have never tasted it. How could reasoned words reform such people? For it is not possible, or easy, to replace by reason what has long since become fixed in the character. (*Nicomachean Ethics*, 10.9, 1179b4–18)

The defect of reason can, however, be corrected by force: "Reason and teaching by no means prevail in everyone's case; instead, there is need that the hearer's soul, like earth about to nourish the seed, be worked over in its habits beforehand so as to enjoy and hate in a noble way. . . . Passion, as a general rule, does not seem to yield to reason but to force" (*Nicomachean Ethics*, 10.9, 1179b23–25). The behavioral substratum of virtue is habit, and habits can be inculcated by force. Aristotle describes law as "reasoned speech that proceeds from prudence and intellect" but yet "has force behind it" (*Nicomachean Ethics*, 10.9, 1180a18). Therefore, the compulsion of the appropriate laws is a great aid in acquiring virtue.

At this point, however, one might object that Aristotle has established only a case for parental, not political, force in moral education. Aristotle admits that only in Sparta and a few other cities is there public education in morals, while "In most cities these matters are neglected, and each lives as he wishes, giving sacred law, in Cyclops' fashion, to his wife and children" (*Nicomachean Ethics*, 10.9, 1180a24–27). Aristotle grants that an education adapted to an individual is better than an education given to a group (*Nicomachean Ethics*, 10.9, 1180b7). But this is an argument against the collective reception of education, not the collective provision. He then argues that such an education is best left to experts, not parents. Just as parents have professional doctors care for their children's bodies, they should have professional educators care for their souls (*Nicomachean Ethics*, 10.9,

1180b14–23). But this does not establish that the professionals should be employees of the state.

Two additional arguments for public education are found in *Politics* 8.1:

> [1] Since the whole city has one end, it is manifest that everyone must also have one and the same education and that taking care of this education must be a common matter. It must not be private in the way that it is now, when everyone takes care of their own children privately and teaches them whatever private learning they think best. Of common things, the training must be common. [2] At the same time, no citizen should even think he belongs to himself but instead that each belongs to the city, for each is part of the city. The care of each part, however, naturally looks to the care of the whole, and to this extent praise might be due to the Spartans, for they devote the most serious attention to their children and do so in common. (*Politics*, 8.1 [5.1], 1337a21–32)

The second argument is both weak and question-begging. Although it may be useful for citizens to "think" that they belong to the city, not themselves, Aristotle offers no reason to think that this is true. Furthermore, the citizens would not think so unless they received precisely the collective education that needs to be established. The first argument, however, is quite strong. If the single, overriding aim of political life is the happiness of the citizens, and if this aim is best attained by public education, then no regime can be legitimate if it fails to provide public education.[2]

Another argument for public moral education can be constructed from the overall argument of the *Politics*. Since public education is more widely distributed than private education, other things being equal, the populace will become more virtuous on the whole. As we shall see, it is widespread virtue that

---

[2] A useful commentary on these and other Aristotelian arguments for public education is Randall R. Curren, *Aristotle on the Necessity of Public Education* (Lanham, Maryland: Rowman and Littlefield, 2000).

makes popular government possible. Popular government is, moreover, one of the bulwarks of popular liberty. Compulsory public education in virtue, therefore, is a bulwark of liberty.

## 2. POLITICS & FREEDOM

Aristotle's emphasis on compulsory moral education puts him in the "positive" libertarian camp. For Aristotle, a free man is not merely any man who lives in a free society. A free man possesses certain traits of character that allow him to govern himself responsibly and attain happiness. These traits are, however, the product of a long process of compulsory tutelage. But such compulsion can be justified only by the production of a free and happy individual, and its scope is therefore limited by this goal.

Since Aristotle ultimately accepted the Socratic principle that all men desire happiness, education merely compels us to do what we really want. It frees us *from* our own ignorance, folly, and irrationality and frees us *for* our own self-actualization. This may be the rationale for Aristotle's claim that, "the law's laying down of what is decent is not oppressive" (*Nicomachean Ethics*, 10.9, 1180a24).

Since Aristotle thinks that freedom from the internal compulsion of the passions is more important than freedom from the external compulsion of force, and that force can quell the passions and establish virtue's empire over them, Aristotle as much as Rousseau believes that we can be forced to be free.

But throughout the *Politics*, Aristotle shows that he is concerned to protect "negative" liberty as well. In *Politics* 2.2-5, Aristotle ingeniously defends private families, private property, and private enterprise from Plato's communistic proposals in the *Republic*, thereby preserving the freedom of large spheres of human activity.

Aristotle's concern with privacy is evident in his criticism of a proposal of Hippodamus of Miletus that would encourage spies and informers (2.8, 1268b22).

Aristotle is concerned to create a regime in which the rich do not enslave the poor and the poor do not plunder the rich (3.10, 1281a13-27).

Second Amendment enthusiasts will be gratified at Aristotle's emphasis on the importance of a wide distribution of arms in maintaining the freedom of the populace (2.8, 1268a16-24; 3.17, 1288a12-14; 4.3 [6.3], 1289b27-40; 4.13 [6.13], 1297a12-27; 7.11 [4.11], 1330b17-20).

War and empire are great enemies of liberty, so isolationists and peace lovers will be gratified by Aristotle's critique of warlike regimes and praise of peace. The good life requires peace and leisure. War is not an end in itself, but merely a means to ensure peace (7.14 [4.14], 1334a2-10; 2.9, 1271a41-b9).

The best regime is not oriented outward, toward dominating other peoples, but inward, towards the happiness of its own. The best regime is an earthly analogue of the Prime Mover. It is self-sufficient and turned inward upon itself (7.3 [4.3], 1325a14-31). Granted, Aristotle may not think that negative liberty is the whole of the good life, but it is an important component that needs to be safeguarded.[3]

### 3. THE ELEMENTS OF POLITICS & THE MIXED REGIME

Since the aim of political association is the good life, the best political regime is the one that best delivers the good life. Delivering the good life can be broken down into two components: production and distribution. There are two basic kinds of goods: the goods of the body and the goods of the soul.[4] Both sorts of goods can be produced and distributed privately and publicly, but Aristotle treats the production and distribution of bodily goods as primarily private whereas he treats the production and distribution of spiritual goods as primarily public. The primary goods of the soul are *moral and intellectual virtue*, which are best produced by public education, and *honor*, the public recognition of virtue, talent, and service rendered to the city.[5] The principle

---

[3] For a fuller discussion of the value Aristotle puts on liberty, see Roderick T. Long, "Aristotle's Conception of Freedom," *The Review of Metaphysics* 49, no. 4 (June 1996), pp. 787-802.

[4] One could add a third category of instrumental goods, but these goods are instrumental to the intrinsic goods of the body, the soul, or both, and thus could be classified under those headings.

[5] As for the highest good of the soul, which is attained by philoso-

of distributive justice is defined as proportionate equality: equally worthy people should be equally happy and unequally worthy people should be unequally happy, commensurate with their unequal worth (*Nicomachean Ethics*, 5.6–7). The best regime, in short, combines happiness and justice.

But how is the best regime to be organized? Aristotle builds his account from at least three sets of elements.

First, in *Politics* 3.6–7, Aristotle observes that sovereignty can rest either with men or with laws. If with men, then it can rest in one man, few men, or many men. (Aristotle treats it as self-evident that it cannot rest in all men.) The rulers can exercise political power for two different ends: for the common good and for special interests. One pursues the common good by promoting the just happiness of all. What makes a regime lawful is aiming at the common good. What makes a regime unlawful is using the state to promote private interests at the expense of the common good.

When a single man rules for the common good, we have kingship. When he rules for his own good, we have tyranny. When the few rule for the common good, we have aristocracy. When they rule for their factional interest, we have oligarchy. When the many rule for the common good, we have polity. When they rule for their factional interest, we have democracy. These six regimes can exist in pure forms, or they can be mixed together.

Second, Aristotle treats social classes as elemental political distinctions. In *Politics* 3.8 he refines his definitions of oligarchy

---

phy, Aristotle's flight from Athens near the end of his life shows that he recognized that different political orders can be more or less open to free thought, but I suspect that he was realist enough (and Platonist enough) to recognize that even the best cities are unlikely to positively cultivate true freedom to philosophize. I would wager that Aristotle would be both surprised at the freedom of thought in the United States and receptive to Tocquevillian complaints about the American tendency toward conformism that makes such freedom unthreatening to the reigning climate of opinion. A cynic might argue that if Americans actually made use of their freedom of thought, it would be quickly taken away.

and democracy, claiming that oligarchy is actually the rule by the rich, whether they are few or many, and democracy is rule by the poor, whether they are few or many. Similarly, in *Politics* 4.11 (6.1) Aristotle also defines polity as rule by the middle class. In *Politics* 4.4 (6.4), Aristotle argues that social classes are irreducible political distinctions. One can be a rich, poor, or middle-class juror, legislator, or office-holder. One can be a rich, poor, or middle-class farmer or merchant. But one cannot be both rich and poor at the same time (1291b2–13). Class distinctions cannot be eliminated; therefore, they have to be recognized and respected, their disadvantages meliorated and their advantages harnessed for the common good.

Third, in *Politics* 4.14 (6.14), Aristotle divides the activities of rulership into three different functions: legislative, judicial, and executive.[6]

Because rulership can be functionally divided, it is possible to create a mixed regime by assigning different functions to different parts of the populace. One could, for instance, mix monarchy and elite rule by assigning supreme executive office to a single man and the legislative and judicial functions to the few. Or one could divide the legislative function into different houses, assigning one to the few and another to the many. Aristotle suggests giving the few the power to legislate and the many the power to veto legislation. He suggests that officers be elected by the many, but nominated from the few. The few should make expenditures, but the many should audit them (2.12, 1274a15–21; 3.11, 1281b21–33; 4.14 [6.14], 1298b26–40).

In *Politics* 3.10, Aristotle argues that some sort of mixed regime is preferable, since no pure regime is satisfactory: "A difficulty arises as to what should be the controlling part of the city, for it is really either the multitude or the rich or the decent or the best one of all or a tyrant? But all of them appear unsatisfactory" (1281a11–13). Democracy is bad because the poor unjustly plun-

---

[6] On the complexities of the executive role in the *Politics*, see Harvey C. Mansfield, Jr., *Taming the Prince: The Ambivalence of Modern Executive Power* (Baltimore: The Johns Hopkins University Press, 1993), chs. 2–3.

der the rich; oligarchy is bad because the rich oppress and exploit the poor; tyranny is bad because the tyrant does injustice to everyone (1281a13–28). Kingship and aristocracy are unsatisfactory because they leave the many without honors and are schools for snobbery and high-handedness (1281a28–33; 4.11 [6.11], 1295b13ff). A pure polity might be unsatisfactory because it lacks a trained leadership caste and is therefore liable to make poor decisions (3.11, 1281b21–33).

## 4. Checks & Balances, Political Rule, & the Rule of Law

Aristotle's mixed regime is the origin of the idea of the separation of powers and "checks and balances." It goes hand in hand with a very modern political realism. Aristotle claims that, "all regimes that look to the common advantage turn out, according to what is simply just, to be correct ones, while those that look only to the advantage of their rulers are mistaken and are all deviations from the correct regime. For they are despotic, but the city is a community of the free" (3.6, 1279a17–21).

It is odd, then, that in *Politics* 4.8–9 (6.8–9) Aristotle describes the best regime as a mixture of two defective regimes, oligarchy and democracy—not of two correct regimes, aristocracy and polity. But perhaps Aristotle entertained the possibility of composing a regime that tends to the common good out of classes that pursue their own factional interests.

Perhaps Aristotle thought that the "intention" to pursue the common good can repose not in the minds of individual men, but in the institutional logic of the regime itself. This would be an enormous advantage, for it would bring about the common good without having to rely entirely upon men of virtue and good will, who are in far shorter supply than men who pursue their own individual and factional advantages.

Related to the mixed regime with its checks and balances is the notion of "political rule." Political rule consists of ruling and being ruled in turn:

> ... there is a sort of rule exercised over those who are similar in birth and free. This rule we call political rule, and the ruler must learn it by being ruled, just as one learns to be a

cavalry commander by serving under a cavalry commander . . . Hence it was nobly said that one cannot rule well without having been ruled. And while virtue in these two cases is different, the good citizen must learn and be able both to be ruled and to rule. This is in fact the virtue of the citizen, to know rule over the free from both sides. (3.4, 1277b7–15; cf. 1.13, 1259b31–34 and 2.2, 1261a32–b3)

Aristotle makes it clear that political rule can exist only where the populace consists of men who are free, i.e., sufficiently virtuous that they can rule themselves. They must also be economically middle-class, well-armed, and warlike. They must, in short, be the sort of men who can participate responsibly in government, who want to participate, and who cannot safely be excluded. A populace that is slavish, vice-ridden, poor, and unarmed can easily be disenfranchised and exploited. If power were entirely in the hands of a free populace, the regime would be a pure polity, and political rule would exist entirely between equals. If, however, a free populace were to take part in a mixed regime, then political rule would exist between different parts of the regime. The many and the few would divide power and functions between them. Not only would members of each class take turns performing the different functions allotted to them, the classes themselves would rule over others in one respect and be ruled in another. In these circumstances, then, checks and balances are merely one form of political rule.

In *Politics* 3.16, Aristotle connects political rule to the rule of law:

> What is just is that people exercise rule no more than they are subject to it and that therefore they rule by turns. But this is already law, for the arrangement is law. Therefore, it is preferable that law rule rather than any one of the citizens. And even if, to pursue the same argument, it were better that there be some persons exercising rule, their appointment should be as guardians and servants of the laws. For though there must be some offices, that there should be this one person exercising rule is, they say, not

just, at least when all are similar. (1287a15-22)

Aristotle's point is simple. If two men govern by turns, then sovereignty does not ultimately repose in either of them, but in the rule that they govern by turns. The same can be said of checks and balances. If the few spend money and the many audit the accounts, then neither group is sovereign, the laws are. If sovereignty reposes in laws, not men, the common good is safe. As Aristotle points out, "anyone who bids the laws to rule seems to bid god and intellect alone to rule, but anyone who bids a human being to rule adds on also the wild beast. For desire is such a beast and spiritedness perverts rulers even when they are the best of men. Hence law is intellect without appetite" (1287a23-31). The greatest enemy of the common good is private interest. The laws, however, have no private interests. Thus if our laws are conducive to the common good, we need not depend entirely on the virtue and public-spiritedness of men.

Aristotle would, however, hasten to add that no regime can do without these characteristics entirely, for the laws cannot apply themselves. They must be applied by men, and their application will seldom be better than the men who apply them. Furthermore, even though a regime may function without entirely virtuous citizens, no legitimate regime can be indifferent to the virtue of the citizens, for the whole purpose of political association is to instill the virtues necessary for happiness.

## Part II: In Defense of Popular Government

### 5. The Good Man & the Good Citizen

Having now surveyed Aristotle's thoughts on the elements and proper aim of politics, we can now examine his arguments for popular government. When I use the phrase "popular government," it should be borne in mind that Aristotle does not advocate a pure polity, but a mixed regime with a popular element.

Aristotle's first case for bringing the many into government can be discerned in *Politics* 3.4. Aristotle's question is whether the virtues of the good man and the good citizen are the same.

They are not the same, insofar as the virtue of the good citizen is defined relative to the regime, and there are many different regimes, while the virtue of the good man is defined relative to human nature, which is one. One can therefore be a good citizen but not a good man, and a good man but not a good citizen. History is replete with examples of regimes that punish men for their virtues and reward them for their vices. Aristotle does, however, allow that the good man and the good citizen can be one in a regime in which the virtues required of a good citizen do not differ from the virtues of a good man.

The chief virtue of a good man is prudence. But prudence is not required of a citizen insofar as he is ruled. Only obedience is required. Prudence is, however, required of a citizen insofar as he rules. Since the best regime best encourages happiness by best cultivating virtue, a regime that allows the many to govern along with the few is better than a regime that excludes them. By including the many in ruling, a popular regime encourages the widest cultivation of prudence and gives the greatest opportunity for its exercise. The best way to bring the many into the regime is what Aristotle calls political rule: ruling and being ruled in turn, as prescribed by law.

As we have seen above, in the passage from *Politics* 3.4 quoted on pages 51–52, Aristotle argues that political rule not only teaches the virtue of prudence to the many, it teaches the virtue of being ruled to the few, who must give way in turn to the many. Since the few aspire to rule but not be ruled, Aristotle argues that they cannot rule without first having been ruled.

Aristotle names justice as a virtue that is learned both in ruling and being ruled. Those born to wealth and power are liable to arrogance and the love of command. By subjecting them to the rule of others, including their social inferiors, they learn to respect their freedom and justly appraise their worth.

### 6. POTLUCKS, CHIMERAS, & JURIES

Aristotle's next case for bringing the many into the regime is found in *Politics* 3.11.[7] Aristotle seeks to rebut the aristocratic

---

[7] For useful discussions of the arguments of *Politics* 3.11, see Mary P.

argument against popular participation, namely that the best political decisions are wise ones, but wisdom is found only among the few, not the many. Popular participation, therefore, would inevitably dilute the quality of the political decision-makers, increasing the number of foolish decisions.

Aristotle accepts the premise that the wise should rule, but he argues that there are circumstances in which the few and the many together are wiser than the few on their own. The aristocratic principle, therefore, demands the participation of the many:

> ... the many, each of whom is not a serious man, nevertheless could, when they have come together, be better than those few best—not, indeed, individually but as a whole, just as meals furnished collectively are better than meals furnished at one person's expense. For each of them, though many, could have a part of virtue and prudence, and just as they could, when joined together in a multitude, become one human being with many feet, hands, and senses, so also could they become one in character and thought. That is why the many are better judges of the works of music and the poets, for one of them judges one part and another another and all of them the whole. (1281a42–b10)

At first glance, this argument seems preposterous. History and everyday life are filled with examples of wise individuals opposing foolish collectives. But Aristotle does not claim that the many are *always* wiser than the few, simply that they *can be* under certain conditions (1281b15).

The analogy of the potluck supper is instructive (cf. 3.15, 1286a28–30).[8] A potluck supper can be better than one provided

---

Nichols, *Citizens and Statesmen: A Study of Aristotle's Politics* (Lanham, Maryland: Rowman and Littlefield, 1992), pp. 66–71, and Peter L. Phillips Simpson, *A Philosophical Commentary on the Politics of Aristotle* (Chapel Hill: University of North Carolina Press, 1998), pp. 166–71.

[8] On the potluck supper analogy, see Arlene W. Saxonhouse, *Fear*

by a single person if it offers a greater number and variety of dishes and diffuses costs and labor. But potluck suppers are not always superior — that is the "luck" in it. Potlucks are often imbalanced. On one occasion, there may be too many desserts and no salads. On another, three people may bring chicken and no one brings beef or pork. The best potluck, therefore, is a centrally orchestrated one that mobilizes the resources of many different contributors but ensures a balanced and wholesome meal.

Likewise, the best way to include the many in political decision-making is to orchestrate their participation, giving them a delimited role that maximizes their virtues and minimizes their vices. This cannot be accomplished in a purely popular regime, particularly a lawless one, but it can be accomplished in a mixed regime in which the participation of the populace is circumscribed by law and checked by the interests of other elements of the population.

Aristotle's second analogy — which likens the intellectual and moral unity of the many to a man with many feet, hands, and sense organs, i.e., a freak of nature — does not exactly assuage doubters. But his point is valid. While even the best of men may lack a particular virtue, it is unlikely that it will be entirely absent from a large throng. Therefore, the many are potentially as virtuous or even more virtuous than the few if their scattered virtues can be gathered together and put to work.

But history records many examples of groups acting less morally than any member on his own. Thus the potential moral superiority of the many is unlikely to emerge in a lawless democracy. But it could emerge in a lawful mixed regime, which actively encourages and employs the virtues of the many while checking their vices.

This process can be illustrated by adapting an analogy that Aristotle offers to illustrate another point: A painting of a man can be more beautiful than any real man, for the painter can pick out the best features of individual men and combine them into a beautiful whole (3.11, 1281b10-11).

---

*of Diversity: The Birth of Political Science in Ancient Greek Thought* (Chicago: University of Chicago Press, 1992), pp. 222-24.

Aristotle illustrates the potential superiority of collective judgment with another questionable assertion, that "the many are better judges of the works of music and the poets, for one of them judges one part and another another and all of them the whole." Again, this seems preposterous. Good taste, like wisdom, is not widely distributed and is cultivated by the few, not the many. Far more people buy rap recordings than classical ones. But Aristotle is not claiming that the many are better judges in all cases. Aristotle is likely referring to Greek dramatic competitions. These competitions were juried by the audience, not a small number of connoisseurs.

A jury trial or competition is a genuine collective decision-making process in which each juror is morally enjoined to pay close attention the matter at hand and to render an objective judgment.[9] Although each juror has his own partial impression, when jurors deliberate they can add their partial impressions together to arrive at a more complete and adequate account. To the extent that a jury decision must approach unanimity, the jurors will be motivated to examine the issue from all sides and persuade one another to move toward a rationally motivated consensus. A jury decision can, therefore, be more rational, well-informed, and objective than an individual one.[10]

The market, by contrast, is not a collective decision-making process. It does not require a consumer to compare his preferences to those of others, to persuade others of their validity or defend them from criticism, or to arrive at any sort of consensus. Instead, the market merely registers the collective effects of individual decisions.[11]

---

[9] I wish to thank M.L.C. for suggesting the model of a jury trial.

[10] For a beautiful description of the deliberative process of a jury, see John C. Calhoun, *A Disquisition on Government*, in *Union and Liberty: The Political Philosophy of John C. Calhoun*, ed. Ross M. Lence (Indianapolis: Liberty Fund, 1992), pp. 49–50.

[11] Friedrich A. Hayek's classic essay "The Use of Knowledge in Society," in his *Individualism and Economic Order* (Chicago: University of Chicago Press, 1948), argues that the market is superior to central planning because it better mobilizes widely scattered information. The market is, of course, larger than any possible jury and thus will always

## 7. Freedom & Stability

Another argument for popular government in *Politics* 3.11 (1281b21–33) is that it is more stable. Aristotle grants the Aristocratic principle that it is not safe for the populace to share in "the greatest offices" because, "on account of their injustice and unwisdom, they would do wrong in some things and go wrong in others." But then he goes on to argue that it would not be safe to exclude the many from rule altogether, since a city "that has many in it who lack honor and are poor must of necessity be full of enemies," which would be a source of instability. Instability is, however, inconsistent with the proper aim of politics, for the good life requires peace. The solution is a mixed regime that ensures peace and stability by allowing the many to participate in government, but not to occupy the highest offices. In *Politics* 2.9, Aristotle praises the Spartan Ephorate for holding the regime together, "since, as the populace share in the greatest office, it keeps them quiet. . . . For if any regime is going to survive, all the parts of the city must want it both to exist and to remain as it is" (1270b17–22; cf. Aristotle's discussion of the Carthaginians in 2.9, 1272b29–32; see also 4.13 [6.13], 1297b6).

In *Politics* 2.12, Aristotle offers another reason for including the populace in government. Solon gave the populace, "the power that was most necessary (electing to office and auditing the accounts), since without it they would have been enslaved

---

command more information.

However, if one were to compare a market and a jury of the same size, the jury would clearly be a more rational decision-making process, for the market registers decisions based on perspectives that are in principle entirely solipsistic, whereas the jury requires a genuine dialogue that challenges all participants to transcend their partial and subjective perspectives and work toward a rational consensus that is more objective than any individual judgment because it more adequately accounts for the phenomena in question.

This crucial disanalogy counts against attempts to justify the market in terms of Gadamerian, Popperian, or Habermasian models and communicative rationality. For the best statement of this sort of approach, see G. B. Madison, *The Political Economy of Civil Society and Human Rights* (New York: Routledge, 1998), esp. chs. 3–5.

and hostile" (1274a4–6). Here Aristotle makes it clear that he values liberty, and he values popular government because it protects the liberty of the many.

## 8. Expert Knowledge

In *Politics* 3.11 Aristotle rebuts the argument that the many should not be involved in politics because they are amateurs, and decisions in politics, as in medicine and other fields, should be left to experts. In response to this, Aristotle repeats his argument that the many, taken together, may be better judges than a few experts. He then adds that there are some arts in which the products can be appreciated by people who do not possess the art: "Appreciating a house, for example, does not just belong to the builder; the one who uses it, namely the household manager, will pass an even better judgment on it. Likewise, the pilot judges the rudder better than the carpenter and the dinner guest judges the feast better than the chef" (1282a19–22). If the art of statesmanship is like these, then the best judge of the quality of a statesman is not the few political experts, but the many political laymen who are ruled by him. The judgment of the populace should not, therefore, be disdained.

## 9. Resistance to Corruption

In *Politics* 3.15 Aristotle argues that popular regimes are more resistant to corruption. Even in a regime in which law ultimately rules, there are particular circumstances that the laws do not anticipate. Where the law cannot decide, men must do so. But this creates an opportunity for corruption. Aristotle argues that such decisions are better made by large bodies deliberating in public: "What is many is more incorruptible: the multitude, like a greater quantity of water, is harder to ruin than a few. A single person's judgment must necessarily be corrupted when he is overcome by anger or some other such passion, but getting everyone in the other case to become angry and go wrong at the same time takes a lot of doing. Let the multitude in question, however, be the free who are acting in no way against law, except where law is necessarily deficient" (1286a33–38). Aristotle's argument that the many may collectively possess fewer vices than the few is merely a mirror image of his earlier collective virtue argument. Here, as elsewhere, Aristotle defends popular government only under delimited circumstances. The populace must be free, not slavish, and they must decide only when the laws cannot.

## 10. Delegation & Diffusion of Power

*Politics* 3.16 is devoted to arguments against total kingship. One of these arguments can be turned into a case for popular government. Aristotle claims that total kingship is unsustainable: "It is not easy for one person to oversee many things, so there will need to be many officials appointed in subordination to him. Consequently, what is the difference between having them there right from the start and having one man in this way appoint them? ... if a man who is serious is justly ruler because he is better, then two good men are better than one" (1287b8–12, cf. 1287b25–29).

Since total kingship is unworkable, kings must necessarily appoint other superior men as "peers" to help them. But if total kingship must create an aristocracy, then why not have aristocracy from the start?

This argument could, however, be pushed further to make a case for popular government. An aristocracy cannot effectively rule the people without the active participation of some and the passive acquiescence of the rest. As we have seen above, Aristotle argues that the best way to bring this about is popular government. But if aristocracy must eventually bring the populace into the regime, then why not include them from the very beginning?

## 11. When Regimes Fail

In *Politics* 4.2 (6.2), Aristotle returns to his list of pure regime types. The three just regimes are kingship, aristocracy, and polity; the three unjust ones are tyranny, oligarchy, and democracy. Aristotle proceeds to rank the three just regimes in terms of the kinds of virtues they require. Thus Aristotle identifies kingship and aristocracy as the best regimes because they are both founded on "fully equipped virtue" (1289a31). Of the two, kingship is the very best, for it depends upon a virtue so superlative that it is possessed by only one man. Aristocracy is less exalted because it presupposes somewhat more broadly distributed and therefore less exalted virtue. Polity depends upon even more widespread and modest virtue. Furthermore, the populace, unlike kings and aristocrats, lacks the full complement of material equipment necessary to fully exercise such virtues as magnificence.

By this ranking, polity is not the best regime, but the least of the good ones. But Aristotle then offers a new, politically realistic standard for ranking the just regimes that reverses their order. Kingship may be the best regime from a morally idealistic perspective, but when it degenerates it turns into tyranny, which is the worst regime. Aristocracy may be the second-best regime from a morally idealistic perspective, but when it degenerates it turns into oligarchy, which is the second worst regime. Polity may be the third choice of the moral idealist, but when it degenerates, it merely becomes democracy, which is the best of a bad lot.

Since degeneration is inevitable, the political realist ranks regimes not only in terms of their best performances, but also in terms of their worst. By this standard, polity is the best of the good regimes and kingship the worst. Kingship is best under ideal conditions, polity under real conditions. Kingship is a sleek Jaguar, polity a dowdy Volvo. On the road, the Jaguar is clearly better. But when they go in the ditch, the Volvo shows itself to be the better car overall.

## 12. THE MIDDLE-CLASS REGIME

Aristotle displays the same political realism in his praise of the middle-class regime in *Politics* 4.11 (6.11): "If we judge neither by a virtue that is beyond the reach of private individuals, nor by an education requiring a nature and equipment dependent on chance, nor again a regime that is as one would pray for, but by a way of life that most can share in common together and by a regime that most cities can participate in . . . ," then a large, politically enfranchised middle class has much to recommend it: "In the case of political community . . . the one that is based on those in the middle is best, and . . . cities capable of being well governed are those sorts where the middle is large . . ." (1295b35–36).

Since the middle class is the wealthier stratum of the common people, Aristotle's arguments for middle-class government are *ipso facto* arguments for popular government. Aristotle makes it clear from the beginning, however, that he is not talking about a purely popular regime, but a mixed one compounded out of a middle-class populace and elements of aristocracy (1295a30–34).

Aristotle's first argument for the middle regime seems a sophistry: "If it was nobly said in the *Ethics* that the happy way of life is unimpeded life in accordance with virtue and that virtue is a mean, then necessarily the middle way of life, the life of a mean that everyone can attain, must be best. The same definitions must hold also for the virtue and vice of city and regime, since the regime is a certain way of life of a city" (1295a35–40).

In the *Nicomachean Ethics*, Aristotle makes it clear that the fact that virtue can be understood as a mean between two vices, one of excess and the other of defect, does not imply either that virtue is merely an arithmetic mean (*Nicomachean Ethics*, 2.2, 1106a26–b8), or that virtue is to be regarded as mediocrity, not as superlative (*Nicomachean Ethics*, 2.2, 1107a9–27). Here, however, Aristotle describes the mean not as a superlative, but as a mediocrity "that everyone can attain." This conclusion follows only if we presuppose that the morally idealistic doctrine of the *Ethics* has been modified into a moral realism analogous to the political realism of *Politics* 4.2.

Aristotle then claims that in a regime the mean lies in the middle class: "In all cities there are in fact three parts: those who are exceedingly well-off, those who are exceedingly needy, and the third who are in the middle of these two. So, since it is agreed that the mean and middle is best, then it is manifest that a middling possession also of the goods of fortune must be best of all" (1295b1–3). Aristotle is, however, equivocating. He begins by defining the middle class as an *arithmetic* mean between the rich and the poor. He concludes that the middle class is a *moral* mean. But he does not establish that the arithmetic mean corresponds with the moral.

Aristotle does, however, go on to offer reasons for thinking that the social mean corresponds to the moral mean. But the middle class is not necessarily more virtuous because its members have been properly educated, but because their social position and class interests lead them to act *as if* they had been.

First, Aristotle argues that "the middle most easily obeys reason." Those who are "excessively beautiful or strong or well-born or wealthy" find it hard to follow reason, because they tend to be "insolent and rather wicked in great things." By contrast, those who are poor and "extremely wretched and weak, and have an exceeding lack of honor" tend to become "villains and too much involved in petty wickedness." The middle class is, however, too humble to breed insolence and too well-off to breed villainy. Since most injustices arise from insolence and villainy, a regime with a strong middle class will be more likely to be just.

Second, Aristotle argues that the middle class is best suited to ruling and being ruled in turn. Those who enjoy, "an excess of good fortune (strength, wealth, friends, and other things of the sort)" love to rule and dislike being ruled. Both of these attitudes are harmful to the city, yet they naturally arise among the wealthy. From an early age, the wealthy are instilled with a "love of ruling and desire to rule, both of which are harmful to cities" (1295b12), and, "because of the luxury they live in, being ruled is not something they get used to, even at school" (1295b13-17). By contrast, poverty breeds vice, servility, and small-mindedness. Thus the poor are easy to push around, and if they do gain power, they are incapable of exercising it virtuously. Therefore, without a middle class, "a city of slaves and masters arises, not a city of the free, and the first are full of envy while the second are full of contempt." Such a city must be "at the furthest remove from friendship and political community" (1295b21-24). The presence of a strong middle class, however, binds the city into a whole, limiting the tendency of the rich to tyranny and the poor to slavishness, creating a "city of the free."

Third, Aristotle argues that middle-class citizens enjoy the safest and most stable lives, imbuing the regime as a whole with these characteristics. Those in the middle are, among all the citizens, the most likely to survive in times of upheaval, when the poor starve and the rich become targets. They are sufficiently content with their lot not to envy the possessions of the rich. Yet they are not so wealthy that the poor envy them. They neither plot against the rich nor are plotted against by the poor.

Fourth, a large middle class stabilizes a regime, particularly if the middle is "stronger than both extremes or, otherwise, than either one of them. For the middle will tip the balance when added to either side and prevent the emergence of an excess at the opposite extremes" (1295b36–40). Without a large and powerful middle class, "either ultimate rule of the populace arises or unmixed oligarchy does, or, because of excess on both sides, tyranny" (1296a3; cf. 6.12, 1297a6ff).

Fifth is the related point that regimes with large middle classes are relatively free of faction and therefore more concerned with the common good. This is because a large middle class makes it harder to separate everyone out into two groups (1296a7–10).

Finally, Aristotle claims that one sign of the superiority of middle-class regimes is that the best legislators come from the middle class. As examples, he cites Solon, Lycurgus, and Charondas (1296a18–21).

## Conclusion: Aristotle's Polity & Our Own

If the proper aim of government is to promote the happiness of the citizen, Aristotle marshals an impressive array of arguments for giving the people, specifically the middle class, a role in government. These arguments can be grouped under five headings: virtue, rational decision-making, freedom, stability, and resistance to corruption.

Popular government both presupposes and encourages widespread virtue among the citizens, and virtue is a necessary condition of happiness. Middle class citizens are particularly likely to follow practical reason and act justly, for they are corrupted neither by wealth nor by poverty. Popular participation can improve political decision-making by mobilizing scattered information and experience, and more informed decisions are more likely to promote happiness. In particular, popular government channels the experiences of those who are actually governed back into the decision-making process.

Popular participation preserves the freedom of the people, who would otherwise be exploited if they had no say in government. By preserving the freedom of the people, popular participation unifies the regime, promoting peace and stability which in turn are conducive to the pursuit of happiness. This is particularly the case with middle-class regimes, for the middle class prevents excessive and destabilizing separation and between the extremes of wealth and poverty.

Popular governments are also more resistant to corruption. It is harder to use bribery or trickery to corrupt decisions made by many people deliberating together in public than by one person or a few deciding in private. This means that popular regimes are more likely to promote the common good instead of allowing the state to become a tool for the pursuit of one special interest at the expense of another. Furthermore, if a popular regime does become corrupt, it is most likely to become a democracy, which is the least unjust of the bad regimes and the easiest to reform.

All these are good arguments for giving the people a role in government. But not just any people. And not just any role.

First, Aristotle presupposes a small city-state. He did not think that any regime could pursue the common good if it became too large. This is particularly true of a popular regime, for the larger the populace, the less room any particular citizen has for meaningful participation.

Second, he presupposes a populace that is racially and culturally homogeneous. A more diverse population is subject to faction and strife. It will either break up into distinct communities or it will have to be held together by violence and governed by an elite. A more diverse population also erodes a society's moral consensus, making moral education even more difficult.

Third, political participation will be limited to middle-class and wealthy property-owning males, specifically men who derive their income from the ownership of productive land, not merchants and craftsmen.

Fourth, Aristotle circumscribes the role of the populace by assigning it specific legal roles, such as the election of officers and the auditing of accounts—roles that are checked and balanced by the legal roles of the aristocratic element, such as occupying leadership positions.

If Aristotle is right about the conditions of popular government, then he would probably take a dim view of its prospects in America.

First and foremost, Aristotle would deplore America's lack of concern with moral education. Aristotle's disagreement would go beyond the obvious fact that the American founders did not make moral education the central concern of the state. America has neglected to cultivate even the minimal moral virtues required to maintain a liberal regime, virtues such as independence, personal responsibility, and basic civility.

Second, Aristotle would predict that multiculturalism and non-white immigration will destroy the cultural preconditions of popular government.

Third, Aristotle would reject America's ever-widening franchise—particularly the extension of the vote to women, non-property owners, and cultural aliens—as a sure prescription for lowering the quality of public decision-making in the voting booth and jury room.

Fourth, Aristotle would be alarmed by the continuing erosion of the American working and middle classes by competition from foreign workers both inside and outside America's borders. He would deplore America's transformation from an agrarian to an industrial-mercantile civilization and support autarky rather than free trade and economic globalization.

Fifth, Aristotle would be alarmed by ongoing attempts to disarm the populace.

Sixth, he would condemn America's imperialistic and warlike policies toward other nations.

Finally, Aristotle would likely observe that since genuine popular government is difficult with hundreds of thousands of citizens it will be impossible with hundreds of millions.

In short, if Aristotle were alive today, he would find himself to the right of Patrick J. Buchanan, decrying America's decline from a republic to an empire. Aristotle challenges us to show whether and how liberty and popular government are compatible with feminism, multiculturalism, and globalized capitalism.

To conclude, however, on a more positive note, although Aristotle gives reasons to think that the future of popular government in America is unpromising, he also gives reasons for optimism about the long-term prospects of popular government in general, for his defense of popular government is based on a realistic assessment of human nature, not only in its striving for perfection, but also in its propensity for failure.

*Counter-Currents,* June 21 & 22, 2012

# OUR MARX, ONLY BETTER:
## VICO & MODERN ANTI-LIBERALISM*

Today I'm going to talk about a topic that's somewhat esoteric. I chose this topic because I was fond of Jonathan Bowden, and I understood that he could get people together to listen to a lecture on Heidegger or Robinson Jeffers or Maurice Cowling. So I thought I'd like to give a lecture on a little-known thinker who I think is very important for our cause and our interests. His name is Giovanni Battista Vico. He was an Italian philosopher.

It's an indication of how little went on in the world of Italian philosophy between the Renaissance and the 20th century that most people think Vico was a Renaissance figure, but actually he was born in 1668, died in 1744, and most of his writings were published in the early 18th century. He is a figure from the Enlightenment, and he's also the first and most fundamental critic of the Enlightenment.

Since we here are interested in a critical appropriation of the Enlightenment, it behooves us to look at the first counter-Enlightenment thinker, and that was Vico. He was a counter-Enlightenment thinker before the Enlightenment was even really up and running. He had already figured out the bugs and written it all down, and he has something to offer us today.

I have been asking myself for years why so few people on the New Right talk about Vico, then it occurred to me that I had not yet given them an introduction. So, I decided to take it upon myself to introduce the New Right to Giambattista Vico.

Vico is sometimes mentioned in footnotes. He gets a few lines in potted histories of Western philosophy as the inventor of the philosophy of history or the philosophy of culture. His goal was to create a universal science of history and culture, which he summarized in his *magnum opus* the *New Science*. The *New Science* is an extension of the Enlightenment. It's an extension of

---

* This text was originally given as a lecture at The London Forum on September 27, 2014, then transcribed by V.S. and heavily edited.

modernity. It's an extension of the use of reason to understand society, to understand human nature. Vico belongs to the Enlightenment in the sense that he uses critical reason. He's extending it from the natural sciences, where it was flourishing with Newton and Galileo, into the human realm. Yet, once he extended natural science into the humanities, he arrived at political conclusions that were diametrically opposed to the liberal progressive policies of the rest of the Enlightenment. So, he is the first counter-Enlightenment thinker, and yet he is a thinker of the Enlightenment.

Vico makes it possible to give a rational defense of man's basic irrationality. He gives a non-religious defense of religion. He gives a non-traditional defense of tradition, an unconventional defense of convention. He's a non-historical defender of historical life, particularity, and identity.

Vico argued that there are three fundamental institutions of society: religion, family, and the burial of the dead. But by the burial of the dead he meant something more than mere inhumation. He meant the sacralization of a particular piece of ground and therefore the origin of settled existence, localism as opposed to nomadism. He also argued for a cyclical theory of history.

Universally, the Left is about progress. The Enlightenment was about progress. The very concept of enlightenment is a process of progressing from darkness, superstition, tradition, religion, and so forth to reason. There is an onward and upward trajectory, a narrative of forward motion. The Left draws upon this pre-existing historical narrative to suggest the next step. It's never enough. We can always progress more. We can always intensify the basic premises of modernity, the basic premises of egalitarianism.

On the Right, we tend to be skeptical of progress, and many of us are enamored of the idea of the cyclical nature of history. Now, both the cyclical idea of history and the progressive idea of history have roots in religion and myth, but in the 18th and 19th centuries the thinkers of the Enlightenment and thinkers like Marx tried to give a rational, scientific foundation for the idea of progress. They were not particularly successful, but they made strong efforts, and they convinced a lot of people that indeed progress is baked into the modern world, and society will continue to progress in the direction of greater human freedom.

Based on Hegel and his interpreter Alexandre Kojève, Francis Fukuyama argued that when Communism collapsed history had ended with the triumph of liberal democracy. These ideas are very powerful to this day. Leftists try to give some kind of foundation for progressivism in history and human nature, whereas we on the New Right, broadly speaking, love to talk about the cycles of time. If you hear "Kali Yuga," more than 90% of the time you're dealing with somebody who's plugged into the New Right. We're virtually the only ones who talk about it today, outside of India.

I use this terminology all the time. I find myths and images to be very powerful ways of organizing and communicating ideas. But if you actually go into the details of what the Traditionalists say about the Golden Age and the decline therefrom, a lot of it is patently untrue. The image of the Golden Age that you get from traditional Hinduism or from Hellenists is of a time of what Vico called "abstruse and recondite wisdom." What does that mean? Basically, being a philosopher: being mentally highly evolved and intuitively in contact with objective truths of nature.

Vico, by contrast, maintained that early man was like children are today: rude and crude and barbarous and dominated by his senses and his imagination. It's only very much later in history that we arrive at abstract and recondite ideas, which are then projected backward on the Golden Age. Vico is criticizing a kind of Traditionalism. That's one of his enemies in the *New Science*.

The other position that Vico is criticizing is Epicureanism, specifically the Epicurean idea of the beginning of history. Like Vico, the Epicureans believed that early man was rude and crude and primitive and barbarous. Their idea of early man and the evolution of man is actually extremely consistent with another faction within the New Right, those who are interested in biological evolution, the people who are interested in sociobiology, ethology, evolutionary psychology, and so forth—the materialist crowd. The Epicureans are the original evolutionary materialists. As we shall see, however, the Epicureans held that the beginning of history is more of a fall for man, whereas for Vico it is a rise.

Vico criticizes the Traditionalists of his time, but he maintains their cyclical view of history, their focus on religion, their interest in religion, arts, and humanities, and their social conservatism. Vico criticizes the materialists of his time, the Epicureans, but he maintains their essentially naturalistic hard-science approach to understanding man. He tries to come up with a synthesis of a Traditionalistic, cyclical view of history, social conservatism, and a critique of the Enlightenment that is also consistent with what is known about man's real evolution, our prehistory and our history.

What Vico did in the 18th century is offer a synthesis that the New Right today dearly needs. Because I know people who, within the space of a single conversation—I include myself in this—will move from talking about what Evola says about the Golden Age, decline, the cyclical nature of history, the regression of the castes, and all that to what Philippe Rushton had to say about genetic similarity theory.

Someday somebody's going to call me on it and say, "Wait a second here. These two worldviews are completely inconsistent. Evola believed that man in the Golden Age was a highly advanced being who devolved, and the whole evolutionary approach believes just the opposite. How do you reconcile these two things?"

A lot of us carry around unreconciled ideas, and Vico is important for the New Right because he offers a way of reconciling the two. So, let me go into a little bit of detail about how he does that.

The Traditionalists in Vico's time were Plato and the Neo-Platonists. When they looked back at Homer and Hesiod and other early Greek writers, they projected the idea of a Golden Age as an age of abstract wisdom where man was intuitively in touch with deep truths, and after the Golden Age, man declines. He declines into a world where opinion rather than truth reigns, where nature is no longer a guide, but rather conventions, customs, and culture spring up. Culture consists of conventions. Nature is the same wherever you go, but conventions change.

Nature is pretty much the same in Wales as it is just across the border in England, but Welsh and English are very different systems of conventions. Languages are conventions, and people who are naturally very similar genetically, who live in similar landscapes, similar environments, even have similar institutions can have radically different conventions like different languages. Nature is always the same across the board. Conventions change from time to time and place to place.

The Platonists looked upon the decline from the Golden Age into the later ages as a decline from the reign of truth—the Age of Truth is what the Hindus call the Golden Age—to living at greater and greater remove from the truth, living in terms of conventions and customs and illusions. It's entering what Plato called "the cave" where you're just looking at opinions rather than the truth. So, the Platonists see history as a fall, as a decline. It's a horrible, ghastly mistake that needs to be erased. It's something from which we need to be redeemed.

The Epicureans, the early materialists, also looked upon the beginning of history as something of a fall, but they had a very different view of man. They believed that man was a simple creature without intellect who is simply driven by his material desires: pleasure and pain. Now, if you just limit yourself to natural desires, it's pretty easy to satisfy them. You need food and shelter and a little bit of companionship. But when you leave the state of nature and enter into society, we acquire artificial desires. We're taught to desire things that we don't really need, and as Eric Hoffer said, "You can never get enough of what you don't really need."

So, the emergence into history is the emergence of the rat race, where people are running themselves ragged to satisfy desires that are entirely artificial, and that is a source of misery. So these early materialists, the Epicureans, looked upon the beginning of history as a fall, as a source of alienation and suffering.

The common denominator between both the Traditionalists of Vico's time and the materialists is they could not accept historical life as good. They both regarded it as a fall, either the fall of the philosopher into the realm of opinion or the fall of the happy brute into the realm of convention and the rat race. They couldn't come up with a defense of what we're interested in: namely, the plurality of different historical communities, our different cultures, our different ways of life. They couldn't defend any identity other than natural identity, either the natural identity of the man who is totally determined by objective truth, which is true for everyone, or the loping, primal, ape-like creature who is totally determined by his natural needs, which are, again, the same. Natural man, whether he's conceived of as an ape or as a kind of semi-divine being, doesn't need and can't even understand the necessity of having four different languages, or five, or millions of them. None of that makes sense. Nature is one. Culture is many, and that's a problem.

Culture, therefore, by this account, is a mistake, and this is why Epicureanism had radical political implications. Back to nature is its basic message. Our happiness lies in nature. If we go back to nature, we have to slough off culture, we have to slough off differences, and we have to slough off our identities.

Now, within the New Right, we have our back-to-nature types, but they are also very attached to their cultural identities and folkways. We do, however, have a contingent of evolutionary psychologists and sociobiologists who seek to explain culture in terms of biology. For instance, Geoffrey Miller has a book called *Spent* which is about consumerism and luxury. It's about the stuff that we don't really need. He tries to come up with a biological explanation for it, and he says buying things you don't really need is a form of signaling fitness to potential mates. So, he's trying to reduce that element of culture into basic biological needs for reproduction. Why? Because there's just a discomfort with the realm of culture as such, and if you can't reduce it down to nature, they regard it as irrational, and they either want to ignore it or get rid of the irrationality of culture.

Vico is a conservative, and that means he's trying to come up with a defense of historical life, a defense of culture, a defense of particular identities. Vico says there really is something golden about the Golden Age. But what was golden about it is not wisdom in the abstract sense. Instead, what is golden about the earliest phase of history is man's vitality and imagination.

Early man was not smart or cultured, but he was vital; he was imaginative. He was a vital savage. He was ruled by his senses and his passions, but he also had a powerful imagination. Vico stressed that all human beings have the same basic nature and also face the same necessities of life. His view was that these crude beings with their powerful imaginations and passions will spontaneously generate culture when they encounter the necessities of life. On this account, culture is not a fall from a primal state of perfection that has to be reversed or redeemed in some way. For Vico, the development of civilization is a process of self-actualization, not just self-alienation.

The animal man is alienated in culture. We have all kinds of rules for governing the satisfaction of our bodily needs. That puts limits on us as animals. But Vico argued that those limitations are more than made up for by the fact that man has a social nature and an intellectual nature. The process of developing civilization actualizes our social and intellectual nature, which slumbers in a primitive state.

Vico calls his account of history a "rational civil theology of divine Providence." Now, that's a big mouthful, but what's he saying? He's saying there's a providential order to history, and he's very careful to say that he's not talking about providence in the Biblical sense. He's not talking about sacred history. He's not talking about the Bible, because of course that's a linear view of history, and he's offering a cyclical one.

In Naples where Vico lived, an institution called the Holy Inquisition had been set up by the Spanish. They looked askance at people who were offering radically different alternative viewpoints to what the Church taught, so Vico was very careful. He said that he's only talking about the Gentile nations, not about sacred history. But he said that within the history of the nations, the Gentiles, there is a kind of providence at work. It's not the providence of the Biblical God, but it's a process of man's self-actualization that justifies history.

History is not merely a fall, but a step up, toward actualizing powers that cannot be actualized in the state of nature. Thus we don't have to look upon culture as something that merely does violence to our nature. It's something that perfects our nature as well. It does violence to our animal nature. It perfects the distinctly human aspects of our nature.

I now wish to discuss Vico's primal institutions and how they come about. I also wish to discuss his scientific analysis of what underlies the cyclical view of history. Again, it's desirable for us to stop using this cyclical view of history as merely a myth or an image but actually find a way of talking about it that's consistent with human evolution, human prehistory, and human history.

I should say that Oswald Spengler does make an attempt to give an account of the cyclical view of history that is not mere myth. Spengler believes that man starts out primitive and rude. There are problems with Spengler's view, but Spengler is basically very consistent with Vico. However, Spengler was not, as far as I can tell, influenced by Vico.

Indeed, one of the most interesting things about Vico is his lack of influence. Vico came up with the counter-Enlightenment 50 years before anybody else. But nobody read him. He died in 1744. His works were unread for almost a hundred years. There are only two thinkers of real first-class merit who could be described as fundamentally influenced by Vico. One is Georges Sorel, the syndicalist who has a lot to say to us, and the other is James Joyce.

As an aside, I once taught a course on Vico's *New Science*, and I began by passing out the first page of *Finnegans Wake* and reading it aloud. My students were shaking their heads and were thinking, "He's gone mad." When I finished, I told them, "I'm not going to comment on this. Just tuck it into the back of the book, and at the end of this class we are going to read this page again." So, at the end of the course, we pulled out the first page of *Finnegans Wake*, and we started reading through it, and as we got into the first sentence people said, "Oh! That's Vico! I see it now!" In the first sentence, Joyce talks about "the commodious Vicus of recirculation." *Vicus* means path; Vico comes from the term for path. Vico's *New Science* is the single most influential text on Joyce's *Finnegans Wake*, and a basic understanding of Vico turns *Finnegans Wake* from schizophrenic leprechaun gibberish to one of the great epic poems of the 20th century. It's a poem about everything, because Vico was really writing about everything, because he's writing about the whole of human history, but the whole of human history touches on everything else. So, I'll commend this to you as an aid for reading Joyce should you ever be tempted to do that as well.

Like Hesiod and the Hindus, Vico talked about four ages: there's an Age of Gods, an Age of Heroes, and an Age of Men, and the fourth age doesn't have a name, but it's an age of dissolution where things fall apart. The Hindus call the first age the Age of Truth, the *Satya Yuga,* and then they have the two other yugas, which are just named the third and second age, basically the *Treta Yuga* and *Dvapara Yuga,* and then the last age is the *Kali Yuga,* the dark age, which is the age of disintegration. With Hesiod, you have the Age of Gold, the Age of Silver, the Age of Bronze, and the Age of Iron. In *Finnegans Wake,* Joyce names the four ages Eggburst, Eggblend, Eggburial, and Hatch-As-Hatch-Can. Eggburst, Eggblend, and Eggburial also refer to Vico's three primal institutions: religion, family, and burial of the dead.

Vico didn't just talk about myth, he used myth. This is Vico's myth about how the primal institutions arose.

He began by bidding us to imagine the world after the flood, because he had to square everything with the Bible. The sons of Ham and Japeth have wandered off to found the Gentile nations, and they have grown rude and crude and unlettered. They've lost language. They've lost culture. They've become solitary, asocial. They've become cyclopean. He actually believed they grew to giant size. So, giants wandered the forests of the Earth after the flood, and these giants would fornicate occasionally if they would bump into a giantess, but they didn't form any families. They didn't have language; they didn't have conventions of any sort; but they had a powerful imagination.

Now imagine what happened after the flood. As the Earth dried out, the atmosphere would start getting humid. Thus there must have been terrible storms all over the world. When the thunder rumbled and the lightning flashed, the giants were terrified. (This is Joyce's "Eggburst.") Their powerful imaginations personified the cause of their fears, and they cried out the word "Jove!" They gave a name to the thunder. This is Vico's account of the origin of the first primal institution, religion.

For Vico, mankind formed language and gods at the same

time. Ernst Cassirer, a 20th-century German-Jewish philosopher of culture, has a book on *Language and Myth* which makes essentially the same point in non-mythical terms. Language and myth have the same beginnings. They start with names. Primitive men name things in order to master things that frighten them. The primal motive behind the creation of religion is coping with things that cause us fear. This is an Epicurean account of the origin of religion. And since we don't want to be ruled by fear, the Epicureans argued we have to get rid of religion. This is part of the implicitly revolutionary aspect of this form of materialism. If religion is caused by fear, then as we grow up as human beings and become modern, we don't want to be ruled by fear anymore. So goodbye to all that.

Vico continued his tale. The giants conceived that the sky was a god. Since the sky is always above us, they imagined that the sky was always watching them, and that made them self-conscious. So, instead of just fornicating with random giantesses they would encounter in the woods, they would drag them off to caves and lairs where they could do their business under cover. This was the beginning of the second primal institution, the family, what Joyce called "Eggblend." The family arrived because the giants felt shame before the gods they imagined into existence.

Since the caves were in one place, the giants ceased to wander. When they fell dead, they did not leave their bodies behind. They had to dispose of them, before they started to stink. Vico believed that the burial of the dead was one of the ways that man invested something in the landscape around him, becoming a settled rather than a nomadic being. Originally, our relationship to land was a sacred one, a relationship of mutual belonging. Property that you just buy and sell was a much later invention.

Vico's account of the origins of the primal social institutions is an attempt to imagine how primitive minds can begin the process of evolving complex institutions that are not consciously designed. Vico's view is radically at variance with one of the most common Enlightenment ideas, namely social contract theory. Culture is a realm of shared conventions. How do you create conventions? Well, you sit down and you agree on things. You agree to drive on the correct side of the road, for instance. There's a *New Yorker* cartoon on the origin of language, and it illustrates the absurdity of the Enlightenment's idea of how conventions come about. A cave man and a cave woman are seated on the ground, back to back. The cave woman says, "We need to talk." The cave man says, "Uh-oh." That's how language came about! We needed to talk, so we talked! The joke, of course, is that language could not have arisen that way, because she was already using it. She already had language to say "We need to talk."

In the same way, conventions cannot be created by a social contract, because such a contract presupposes that society, language, civility, mutual trust, and contracts already exist. Therefore, the idea that governments are instituted by contract to secure natural rights — as we see in the US Declaration of Independence — is preposterous. Governments never were instituted like that. But of course revolutions can be.

On Vico's account, governments grew from patriarchal family relationships and extended tribes. This process, moreover, took place by the trial and error of primitive and irrational beings, not conscious reasoning and design. These were very crude people. Language developed slowly over time. The ability to reflect critically came about very late. Even today, it hardly exists at all in some people. Most people are passive followers, even really smart people. So, the idea that critical reason is at the root of society is preposterous.

The Enlightenment attitude that institutions should be founded on reason leads to the conclusion that existing institutions that can't give a rational account of their utility should be done away with. For Vico, this is basically a kind of nihilism that will dissolve society. So, for Vico, the fourth age is one in which the early "barbarism of sense," as he calls it, is replaced by a new barbarism, the "barbarism of reflection." The barbarism of reflection strives to make the world a better place. But it ultimately dissolves the bonds of sociality, and therefore society returns to chaos.

To sum up, the Age of Gods is the first age when religion,

family and settled life begin. The Age of Heroes is the second age where you have the rise of aristocratic societies. It's the Homeric Age. The Age of Men is the age of popular government, democracy, and in the fourth age, Hatch-As-Hatch-Can, the *Kali Yuga*, the dissolution comes about when, within these democratic societies, skepticism and materialism and the barbarism of reflection take over and dissolve the constituent bonds of society.

Now with this in mind, I want to read a couple of passages from the end of *The New Science*. And as you will see, I think we should read Vico not only for the light that he shines on society, but also for the beauty of his words, for he was a professor of eloquence. Perhaps the biggest impediment to reading Vico is that his illustrations presuppose too much familiarity with Roman history. If he were alive today, he'd no doubt be citing examples from *Star Trek*.

> As the popular states, democracies, became corrupt so also did philosophies. They descended to skepticism. Learned fools fell to calumniating the truth. Thence alone arose a false eloquence ready to uphold either of the opposed sides of a case indifferently. Thus it came about that by abuse of eloquence like that of the tribunes of the plebs of Rome and the citizens who were no longer content with making wealth the basis of rank . . . [Here he goes off into Roman history. I'm going to skip forward.] Thus, they caused the commonwealths to fall from the perfect liberty into the perfect tyranny of anarchy or the unchecked liberty of the free peoples.[1]

Vico is talking about how demagogues whip up democracies and install themselves as tyrants. So, the fourth age really is the Age of the Tyrant. Then he says:

> To this great disease of cities, Providence applies one of

---

[1] *The New Science of Giambattista Vico*, Revised Translation of the Third Edition (1744), trans. Thomas Goddard Bergin and Max Harold Fisch (Ithaca: Cornell University Press, 1968), Conclusion, pp. 417–26.

three great remedies in the following order of human civil institutions: First, it ordains that there be found among these peoples a man like Augustus to arise and establish himself as a monarch and by force of arms take in hand all the institutions and all the laws which, though sprung from liberty, no longer avail to regulate and hold it within bounds. On the other hand, Providence ordains that the very form of the monarchic state shall confine the will of the monarchs in spite of their unlimited sovereignty within the natural order of keeping the peoples content and satisfied with both their religion and their natural liberty.

This is what Spengler calls Caesarism, and that's the best outcome. The next best outcome is this:

Then if Providence does not find such a remedy within, it seeks it outside and since people so far corrupted have already become naturally slaves of their unrestrained passions of luxury, effeminacy, avarice, envy, pride and vanity and in pursuit of the pleasures of their dissolute life are falling back into all of the vices characteristic of the most abject slaves, having become liars, tricksters, thieves, cowards and pretenders, Providence decrees that they become slaves by the natural law of the *gentes* which spring from the nature of nations and that they become subject to better nations, which, having conquered them by arms, preserve them as subject provinces. Herein the two great lights of natural order shine forth.

This is very interesting: first, that he who cannot govern himself must let himself be governed by another who can, and second, the world is always governed by those who are naturally fittest. This is a long time before Darwin, much less Social Darwinism, came along, but this is in Vico.

If a corrupt society is unlucky enough to find a Caesar from within or from without, then society goes to perdition. This is Vico's description of perdition:

> But if the peoples are rotting in that ultimate civil disease and cannot agree on a monarch from within and are not conquered and preserved by better nations from without then Providence for their extreme ill has its extreme remedy at hand. For such peoples like so many beasts have fallen into the custom of each man thinking only of his own private interests, but have reached the extreme of delicacy, or better of pride in which like wild animals they bristle and lash out at the slightest displeasure.

Sounds like the internet to me.

> Thus, no matter how great the throng and press of their bodies they live like wild beasts in a deep solitude of spirit and will, scarcely any two being able to agree since each follows his own pleasure or caprice.

Sounds like the New York subway, where there's this great press of people who are sunk in the solitude of individualism. There's nothing that holds them together except the press of their bodies and the tube that they're going through.

> By reason of all this, Providence decrees that through obstinate factions and desperate civil wars they shall turn their cities into forests and the forests into dens and lairs of men. In this way, through long centuries of barbarism rust will consume the misbegotten subtleties of malicious wits that have turned them into beasts made more inhuman by the barbarism of reflection than the first men had been made by the barbarism of sense. For the latter displayed a generous savagery against which one could defend oneself or take flight or be on one's guard, but the former with a base savagery and soft words and embraces plots against the life and fortunes of friends and intimates. Hence, people who have reached this point of premeditated malice when they receive this last remedy of Providence are thereby stunned and brutalized, are sensible no longer of comforts, delicacies, pleasures, and pomp but only of the sheer necessities of life.

Vico believed that there's a single human nature. He calls this our common mental dictionary. He's a universalist in that sense. He's not a cultural relativist. What underlies culture is a universal human nature that, under the impress of natural necessity, will give rise to culture again and again. So if we return to the barbarism of sense, we won't tarry there long, because the self-actualization of man requires that history begin over again.

This is an account of a cyclical view of history grounded in an understanding of human nature. Primitive men are crude but vital and imaginative. Imagination, spurred by vitality and natural necessities, gives rise to institutions. As mankind becomes more reflective and intellectual, however, we become alienated from vitality and from historically evolved institutions. Reflection dissolves our participation in society, our identity with society. We become selfish, individualistic, and deracinated. But such people cannot maintain a civilization. So civilization collapses from the barbarism of reflection. Men return to the barbarism of sense, and the process begins all over.

Thus Vico takes an account of human nature that's consistent with natural science and combines it with an account of history and culture that leads to conclusions that people on the New Right support.

That's my brief for Vico. Giorgio Almirante, the founder of the neo-fascist Italian Social Movement, once said that Julius Evola was "our Marcuse, only better." So I give you Giambattista Vico: our Marx, only better.

*Counter-Currents*, April 11, 2019

# ROUSSEAU AS CONSERVATIVE:
## THE THEODICY OF CIVILIZATION

In 1762, Immanuel Kant did something unprecedented. He missed his daily walk. He stayed home to read Jean-Jacques Rousseau's new book *Emile*, a philosophical novel on education that was to exercise a profound and revolutionary influence on his thought.[1] In one of his notes on Rousseau, from 1764–1765, Kant writes:

> Newton was the very first to see order and regularity bound up with the greatest simplicity, where before him disorder and mismatched heterogeneity were to be met with, whereas since then comets run in geometric paths.
>
> Rousseau was the very first to discover under the heterogeneity of the assumed shapes of humanity its deeply hidden nature and the concealed law according to which providence through his observation is justified. Formerly the objections of Alfonso and Mani were still valid. After Newton and Rousseau, God is justified and Pope's thesis is henceforth true.[2]

Here Kant, who was a great admirer of Newton, lauds Rous-

---

[1] In the 1970s, at the University of Toronto's Law School, there occurred a remarkable panel on Plato's *Republic*, the principal members of which are numbered among the 20th century's greatest Plato interpreters: Hans-Georg Gadamer, Eric Voegelin, and Allan Bloom. Bloom prefaced his remarks on the *Republic* with a remarkable claim about Kant and Rousseau. He said, if memory serves, that "Kant was an absolutely extraordinary interpreter of Rousseau, perhaps the greatest interpreter of Rousseau who ever lived." I find this claim interesting for many reasons, not the least of which is this: If Bloom's estimation of the profundity of Kant's reading is correct, then some of what Bloom himself says about Rousseau has to be wrong.

[2] Immanuel Kant, *Bemerkungen in den "Beobachtungen über das Gefühl des Schönen und Erhabenen,"* ed. Marie Rischmüller (Hamburg: Felix Meiner, 1991), p. 48; my trans.

seau as the Newton of the human world. He also indicates the central problem that any Newton of the human world must face: the objections of Alfonso and Mani. What Alfonso and Mani are objecting to is the idea of divine providence.

King Alfonso X of Castile reportedly declared, "Let justice triumph though the world may perish," implying that in this world there is no justice; he also reportedly said, upon inspecting the Ptolemaic system of the heavens, that "If I had been the creator of the world, I should have made the thing better."[3]

Both claims imply that the created world is not ruled by a benevolent divine providence, but by the forces of evil, which is the position of Mani, the founder of Manicheanism.

To answer the objections of Alfonso and Mani, we must solve the problem of evil, i.e., we must produce a theodicy. We must show that the evils of the world are consistent with an omnipotent, omniscient, omnibenevolent, provident God—either by showing that the evils of the world are illusory, or by showing that they are the unavoidable characteristics of the best of all possible worlds, which is the thesis of Alexander Pope's *Essay on Man* and Leibniz's *Theodicy*, the thesis known as "optimism."

Now, at first glance, it seems odd to attribute an optimistic solution to the problem of evil to Rousseau, for although Rousseau thought that the natural world is good, the same was not true of society. Consider this passage from *Emile*:

> . . . when . . . I seek to know my individual place in my species, and I consider its various ranks and the men who fill them, what happens to me? What a spectacle! Where is the order I had observed [in nature]? The picture of nature had presented me with only harmony and proportion; that of mankind presents me with only confusion and disorder! Concert reigns among the elements, and men are in chaos! The animals are happy; their king alone is miserable! O

---

[3] My source for the second anecdote is Ernst Cassirer, *Rousseau, Kant, Goethe: Two Essays*, trans. James Gutmann, Paul Oskar Kristeller, and John Hermann Randall, Jr. (Princeton: Princeton University Press, 1945), p. 18, n22.

wisdom, where are your laws? O providence, is it thus that you rule the world? Beneficent Being, what has become of your power? I see evil on earth. (*Emile*, p. 278)[4]

Indeed, the overall tenor of Rousseau's *Discourse on the Sciences and the Arts* (First Discourse, 1750[5]) and his *Discourse on the Origins of Inequality* (Second Discourse, 1754[6]) was so darkly pessimistic that Voltaire, who was himself no defender of optimism, declared them "books against the human race."

The First Discourse argues that the progress of the arts and sciences from the Renaissance to the Enlightenment has served to corrupt rather than to improve morals. The advancement of civilization causes the decay of humanity.

The Second Discourse argues that civilization as such is absurd and evil—absurd because it arises from sheer Epicurean contingency rather than through providence or natural teleology, both of which aim at the good—and evil because it alienates us from our natural goodness, our natural freedom, and our natural sentiments of self-love and pity.

What, then, was Kant thinking when he attributed a theodicy of the human world to Rousseau? How did he read Rousseau as an optimist? There are three Rousseauian texts that can support Kant's optimistic reading: *Emile*, *Of the Social Contract* (1762), and the famous letter to Voltaire of August 18, 1756,[7] which was published without Rousseau's permission and may have

---

[4] Jean-Jacques Rousseau, *Emile, or On Education*, trans. Allan Bloom (New York: Basic Books, 1979).

[5] Jean-Jacques Rousseau, *Discourse on the Sciences and Arts (First Discourse) and Polemics*, ed. Roger D. Masters and Christopher Kelly, *The Collected Writings of Rousseau*, vol. 2 (Hanover and London: Dartmouth College/University Press of New England, 1992).

[6] Jean-Jacques Rousseau, *Discourse on the Origins of Inequality (Second Discourse), Polemics, and Political Economy*, ed. Roger D. Masters and Christopher Kelly, *The Collected Writings of Rousseau*, vol. 3, ed. Roger D. Masters and Christopher Kelly (Hanover and London: Dartmouth College/University Press of New England, 1992).

[7] Jean-Jacques Rousseau, Letter to Voltaire, August 18, 1756. Trans. Terence E. Marshall, in *The Collected Writings of Rousseau*, vol. 3.

reached Kant. (I should also note that the following discussion is partial, for it abstracts from the crucial topic of Rousseau's denial of original sin and assertion of the natural goodness of man.)

In his letter to Voltaire, Rousseau responds to Voltaire's "Poems on the Lisbon Disaster," an attack on optimism occasioned by the series of great earthquakes that destroyed much of Lisbon in 1755. Rousseau explicitly defends the optimism of Leibniz and Pope.

Furthermore, he makes it clear that he is an optimist about both the human and the natural worlds, arguing that the First and Second Discourses, contrary to the pessimistic impression they create, actually vindicate God's providence by showing that God is not the author of mankind's miseries. Man himself is their author.

> Because mankind is free, we are the author of all of our moral miseries, and, because we have the freedom to avoid or minimize most of our physical miseries, to the extent that we fail to do so, we are their authors as well. God is blameless.[8]

In *Of the Social Contract*, the project of a theodicy of the human world is apparent in the famous opening paragraph of Book I, Chapter 1:

> Man is born free and everywhere he is in chains. One believes himself the master of others, and yet he is a greater slave than they. How has this change come about? I do not know. What can render it legitimate? I believe that I can settle this question.[9]

In the state of nature, man is free. In the civil condition, he is in chains, but the chains are not merely the iron fetters of slaves, but the fetters of vanity (*amour-propre*) that bind the masters as

---

[8] Letter to Voltaire, pp. 109–10, 111–12; cf. *Emile*, pp. 281–82, 293.

[9] Rousseau, *Of the Social Contract*, trans. Charles M. Sherover (New York: Harper and Row, 1984), p. 4.

well. How did man pass from the state of nature to the civil state? Rousseau claims he does not know.

Now this is a startling claim, for Rousseau's Second Discourse is precisely an account of man's passage from the state of nature to the civil state. Apparently, whatever kind of account it is, it does not in Rousseau's eyes constitute *knowledge*. This is an important point, to which we will return later.

Rousseau's next question, "What can render it legitimate?" introduces the question of justice. Rousseau's goal is to show us that the chains of civilization are legitimate, that they are justified.

It is not possible to offer a complete interpretation of Rousseau's General Will doctrine here, so let me simply assert that for Rousseau the civil state is not good because we choose it; rather we ought to choose it because it is good.

Furthermore, Rousseau does not think that only the ideal state of the Social Contract is preferable to the state of nature. He thinks that all really-existing civil states, save the most corrupt, are more choiceworthy than the state of nature; the civil state as such is better than the state of nature.

And why is the civil state good? Rousseau's most explicit answer is Chapter 8 of Book I: "Of the Civil State":

This transition from the state of nature to the civil state produces in man a very remarkable change, by substituting in his conduct justice for instinct, and by giving his actions a morality that they previously lacked. It is only when the voice of duty succeeds physical impulsion, and right succeeds appetite, that man, who till then had only looked after himself, sees that he is forced to act on other principles, and to consult his reason before listening to his inclinations. Although in this state he is deprived of many advantages he holds from nature, he gains such great ones in return, that his faculties are exercised and developed; his ideas are expanded; his feelings are ennobled; his whole soul is exalted to such a degree that, if the abuse of his new condition did not often degrade him to below that from which he has emerged, he should ceaselessly bless the happy moment that removed him from it forever, and transformed him from a stupid and ignorant animal into an intelligent being and a man.[10]

Now, in the context of *Of the Social Contract*, the alternative title of which is "Principles of Political Right," it is only natural to construe the question of the legitimacy of the civil state as a matter of political or human justice. But the "happy moment" when man passed from the state of nature into the civil state marks the beginning of historical life; it is not the same as the moment in history when man passed from primitive and warlike society (Hobbes' state of nature) to law-governed political society; rather it is the moment when the human world itself comes into existence.

The transition from warlike society to political society can be guided and illuminated by principles of political right. But the transition from nature to history is *pre-political*, and if we are to "ceaselessly bless" this moment, it is not in virtue of its political justice, but in virtue of a natural justice — a natural justice that in *Emile* is revealed to be a divine justice.

In *Emile*, particularly the "Profession of Faith of a Savoyard Vicar" in Book IV, Rousseau offers an explicit theodicy of the human world, arguing that man's fall from nature into history is a *felix culpa*, even if it does violence to our natural freedom and sentiments, because it creates the conditions for the development of our moral and spiritual natures. Providence, therefore, is vindicated.

First, Rousseau argues that, although man chooses most of his miseries and is therefore responsible for them, the very freedom that creates these miseries is also the condition for his moral dignity:

> To complain about God's not preventing men from doing evil is to complain about His having given him an excellent nature, about His having put in man's actions the morality which ennobles them, about His having given him

---

[10] *Of the Social Contract*, p. 18.

the right to virtue. The supreme enjoyment is in satisfaction with oneself; it is in order to deserve this satisfaction that we are placed on Earth and endowed with freedom, that we are tempted by the passions and restrained by conscience. (*Emile*, p. 281)

Second, Rousseau argues that civilization makes possible the development of man's rational faculties, whereas savages and peasants, although bright and active during childhood, become mentally dull and placid as adults. During childhood, young Emile, whose education is the subject of the book, is given all the freedom of young savages and peasants. But Emile will be taught to think, and thinking is an activity that presupposes the development of civilization. Therefore, the full development of Emile's intellectual faculties requires that he leave the state of nature for the civil state. Thinking is good, and civilization, because it cultivates thinking, is good as well (*Emile*, pp. 315–16).

Third, the cultivation of taste adds a great deal to the agreeableness of life; it teaches us to find pleasures virtually anywhere and to minimize pain and suffering (*Emile*, p. 344); it also makes us more finely attuned to the objective differences in the world around us; and it encourages us to take pleasure in reflection and discussion, thus creating the conditions for philosophy. The ideal place to cultivate taste, however, is not Arcadia or Sparta or Geneva, but decadent Paris:

> If, in order to cultivate my disciple's taste [speaks the preceptor, the narrator of *Emile*], I had to choose between taking him to countries where there has not yet been any cultivation of taste and to others where taste has already degenerated, I would proceed in reverse order. . . . taste is corrupted by an excessive delicacy which creates a sensitivity to things that the bulk of men do not perceive. This delicacy leads to a spirit of discussion, for the more subtle one is about things, the more they multiply. This subtlety makes feelings more delicate and less uniform. Then as many tastes are formed as there are individuals. In the disputes about preferences, philosophy and enlightenment

are extended, and it is in this way that one learns to think. (*Emile*, p. 342)

Even the theater, Geneva's ban on which Rousseau defended, is lauded as a school of taste (*Emile*, p. 344).

Finally, in book five of *Emile*, the political institutions that so frequently do violence to our natural freedom and sentiments are defended as necessary conditions for the development of our moral and spiritual nature:

> If he [Emile] had been born in the heart of the woods, he would have lived happier and freer. But he would have had nothing to combat in order to follow his inclinations, and thus he would have been good without merit; he would not have been virtuous; and now he knows how to be so in spite of his passions. The mere appearance of order brings him to know order and to love it. The public good, which serves others only as a pretext, is a real motive for him alone. He learns to struggle with himself, to conquer himself, to sacrifice his interest to the common interest. It is not true that he draws no profit from the laws. They give him the courage to be just even among wicked men. It is not true that they have not made him free. They have taught him to reign over himself. (*Emile*, p. 473)

It is important to note that Rousseau is not talking about the good laws of the ideal state described in *Of the Social Contract*, but about the bad laws of any and all really-existing states. For Rousseau, even bad laws are better than no laws at all, for laws as such awaken and actualize potencies of the soul that slumber in the state of nature. In particular, laws that prescribe actions contrary to our inclinations awaken our free will; such laws open up the latent distinction between the soul and the body (the soul understood as our moral personality, the body understood as the desires, drives, and inclinations of our physical frame), and finally such laws offer us occasions for virtue, understood as self-mastery.

Man in the state of nature is unreflective and therefore experiences no distinction between the self and its desires and inclinations. Freedom in the state of nature is experienced as the free play of inclination. It is only when a human being is presented with the choice of two incompatible courses of action, one determined by his inclinations and the other by the commandments of the law, that he becomes aware of his moral freedom, i.e., his capacity not simply to follow his impulses, but actively to choose his actions—and not simply to choose particular actions, but to choose the ultimate grounds for determining his actions.

When a human being is presented with the choice of acting upon the desires and incentives of the economy of nature or upon human laws—even absurd and unjust commands—if he chooses to suppress his natural inclinations to obey human laws, then he experiences a sublime elevation of his moral personality above his own body, and above the economy of nature in general, as well as a sense of pride in his moral strength and self-mastery.

Rousseau is fully cognizant of the cruelty of civilization, of its tendency to mortify and mutilate our natural freedom, our natural goodness, and our natural sentiments of self-love and pity. But even at its worst, civilization is justified by the fact that it awakens our distinctly human capacities to exercise moral freedom, to master our inclinations, to take responsibility for our actions. Civilization brings us to know and esteem ourselves as creatures who are not merely cogs in the clockwork of nature, but its masters and possessors. Therefore, civilization—even at its worst—is better than the state of nature. Therefore, the providence that brought us from nature to history is vindicated.

This, I think, is a plausible reconstruction of how Kant read Rousseau's project as a theodicy of the human world. Now I wish to deal with an objection to this interpretation.

The Kantian interpretation of Rousseau can be characterized as theistic and dualistic, whereas most contemporary interpretations of Rousseau, particularly those influenced by Marx and Leo Strauss tend to treat Rousseau as a modern Epicurean, i.e., as an atheist and a materialist. The Epicurean interpretation of Rousseau is based primarily upon the Second Discourse, and I think that James H. Nichols, Jr. is correct to suggest that,

> in this particular work Rousseau is most obviously influenced by Lucretius: the analysis of man's primitive condition, and of the subsequent steps of development out of it; the character of prepolitical society; and thereafter the movement via disorder and violence to the institution by compact of political society with coercive laws—on all these points Rousseau follows the main lines of the Lucretian account.[11]

Both Rousseau and Lucretius regard man as naturally independent, self-sufficient, limited in his desires, and therefore as happy.

Both regard society as a realm of vanity, false opinions, and artificial desires that trap us in an alienating web of interdependence with other persons and external things, leading to competition, enmity, violence, oppression, and misery.

Finally, both Lucretius and Rousseau offer a non-teleological and non-providential account of man's passage from nature into history.

Epicureanism is to this day the main alternative to teleological and theistic accounts of the origins of order. According to Epicurus, the appearance of order can be explained without reference to teleology or design, simply as the product of random material collisions that, over a very long time, accidentally produce pockets of order that can maintain and replicate themselves within the environing chaos.

On such an account, man does not leave the state of nature because of the inner promptings of his nature. Nor does he leave it under the guidance of providence to fulfill a divine plan. Man leaves the state of nature simply because of the accumulation of a large number of essentially contingent and absurd events, such as volcanic eruptions, tectonic upheavals, and even—in the *Essay on the Origin of Language*—the sudden shifting of the earth's axis

---

[11] James H. Nichols, Jr., *Epicurean Political Philosophy: The* De rerum natura *of Lucretius* (Ithaca: Cornell University Press, 1976), pp. 198–99.

of rotation away from the perpendicular of the plane of its orbit.

Rousseau makes no reference to natural teleology. And save for one reference, appeals to providence are conspicuously absent. Indeed, Rousseau's account of man's passage from the state of nature is even more Epicurean than Lucretius's account, for Lucretius offers a harsher view of prehistoric life than Rousseau and therefore makes the passage from prehistory to history seem far more natural, whereas Rousseau paints an idyllic picture of prehistoric life, which makes the transition from nature to history seem all the more jarring and inexplicable.

Since the perspective of the Second Discourse is clearly Epicurean, i.e., atheistic and materialistic, if one accepts the Second Discourse as a statement of Rousseau's metaphysical convictions, one is obligated to explain away Rousseau's theistic and dualistic pronouncements—as well as his explicit critique and rejection of Epicureanism—in *Emile*, the letter to Voltaire, and elsewhere.

The strategy of Leo Strauss and Allan Bloom seems to be to assimilate the credo of the Savoyard vicar to Rousseau's account of civil religion in *Of the Social Contract*. To put it crudely, the vicar's credo is a salutary noble lie—something to be believed by Emile, but not by Rousseau himself.

Roger D. Masters, although he is a student of Strauss, rejects this approach—in my opinion quite rightly. Rousseau's substantial agreement with the vicar's credo is indicated by the fact that its language and arguments appear in texts written in Rousseau's own name, such as the letter to Voltaire of August 18, 1756, the letter to Jacob Vernes of February 18, 1758, the *Letters written from the Mountain*, and the *Reveries*. Rousseau also adds his own approving notes to the Profession itself.[12] On the basis of such evidence, Masters concludes that Rousseau's private convictions were theistic and dualistic, although he maintains that these private convictions are "detachable" from Rousseau's public philosophy, which remains atheistic and materialistic.

By contrast, the Kantian interpretation of Rousseau I wish to

---

[12] Roger D. Masters, *The Political Philosophy of Rousseau* (Princeton: Princeton University Press, 1968), ch. 2.

defend maintains that both Rousseau's private convictions and his final philosophic system are dualistic and theistic.

But to maintain this thesis, I must explain, or explain away, the apparent Epicureanism of the Second Discourse. I wish to suggest that the Second Discourse really is an Epicurean account of man's nature and his passage into history, but that it does not represent Rousseau's final metaphysical position.

I do not, however, wish to argue that it represents an Epicurean "stage" in Rousseau's "philosophical development." Instead, I wish to suggest that the Epicureanism of the Second Discourse is merely *hypothetical* and *provisional*. This is, I think, the clear sense of the following passage:

> Let us . . . begin by setting all the facts aside, for they do not affect the question. The researches which can be undertaken concerning this subject must not be taken for historical truths, but only for hypothetical and conditional reasonings better suited to clarify the nature of things than to show their true origin, like those of our physicists make every day concerning the formation of the world. Religion commands us to believe that since God Himself took men out of the state of nature immediately after creation, they are unequal because He wanted them to be so; but it does not forbid us to form conjectures, drawn solely from the nature of man and the beings surrounding him, about what the human race might have become if it has remained abandoned to itself. That is what I am asked and what I propose to examine in this Discourse.[13]

Those who wish to treat Rousseau as something more than a hypothetical and conditional Epicurean can, of course, treat this passage as merely an attempt to placate possible Christian censors by casting what is meant to be a true account of man's nature and history as merely suppositious.

---

[13] Jean-Jacques Rousseau, *The First and Second Discourses*, ed., Roger D. Masters, trans. Roger D. Masters and Judith R. Bush (New York: St. Martin's Press, 1964), p. 103.

I think that this is clearly part of Rousseau's intention. But I see no reason to conclude that his statement is also insincere, especially because I can offer good philosophical reasons for why Rousseau might have adopted a hypothetical Epicureanism, and as a rule I think that we should always prefer philosophical explanations of a given passage instead of, or in addition to, extrinsic political explanations, and we should always prefer taking an author's statement as sincere unless and until it resists such treatment.

What, then, is the philosophical explanation for Rousseau's provisional adoption of a position he regards as ultimately false? I wish to suggest that the purpose of the Second Discourse is to lay the groundwork for a total critique of civilization. To offer a total critique of civilization, we must find a standpoint outside of civilization from which we can take the totality of civilization into view. This standpoint is the state of nature.

But why an Epicurean as opposed to, say, an Aristotelian account of the state of nature? Because for Aristotle, man is by nature both rational and political; for Aristotle, the actualization of man's nature requires civilization; therefore, Aristotelian nature cannot provide a critical standpoint outside of civilization. Epicurean nature, however, can.

In the Second Discourse, man is by nature neither rational nor political. He is a simple, unreflective, undivided material being, wholly content with his lot. Civilization, when viewed from the state of nature, thus seems to be nothing more than a ghastly spectacle of suffering, and we are left to conclude that there's nothing in it for us; we feel with a pang that our hearts are just not in it.

Given the choice, we would never have left the state of nature. Instead, we were forced out of it by mere accidents. Civilization as such, therefore, is both evil and absurd.

But why does Rousseau mount a total critique of civilization? Rousseau's critique is not an end itself. Nor is it the prelude to a total revolutionary reconstruction of society. Instead, it is a prelude to an essentially conservative project of reconciliation—the reconciliation of man with civilization and with divine providence. It is a theodicy of the human world.

Rousseau constructs the strongest possible critique of civilization in order to oppose it with the strongest possible defense.

To mount this defense, however, we must recognize that the sense of complete alienation from civilization produced by the Second Discourse is a product of its essentially atheistic and materialistic perspective.

Rousseau claims that civilization is based upon man's internal dividedness against himself. Epicureanism, as a one-dimensional materialism, can conceive of man only as a unified being. Therefore, from the Epicurean point of view, the dividedness of civilization—any civilization—is a violent deformation of our nature.

Civilization would, however, be justified if man really is a divided being. If man really is divided into body and soul, then the only way to heal the violent dividedness of vanity is with the natural dividedness of virtue.

It is only by adopting a dualistic account of human nature and a theistic and providential metaphysics that we can reconcile ourselves to civilization.

This does not, of course, imply that Rousseau was uninterested in social and political reform. What it does imply is that Rousseau accepted the essentially conservative principle that although bad laws ought to be changed, bad laws are still better than no laws at all; therefore, we should be cautious lest we discover we are more capable of destroying bad laws than creating better ones.

*Counter-Currents*, October 23, 2010

# NOTES ON PHILOSOPHICAL DIALECTIC

The concept of philosophical dialectic is quite mysterious and intimidating. Even among professional philosophers, dialectic often has connotations of mysticism, obscurantism, and sleight of hand. I wish to dispel this aura. I will lay out the elements of philosophical dialectic by looking at specific arguments in Plato's *Republic*[1] and Hegel's *Philosophy of Right*[2] and then employ Heidegger's account of the hermeneutic circle in *Being and Time* and Husserl's account of the logic of parts and wholes in his *Logical Investigations* to clarify the dialectical process.

## 1. DIALOGUE & DIALECTIC IN PLATO'S *REPUBLIC*, BOOK 1

For Plato, philosophy is the love—meaning the pursuit—of wisdom. For Plato, wisdom is not an art, but the pursuit of wisdom is an art, and the name of that art is dialectic. Philosophical dialectic is a process of articulating and defining a concept, such as piety in the *Euthyphro* or justice in the *Republic*.

Let us look at two examples of Plato's dialectic in *Republic*, Book 1, where Socrates examines three definitions of justice: Cephalus says that justice is honesty in word and deed and paying what one owes (331a–b), Polemarchus holds that justice is helping friends and harming enemies (332d), and Thrasymachus claims that justice is the advantage of the stronger (338b). I wish to focus on Socrates's treatment of the first two definitions.

Let's begin with Cephalus' definition. Cephalus claims that money helps one to be just because:

> The possession of money contributes a great deal to not having to cheat or lie to any man against one's will, and, moreover, to not having to depart for that other place

---

[1] Plato, *Republic*, trans. Allan Bloom (New York: Basic Books, 1968), henceforth cited by Stephanus number(s).
[2] G. W. F. Hegel, *Philosophy of Right*, trans. T. M. Knox (Oxford: Clarendon, 1952).

frightened because one owes some sacrifices to a god or money to a human being (331a–b)

Socrates, however, doubts that this can be an adequate account of justice, saying "[A]s to justice, shall we so simply assert that it is the truth and giving back what a man has taken from another, or is to do these very things sometimes just and sometimes unjust?" (331c).

First, there is a concept, justice, which is to be articulated in concrete terms. Second, a possible articulation is put forward by Cephalus. Third, Socrates *provisionally totalizes* this articulation, asking if Cephalus' account is *all* there is to justice. Fourth, using his imagination, Socrates constructs a scenario in which Cephalus' account is "clearly seen" as inadequate:

Take this case as an example of what I mean: everyone would surely say that if a man takes weapons from a friend when the latter is of sound mind, and the friend demands them back when he is mad, one shouldn't give back such things, and the man who gave them back would not be just, and, moreover, one should not be willing to tell someone in this state the whole truth. (331c–d)

Here Socrates puts forward a situation in which "everyone would surely say" that justice cannot be identified with returning what one borrows or telling the truth. Granted, these are *parts* of justice, but they are not the whole thing.

But how do we know this? By what criterion does this counterexample gain universal assent? Clearly, the argument presupposes that *we always-already know what justice is*, albeit in an inarticulate way, but we can still use this tacit knowledge to judge the adequacy of our attempts to explicitly articulate it.

Having assented to Socrates's refutation, Cephalus bows out in order to pay his debts to the gods, allowing his son and heir Polemarchus to inherit the discussion.

Polemarchus too sees the inadequacy of his father's account and seeks to supplement it by recasting it in terms that are not subject to the same counterexample. His new formulation is: Justice is helping one's friends and harming one's enemies.

Socrates responds to this formulation as follows. First, he draws out of Polemarchus the premise that each art pursues its particular good. The doctor is good at curing, the shoemaker at making shoes, the pilot at steering a ship. Each man is good at these things *qua* member of his profession, not just *qua* man. What, then, asks Socrates, is a just man good at *qua* just man? Polemarchus answers that the just man is good at safeguarding the wealth of his friends. Clearly, though, Socrates says, this makes justice rather trivial. And clearly it does. Polemarchus readily assents.

Socrates then goes on to argue further that, if the just man *qua* just man is good at guarding treasure, then his same expertise would also make him good at stealing treasure. This follows from the commonplace belief among the Greeks that any art gives one command over contraries: Medical knowledge, for instance, can be used both to cure and to kill, to alleviate pain and to inflict it. But again, Socrates points out, this is clearly an inadequate account of justice, and Polemarchus assents, saying "I no longer know what I did mean. However, it is still my opinion that justice is helping friends and harming enemies" (334b).

Socrates then presses forward, introducing a distinction between true and false friends and true and false enemies.

True friends are just and true enemies unjust. False friends, however, are unjust and false enemies are just (or at least they have never done any harm). On Polemarchus' account, though, justice as helping friends and harming enemies might lead to helping false friends who are not just and harming false enemies who have done nothing unjust. But this means that justice can consist in rewarding injustice and harming those who have done no wrong. Justice on Polemarchus' account can, in short, involve doing injustice. But clearly this cannot be the case; clearly this cannot be the whole story. Polemarchus, therefore, revises and supplements his account to make it invulnerable to this objection. Socrates sums up Polemarchus' supplementation of his earlier account as follows.

> You order us to add something to what we said at first

about the just. Then we said that it is just to do good to the friend and harm to the enemy, while now we are to say in addition that it is just to do good to the friend, if he [really] is good, and harm to the enemy, if he [really] is bad. (335a)

Socrates responds to this revised account as follows. If justice is doing harm to those who are truly bad—and if doing harm to the truly bad makes the bad worse—then justice consists in making the unjust even less just *through justice*. But, again, this is clearly a bad account of justice. Justice *qua* justice surely cannot make the unjust even more unjust. This is analogous to saying that the art of music *qua* music can make the unmusical even less musical, and the art of medicine *qua* medicine can make the sick even more sick.[3] Clearly, in these cases, we would say that the arts of music and medicine had miscarried; they went out of commission and were replaced by their opposites.[4] The same is true for justice. Justice can make the unjust more unjust not *qua* justice, but only *qua* miscarriage of justice, i.e., injustice. To claim, therefore, that justice involves harming the unjust is simply a contradiction. Polemarchus' account, therefore, is clearly inadequate. At this point, Polemarchus gives up, Thrasymachus leaps in, and we break off.

To sum up, Platonic dialectic is the following process.

1. We begin with an inarticulate grasp of an idea or concept. The goal of dialectic is to fully articulate this knowledge.
2. Then we venture a provisional articulation.
3. We then test this articulation by comparing it to our

---

[3] But does this not follow from the commonplace belief that an art gives one mastery over contraries?

[4] What Plato is pointing out here is the impossibility of reducing moral questions to technical questions. *Techne* gives us the mastery over contraries. Medicine gives us the power to cure and to kill. But this power does not determine whether or not we *should* cure or kill. This is a distinctly moral—or, better, ethical—question, a question that refers us ultimately to the possibilities of the souls in which arts inhere.

inarticulate grasp. We have the capacity to simply "see" whether an articulation is adequate or not. Any serious attempt to articulate an idea we already possess implicitly will be at least *partially* true. Thus the way to test it is by *totalizing* it, by asking whether or not the proffered definition is not just *part* but the *whole* of justice, piety, etc. The way to test such a totalized definition is to use one's knowledge of history, literature, and common sense to generate *counterexamples*: instances or scenarios that perfectly exemplify the definition that we are testing, but which reveal the definition to be incomplete in light of the very inarticulate grasp that we are trying to put into words.
4. Then, as each account is shown to be inadequate, it is then *supplemented* by additional distinctions or elements—finer and finer articulations.
5. This process can be repeated, until, it is hoped, we finally approach a complete articulation of the concept at hand, at which time dialectic grinds to a halt because no problems can be generated in terms of which the final account can be shown to be inadequate.

## 2. Hegel's *Philosophy of Right*

Now let us compare the dialectic of Hegel's *Philosophy of Right* to Plato's. In the *Philosophy of Right*, Hegel states that "The subject-matter of the philosophical science of right is the Idea (*Idee*) of right, i.e., the Concept (*Begriff*) of right together with the actualization of that Concept" (PR, p. 14).[5]

Concept + Concrete Actualization = Idea.

What Hegel means by the "actualization" of the Concept of right is its concrete realization in social institutions and practices. For Hegel, therefore, an Idea is nothing abstract. Concepts are

---

[5] Throughout this essay, I shall capitalize the words Idea and Concept when they refer specifically to Hegel's technical conceptions of *Idee* and *Begriff*.

abstract, but Ideas are the concrete actualization of Concepts—the world transformed in light of Concepts. Hegel sees history as the process by which Concepts like freedom are realized concretely through human action, including the scientific and technological conquest of nature and the creation of an increasingly man-made, artificial world. The implicit logic of the process of actualizing Concepts is dialectic. In the *Philosophy of Right*, Hegel seeks to articulate the dialectical logic by which the modern state emerged.

Hegel considers the abstract Concept of right to be empty, indeterminate, and infinite. It has no parts, or joints between parts. Hegel considers the Idea of right to be fully determinate and finite, as well as concrete. It is fully articulated into all of its parts, and the boundaries between them are clearly delimited.

The concepts of articulation, finitude, and determinacy are related, for articulation means the breaking up of something into parts along "joints." In the same way, finitude means having bounds or limits; finitude breaks up the unlimited and unbounded—the infinite—into distinct parts, along joints. So too does determinacy, which means having defined limits, and which breaks up the unlimited and unfixed—the inarticulate, the infinite—into distinct parts, with defined limits, along joints.

The process of dialectic, therefore, is the process whereby the indeterminate, infinite, inarticulate, and abstract Concept becomes progressively articulated, defined (finitized), and determined—and then concretely realized—until one reaches the Idea.

It is often claimed that Hegel's phenomenology is not "reflective" but "speculative," meaning that the Hegelian phenomenologist does not *turn inward* and reflect upon how things show up to us, or our ways of involvement with the world, but rather he simply *looks outward* at the Concept's self-generation of determinations.

It is also commonly claimed that Hegel's phenomenology is *presuppositionless*, i.e., that it presupposes no determinate content, but simply the indeterminate Concept, which then generates determinations of its own internal "motion" without any external input on the part of the investigator.[6]

I wish, however, to argue that Hegel's dialectic is actually much more "transcendental" than either he or his anti-foundationalist followers have claimed. Specifically, I wish to argue that a careful examination of actual dialectical arguments indicates that Hegel's speculation is actually a form of reflection, i.e., (1) that all of the determinations of the Idea are latent in the Concept, such that Hegel's dialectic can also be understood as explicative, as moving from the implicit to the explicit, and (2) that the implicit Concept is "possessed" by the dialectical investigator in such a way that dialectic is not the self-explication of the Concept, but rather the self-explication of the implicit knowledge of the dialectical investigator himself.

I also will argue that that Hegel's dialectic is not presuppositionless at all, but rather represents the most advanced possible form of "dogmatism" or "positivism," i.e., Hegel does not simply presuppose as "given" the rather innocuous determinate contents discussed by various empiricists—i.e., sense data, percepts, etc.—but rather Hegel presupposes all the contents of his philosophical system are given, but they are given implicitly in the history of Western civilization, including both commonsense knowledge and the heights of our traditions of art, religion, philosophy, science, and jurisprudence.

I should, however, note that Hegel's approach is indeed presuppositionless, *if* one narrows the meaning of the word "presupposition" to refer only to *explicit* presuppositions, i.e., articulated premises. If, however, one uses "presupposition" as I do, to refer to all suppositions, articulate and inarticulate, then Hegel's method is definitely not presuppositionless. The point, of course, though, is not to get bogged down in debates about what words like "presupposition" "really" mean, but rather to stipu-

---

[6] For forceful statements of these positions, see any number of works by Richard Dien Winfield, such as "The Route to Foundation-Free Systematic Philosophy," and "Hegel Versus the New Orthodoxy," in his *Overcoming Foundations: Studies in Systematic Philosophy* (New York: Columbia University Press, 1989) and "Hegel's Remedy for the Impasse of Contemporary Philosophy," *Reason Papers* 16 (1991): 115-32.

late a defensible usage for the word and stick to it consistently.

Consider, first, the dialectic of the will in the Introduction to the *Philosophy of Right*. Hegel sets his dialectic in motion by observing a seeming paradox in the free will. A will is intentional; in order to be a will, it must will something determinate. But insofar as it wills something determinate, it is in turn determined by that object. The will becomes the will-to-X. It seems, however, that the freedom of the will consists in its indeterminacy, its non-identification with any particular object, its refusal to be tied down. Hence we arrive at the paradox of the free will. In order to be, the will must will something; but in order to be free, it must not will anything in particular. The way out of this paradox is to specify determinate conditions for freedom itself. The only determinate objects that a will can will and yet remain free are the determinate conditions of freedom itself. Articulating the conditions of freedom — the whole set of institutions and practices that concretely realize the Concept freedom in the world — i.e., the Idea of freedom — is the task of the *Philosophy of Right*.

Hegel's question is: What is a free will? This is neither a merely conceptual question nor a merely empirical one. It does not ask simply about the Concept of the free will. Thus it cannot be answered adequately by giving a simple definition or "linguistic analysis" of the words "free" and "will." Nor does it ask simply about the concrete existence of the free will, thus it cannot be answered adequately by simply pointing to a concrete instance of a free will. Rather, the question asks after the *Idea* of the free will, meaning a full articulation of the elements of a free will and the concrete conditions for its actualization.

In order to answer this question, Hegel puts forth several possible accounts of the concrete conditions for the actualization of a free will. But Hegel's exposition is deeply frustrating. On the one hand, we know that Hegel has something called a "dialectic," which is the logic of the transitions between the different positions of his system. But on the other hand, when we look at Hegel's page, we see a list of different concepts, with various elucidations, asides, and additions. But the transitions between them are not very clear. But then nothing in Hegel is very clear.

Hegel's text comes to life, however, if we, in effect, imagine how Socrates might get from one step to another. In short, we have to enter into Hegel's text, drawing upon our pre-existing although inarticulate knowledge of freedom, and generate counter-examples based on history, literature, and common sense.

So, for instance, Hegel's first account of freedom draws upon a real aspect of a free will: the sensuous immediacy of feeling, emotion, and appetite. This is what Hegel calls the *natural will*. Is the natural will an adequate account of the Idea of freedom? Does it fully articulate the moments of the Idea? Granted, it captures a part of the story, but does it capture the whole story? How do we know that it captures a part? How do we verify Hegel's assertion? The answer: through our own experience of being creatures who will.

In order to determine the adequacy of the natural will as an account of the free will, one cannot simply "look on" at the self-development of the Concept. Rather, one must intervene, so to speak, in Hegel's text. One must first and provisionally take the natural will to be a *complete* account of the free will, and then ask whether or not this generates any problems. If we range over our past experiences and our knowledge of literature and history and then augment them with our imaginations, we can generate plausible situations in which the natural will can be seen clearly to fail to account adequately for the free will.

For instance, it is clearly possible to conceive of a situation in which a human being is enslaved through a combination of blind fear and the appetite for the basic requirements of life: food, clothing, shelter, etc. Also, it is clearly possible to conceive of situations in which one's impulses conflict with one another, paralyzing one's ability to act. Furthermore, it is possible to have so many different desires that one is paralyzed in their face. In such cases the natural will leads us to slavery, not to freedom; therefore, the natural will cannot be anything more than a *part* of an adequate account of freedom. It is not the *whole* story; therefore, it needs to be *supplemented* by other factors to yield a more adequate account. And how do we know that an account is fully adequate? When its concrete realization is stable and self-sufficient, rather than unstable and requiring supplementation from outside. The idea of freedom, therefore, is an enduring concrete social whole, a substance that stands on its own rather than needing external props. But the natural will cannot stand on its own. It cancels itself out.

Thus we move forward to Hegel's next account: the arbitrary will. Following one's feelings is an inadequate account of freedom, because one's feelings can also lead one into slavery. Thus we have to do more than *feel*. We have to *think* about the consequences of our actions and *choose* the feelings we follow and the feelings we ignore. Thus we arrive at the idea of the arbitrary will, the will that chooses. Hegel's notion of the arbitrary will is basically modern economic man, who uses reason (instrumental reason and the power to choose) to maximize his enjoyment of his "given preferences" (one's feelings, one's natural will).

But we have to ask: Is economic man really free? Obviously, there are circumstances in which economic men can make deals and sign contracts by which they lose their freedom. Beyond that, the answer hinges on the status of the "given preferences" one seeks to satisfy. Is one really free if one's reason and choices are confined solely to maximizing one's enjoyment of preferences that are *just there*? Our given preferences are either natural or conventional, but in both cases, if they are simply *given* to us by nature or society, are we really free if reason and choice are in effect slaves to preferences that we do not choose? We may choose *among* them. We may suppress *some* altogether. But that is only to better pursue *other* given preferences. But what if the values that are sold to us are concocted to degrade, enslave, or destroy us? What if our ideas of what is cool or fashionable or moral are produced by people who resent, despise, and wish to harm us? Obviously, maximizing our enjoyment of such values is not freedom, but a sick form of bondage in which we take pride in pursuing our own destruction.

Thus the economic model fails to be true freedom, because according to that model, we do not *choose* our preferences. They are simply *given* to us. To be truly free, we must choose *what* we value, not merely *how* to gain or keep given values. True freedom involves the choice of ends, not merely the choice of means. We need to know that our given preferences *really are good*. Thus we arrive at the next step of Hegel's dialectic, which holds that true freedom is *willing what is objectively good*, what we *ought* to want, rather than what we simply *think* we want. Now, Plato, Rousseau, and Kant give differing accounts of basically the same viewpoint, but in Hegel's case, the true object of the free will is the Idea of freedom, which is the social and political system set forth in the *Philosophy of Right*.

Now these transitions between different accounts of freedom aren't actually in Hegel's text, but they are suggested by it. They are also consistent with Hegel's ideas and methods, and they actually get us to the next stage of the argument. In sum, the following elements are present in Hegel's dialectic. There is (1) the Concept of freedom which is being articulated into (2) the Idea of freedom. There is then (3) an attempt to articulate the Concept of freedom as the natural will. This account is then tested by (4) *totalizing* it provisionally in order to (5) determine whether or not it can stand on its own or if it fails. Then (6) a hypothetical situation is generated using personal experience, history, and imagination in which the natural will can be *clearly seen* to be an incomplete account of the free will. At this point, the incomplete account is (7) *supplemented* by other factors to yield a new, more complete and stable account that is then put to the test as in (4).

My question is: In virtue of what can the natural will or the arbitrary will be "clearly seen" to be inadequate accounts of the free will? How do we know this? What is the criterion that is being evoked? Why do we not instead simply say that what appears to be slavery must "really" be freedom, because acting on the dictates of the natural will or the arbitrary will *just is* freedom, whether one is cowering before a whip or lolling around on heroin or actively maximizing one's ingestion of poisonous pseudo-values?

I submit that we can "clearly see" that X is an inadequate account of free will only if *we always-already know what a free will is*. But we do not, of course, know it *explicitly* (or we would not be groping for a definition), but "implicitly." By "implicit" knowledge I do not mean any sort of articulate or "conceptual" knowledge. Rather, by implicit knowledge, I mean an inarticulate, pre-conceptual knowledge: things that we know but have not said. In this case, we are able to judge concepts of free will simply because human beings have free wills. The Concept of a free will does not, therefore, stand apart from the investigator. Rather, the Concept is simply Hegel's name for the pre-reflective, inarticulate grasp of the human condition that we all have because we are human.

And, since for Hegel human being is *historical* being, our grasp of being human includes our tacit understanding of the cultures and traditions that are part of us. And if the Concept of the free will does not stand apart from the investigator, then the speculative investigator does not simply gaze outward at the self-articulation of the Concept. Rather, he reflectively turns inward and articulates the Concept that is part of who he is. The Concept is self-articulating only insofar as it is part of a self striving for self-understanding.

I believe that this basic structure is present throughout the *Philosophy of Right*: through the dialectic of the will in the Introduction, in the progression from abstract right to morality to ethical life, and in the internal articulation of ethical life into the moments of family, civil society, and state. At each step of the dialectic a partial articulation of the Concept can be tested against our tacit knowledge of it by using reflection, history, science, and imagination to generate scenarios in which the inadequacy of the account in question is demonstrated. The inadequate account is then supplemented by other elements, and the resulting new account is tested again until, finally, the Concept is wholly explicated into the Idea, which is not just a system of Concepts, but a concrete social and political whole that is complete, stable, and does not need to be patched or propped up from outside.

### 3. THE HERMENEUTIC CIRCLE IN HEIDEGGER'S *BEING & TIME*

Heidegger's purpose in *Being and Time*[7] is to explore the ques-

---

[7] Martin Heidegger, *Sein und Zeit*, 10th ed. (Tubingen: Niemeyer, 1927), henceforth cited as SZ; *Being and Time*, trans. John MacQuarrie and Edward Robinson (New York: Harper and Row, 1962), henceforth cited as BT. I shall also use Joan Stambaugh's translation of the Introduction to *Being and Time* in Martin Heidegger, *Basic Writings*,

tion of the sense (*Sinn*) of Being (*Sein*). By "Being" Heidegger means the *meaningful presence* of beings to a knower. By the "sense of Being," Heidegger refers to the meaningful presence of *meaning itself*. The "sense" of Being has nothing to do with sense perception, but rather sense and nonsense, the whole realm of meaning. The sense of Being is what makes it possible for us to think about the meaningful presence of beings, the fact that we experience a world of meaning rather than a meaningless assemblage of mere things. So for Heidegger, there are *things* (beings), the *meaningful presence* of beings (Being), and the *meaningful presence of meaning itself* (the sense of Being).

Meaning is not just the *meaning of* things, it is also *meaning to* a knower, which Heidegger calls *Dasein*. *Dasein* is a German word for existence, but Heidegger hears it as a compound of *da* (here and there, in the sense of location) and *Sein* (Being). Thus Heidegger does not speak of the human *subject* or *consciousness*. Instead, he speaks of *Dasein*, the "place" or "location" where beings become meaningful.

For Heidegger, *Dasein* and *Sein*, man and meaning, have a reciprocal relationship. There cannot be man without meaning, or meaning without man. Because man and meaning, *Dasein* and Being, belong together, it is natural to employ our knowledge of who we are in order to understand the sense of Being:

> Thus to work out the question of Being adequately, we must make a being — the enquirer — transparent in his own Being.... The explicit and transparent formulation of the question of the meaning of Being requires a proper explication of a being (*Dasein*) with regard to its Being. (SZ, p. 7; BT, p. 27; BW, p. 48)

As in Hegel and Plato, so too in Heidegger, philosophical investigation is ultimately a matter of self-knowledge and self-explication. This gives rise to the hermeneutic method of *Being and Time*:

---

ed. David Farrell Krell (New York: Harper and Row, 1976), henceforth cited as BW.

Inquiry, as a kind of seeking, must be guided beforehand by what is sought. So the sense of Being must already be available to us in some way. As we have intimated, we always conduct activities in an understanding of Being.... We do not know what "Being" means. But even if we ask, "What is Being?," we keep within an understanding of the "is," though we are unable to fix conceptually what that "is" signifies. We do not even know the horizon in terms of which that sense is to be grasped and fixed. But this vague average understanding of Being is still a fact. (SZ, p. 6; BT, p. 25; BW, pp. 45–46).

Heidegger claims that "What we seek when we inquire into Being is not something entirely unfamiliar, even if at first we cannot grasp it at all" (SZ, p. 6; BT, p. 25; BW, p. 46). Heidegger then asks, "But does not this undertaking fall into an obvious circle?" (SZ, p. 7; BT, p. 27; BW, p. 48).

If we must first define a being (*Dasein*) in its Being, and if we want to formulate the question of Being only on this basis, what is this but going in a circle? In working out our question, have we not "presupposed" something which only the answer can bring? (SZ, p. 7; BT, p. 27; BW, p. 48)

The logical fallacy of circular argument, or begging the question, means using the conclusion one seeks to establish as one of the premises of the argument. If we have to presuppose that we know the sense of Being in any attempt to elucidate it, is this not a circular argument? Having raised this problem, Heidegger then goes on to answer it:

Factically though there is no [vicious] circle at all in formulating our question as we have described. One can determine the nature of beings in their Being without necessarily having the explicit concept of the sense of Being at one's disposal.... This "presupposing" of Being has rather the character of taking a look at it beforehand, so that in the light of it the entities presented to us get provisionally articulated in their being.... Such "presupposing" has nothing to do with laying down an axiom from which a sequence of propositions is deductively derived. It is quite impossible for there to be any "circular argument" in formulating the question about the sense of Being; for in answering this question, the issue is not one of grounding something by such a derivation; it is rather one of laying bare the grounds for it and exhibiting them. (SZ, pp. 7-8; BT, pp. 27-28; BW, p. 49)

The Heideggerian solution to this problem is that we always-already know the sense of Being, *but in a vague and tacit way*. This makes inquiry possible. But we wish to know clearly and explicitly. Thus the vagueness and tacitness of our knowledge makes inquiry necessary. Thus inquiry is a process of explication or interpretation (*Auslegung*) in which an implicit, tacit knowledge is made explicit and articulate. This is not a vicious circle, for we are not deducing a conclusion from a ground, but rather descriptively laying bare the ground from which a deduction can proceed. It is, loosely speaking, an "inductive" not a deductive process.

Heidegger does, however, call it a *hermeneutical* circle. A hermeneutical circle is a process in which each part of a text being interpreted is understood in the context of the whole, while at the same time our understanding of the whole is being slowly constructed out of the parts. Heidegger's process wherein the inarticulate is rendered articulate could be interpreted as a hermeneutical circle as follows. First, one advances a tentative articulation of one's subject matter. Then one circles back, testing this account against one's inarticulate grasp of the matter to be articulated, progressively supplementing each new account to accord better with the matter to be articulated.

But this is precisely what both Hegel and Plato—as I have construed them—are doing. Hegelian and Platonic dialectic both are a process whereby tacit, inarticulate knowledge is rendered explicit and articulate. Hegelian-Platonic dialectic moves within a hermeneutical circle.

But if Plato and Hegel can be read as hermeneutical thinkers, does this mean that Heidegger is a dialectical thinker? The answer is yes. Heidegger does not, of course, describe himself as a dialectical thinker. The early Heidegger calls his activity phenomenology (which is couched in the language of reflection and description), and the later Heidegger calls it simply "thinking." But, as we shall see in our discussion of Husserl on parts and wholes, there is a sense in which phenomenology is dialectical as well as reflective and descriptive. To put it paradoxically, "dialectic" is a better description of the activity of phenomenology than description itself. Beyond that, Heidegger's "thinking" is always attuned to what is missing from the standard positions in the history of philosophy, the larger hidden contexts in which these ideas make sense, and this is essentially the activity of dialectic.

## 4. Parts & Wholes in Husserl's Third *Logical Investigation*

Edmund Husserl's treatment of the logic of parts and wholes in the *Logical Investigations*,[8] Investigation Three, "On the Theory of Parts and Wholes," offers resources for a fairly rigorous account of the structure of dialectic as it plays itself out within the hermeneutic circle.[9] Husserl articulates the *a priori* laws governing the modes of givenness of various kinds of parts and wholes.

---

[8] Edmund Husserl, *Logical Investigations*, 2 vols., trans. J. N. Findlay (New York: Humanities Press, 1970).

[9] For two very useful accounts of this investigation, see Robert Sokolowski, "The Logic of Parts and Wholes in Husserl's *Logical Investigations*," *Philosophy and Phenomenological Research* 28 (1967–68): 537–53, and Jay Lampert, "Husserl's Theory of Parts and Wholes: The Dynamic of Individuating and Contextualizing Interpretation — *Übergehen, Abheben, Ergänzungsbedürftigkeit*," *Research in Phenomenology* 19 (1989): 195–212. Lampert's article is especially useful in bringing out the implications of Husserl's account for dialectic, although he is unfair in accusing Sokolowski of being unaware of these implications. Sokolowski does demonstrate an awareness of the issue, though he does not make it a central theme of his paper. Sokolowski makes more of this issue in chapter 1, "Parts and Wholes," of his *Husserlian Meditations: How Words Present Things* (Evanston: Northwestern University Press, 1974).

I shall focus only on his key distinction between two kinds of parts: *pieces* and *moments*.

Pieces are parts that can be given in separation from their wholes. Examples would be a horse's head or a human hand. (Husserl notes that although these can be given apart from their proper wholes, they cannot be given in complete separation. They must, at the very least, be given as figures against a background.) Moments are parts that cannot be given separate from their proper wholes. For instance, a physical body—say a soccer ball—may show up as a self-sufficient whole against the backdrop of the soccer field. But the ball is given through a number of non-independent moments: extension, surface, color, texture, etc. Texture cannot be given apart from a surface, and surface cannot be given apart from some texture. Surface and texture are interpenetrated with one another, and in virtue of this, they cannot be given in separation.

But what if one were to attempt to give a moment in separation? What if, for instance, an Italian futurist such as Balla were to decide to give a painted or plastic representation of brightness, sound, or speed? Take brightness. Let us begin at the stage of the creative process in which the artist merely considers his object hypothetically, turning it over and over in his imagination, trying to picture it in his head. In considering the attempt to represent brightness alone he would discover, by the inexorable *a priori* laws governing the givenness of brightness, that brightness can be given concretely only along with color. Brightness is the brightness *of* a color. (Let us limit the example to pigment, rather than to light.)

Brightness, in short, demands the supplementation or horizon of color if it is to be given. But color itself demands a certain supplementary horizon if it itself is to be given: surface. Color is the color *of* a surface. Surface itself, however, demands its own supplementation: an extended body. Surfaces are the surfaces *of* a body. And an extended body in turn requires a background if it is to be given. Finally, to give an extended body against a background demands the ultimate supplementation: a subject to whom it can be given. But with an extended body given against a background to a subject we have arrived at a self-sufficient whole.

The pattern is as follows. Each moment, when considered in terms of the concrete conditions necessary to actualize and give it, reveals within itself an essential "demand for supplementation" (*Ergänzungsbedürftigkeit*) — a demand for an appropriate horizon — if it is to be given. The process of supplementation continues, each incomplete moment tendering its demand for its proper supplements, until one has ascended to a self-sufficient whole, a whole that can be given without further supplementation.

The example that I have chosen begins with a pregiven, well-known, and ordinary kind of whole: a physical object given to a subject against a backdrop. For the sake of my example, this whole was deconstructed into, and then reconstructed from, its moments. But it is also, it seems, possible to work one's way up from moments to a whole that has not been given "in person" beforehand — although, of course, such a process would at every step of the way be guided by a pre-intuition of the whole toward which one is ascending. One would take a hypothetical moment and consider it in terms of its requirements for concrete realization, disclosing its necessary supplementations. At each step, the progressive accretion of supplementations would allow one to revise one's pre-intuition of the whole, in turn allowing one to tack back from the whole to its progressively accreting moments, lighting them up and allowing the further disclosure of necessary supplementations, until one has arrived at and made present — or at least progressively approached — the pre-intuited whole.

Two essential features of this process must be noted.

First, the process of supplementing a moment, thereby incorporating it into its proper whole, should be understood as both *founding* or *grounding* the moment, and as *limiting* or *binding* it. This limitation, however, is a special, originary form of limitation. It is not the imposition of an external limit upon a pregiven, self-sufficient phenomenon, such as slicing up a pie. Rather, it is an imposition on something that is precisely *not* pregiven and self-sufficient, but that is only a hypothetically ventured candidate for a phenomenon. This limitation is not, therefore, a diminishment of the hypothetical phenomenon, but rather that which lifts it from being merely hypothetical and non-given possibility to being a given actuality. By limiting or binding the hypothetical phenomenon into its proper horizon of supplementations, it becomes actual; it becomes given; it comes into existence. The originary limitation is, in short, identical to the process of founding. It is a limitation that brings that which it limits into being, rather than diminishing its being.

Consider, for instance, the drawing of any geometrical figure. It would be madness to consider the outlines of a geometric figure to be diminishments or impositions on the figure, as if the figure would be improved by abolishing its outer limits. Quite the contrary. The abolition of a figure's limits is the abolition of the figure itself.

Second, the process by which we move from hypothetically entertained moments through supplementation to their proper wholes is not in any sense a deductive process through which pre-given meanings are simply "unpacked." Nor, however, is it an inductive process—at least in the sense of induction as a reasoning process by which conclusions are drawn from—but strictly limited to—the enumeration and aggregation of particulars. What both induction and deduction have in common—in contradistinction to the process in question—is that in originating their conclusions they are both confined to the available evidence.

The process of ascending through supplementation from moments to their proper wholes is, by contrast, an essentially originative procedure, a process of discovery wherein the mind leaps over pregiven meanings and ahead of the enumeration and aggregation of particulars to grasp more and more adequately—and in an essentially originary insight—the nature of a whole.

*Counter-Currents*, December 26 & 27, 2016

# WHY READ HEGEL?
## NOTES ON THE "END OF HISTORY"*

Georg Wilhelm Friedrich Hegel (1770–1831) has had a tremendous influence on the modern world, not only in the history of ideas, but in the political realm as well. How big an influence? Without Hegel, there would have been no Marx; without Marx, no Lenin, no Mao, no Castro, no Pol Pot. Reflect just a moment on the difference that Communism has made in the modern world, even in non-Communist countries, whose policies were deeply motivated by the desire to defeat Communism. Communism is without a doubt the most important and influential, not to mention deadly, political innovation in the 20th century; and, before Marx, some of its intellectual foundations were laid by Hegel.

I should add, however, that Hegel would have rejected Marxism and thus cannot be held responsible for the lesser minds influenced by him; furthermore, not all aspects of his cultural and political legacy are so negative; and, rightly understood, Hegel has the potential to exercise an immensely positive influence on modern politics and culture.

Outwardly, Hegel did not live a particularly interesting life. He was born in 1770 in Stuttgart, to an educated, middle-class family of lawyers, civil servants, and Lutheran pastors. He was educated at the University of Tübingen, first as a seminarian. He shared rooms with Friedrich Wilhelm Joseph Schelling and Friedrich Hölderlin, who also made huge contributions to German philosophy and letters. Having completed the equivalent of a Ph.D. in philosophy, he held a series of tutoring positions, collaborated on a couple of journals, inherited and spent his patrimony, and found himself broke and approaching his middle thirties.

Salvation came in the form of a book contract with a healthy advance but a draconian penalty for lateness. Hegel started

---

* This is the opening lecture of an adult education class on "The End of History" given in Atlanta in the mid-1990s.

writing . . . and writing . . . and writing. His outlined work got out of hand; each chapter became bigger than the last, and Hegel found himself dangerously close to his deadline, writing feverishly to finish his work, while outside Jena, the city where he resided, Napoleon fought and defeated the Prussian army. In the midst of the chaos, as French troops were occupying the city, Hegel bundled up the only copy of his manuscript and put it in the mail. It reached the publisher, and the next year, in 1807, Hegel's most celebrated work, the *Phenomenology of Spirit*, was published.

The *Phenomenology of Spirit* is one of the classic works of German idealism: more than 500 prolix, rambling, tortured, and mind-bogglingly obscure pages. My copy is covered with dents from the times I hurled it against the wall or floor in frustration. Hegel is, without a doubt, the worst stylist in the history of philosophy. Unlike Kant, who could write well when he wanted to (but often chose not to), Hegel could not write a clear sentence to save his life. Heinrich Heine reports that on his deathbed, Hegel is said to have sighed, "Only one man has understood me." But then, a few seconds later, he added fretfully, "And even he did not understand me." Never has so much been misunderstood by so many.

The *Phenomenology of Spirit* laid the foundations for Hegel's philosophical system and for his academic career and reputation, but it was only after 10 years that he received an academic position. For the rest of his life he lectured, he wrote, and he published. And then, in 1831, he died.

Now, at this point, with any other author's story, I would conclude by saying, "and the rest is history." But, as we shall see, it is not so simple.

### THE *PHENOMENOLOGY OF SPIRIT*

Given its formidable difficulties, why would anyone try to read a book like the *Phenomenology of Spirit*? Because, as Alexandre Kojève famously claimed, if Hegel is right, then world history comes to an end with the writing of his book. Specifically, the Battle of Jena brought world history to an end in the concrete realm because it was the turning point in the battle between the principles of the French Revolution—liberty, equality, fraternity, secularism, and progress—and the principles of traditional absolutism, the so-called throne-altar alliance.

Napoleon was, for Hegel, the World Spirit made incarnate, on a horse. Napoleon did not, however, *understand* his own significance. But Hegel did. And when Hegel understood the world-historical significance of the principles of the French Revolution and their military avatar, Napoleon, and wrote it down in the *Phenomenology of Spirit*, he believed that the underlying purpose of history had been fulfilled. Just as Christ was the incarnation of the divine logos, so is the historical world—and the book—brought about by the French Revolution the incarnation of the logos of human history, and Hegel and Napoleon played the role of the Holy Spirit, mediating the two, making the ideal (the concept) concrete.

Now, at first glance—and maybe at second glance—all of this must seem quite mad. There is more madness to come. But I think that if your experience is like mine, you will find that these claims, which initially seem so mad, have a certain method to them, and even a logic. Hegel and his most charismatic expositor Alexandre Kojève exercise a strange fascination that I hope you will come to share. If they were mad, then I hope to convince you that they had cases of divine madness.

## WHAT IS "HISTORY"?

The main reason for reading Hegel is that he provides deep insights into the philosophy of history and culture. But what does Hegel mean by "history"? If history is something that can come to an end through a battle and a book, then Hegel must have a very specific—and very peculiar—conception of history in mind. This is true.

History, for Hegel, is the history of fundamental ideas, basic interpretations of human existence, interpretations of mankind and our place in the cosmos; basic "horizons" or "worldviews." History for Hegel is equivalent to what Heidegger calls the "History of Being"—"Being" to be understood here as fundamental and hegemonic worldviews. For uniformity's sake, I shall say that Hegelian history is the history of "fundamental interpretations of human existence." When these interpretations are explicitly articulated in abstract terms, they are what we call philosophies.

But it would be a mistake to think of these fundamental interpretations of human existence merely as abstract philosophical positions. They can also be found in less abstract articulations, such as myth, religion, poetry, and literature. And they can be concretely embodied: in the form of art and architecture and all other cultural productions, as well as in social and political institutions and practices.

Indeed, Hegel holds that these fundamental interpretations of existence are found for the most part in concrete, rather than abstract form. They exist as "tacit" presuppositions embedded in language, myth, religion, custom, etc. Although these can be articulated at least in part, they need not be and seldom fully are. These fundamental interpretations of existence are what Nietzsche calls "horizons": unspoken, unarticulated, unreflective attitudes and values that constitute the bounding parameters and vital force of a culture.

History for Hegel does include more concrete and mundane historical facts and events, but only insofar as these embody fundamental interpretations of human existence—and there are few things in the world that do not embody such interpretations. Even the stars, which would seem to fall into the realms of natural science and natural history, fall into human history and the human world, insofar as they are construed from the point of view of the earth, and through the lenses of different myths and cultures, as constellations, portents, or even gods. Indeed, since all of the sciences are themselves human activities, and the sciences interpret all of nature, all of nature falls within the human world.

## The "Human World"

I have been using the expression "the human world." What does this expression mean? The human world means the world of nature as *interpreted* by human reason and as *transformed* by human work. The human world comes into being when men appropriate nature, when we make it our own by endowing it with meaning and/or transforming it through work, thereby integrating it into the web of human concerns, human purposes, and human projects.

This process can be quite simple. A rock in your driveway is simply a chunk of nature. But it can be brought into the human world by endowing it with a purpose. One can use it as a paperweight; or one can use it as an example in a lecture. By doing this, I have appropriated the rock, lifting it out of the natural world, where it has no purpose and no meaning, and bringing it into the human world, where it has purpose and meaning. Hegel's primary concern as a philosopher is with the human world.

Hegel is known as an "idealist." Idealism is generally held to be a thesis that the world is made of "idea stuff." And "idea stuff" is supposed to be something ghostly, numinous, immaterial, mental. Does this mean that Hegel held that the human world is somehow numinous and abstract?

No, Hegel is not that kind of idealist. Hegel has a very peculiar way of using the world "idea" (*Idee*). When Hegel talks about ghostly, immaterial abstract mental "ideas" he uses the German word "*Begriff,*" which is well-translated "concept." And concepts are distinct from Ideas, though related to them. Hegel's understanding of the distinctness and the relatedness of concepts and Ideas can be expressed by the following equation:

$$\text{Concept} + \text{Concrete} = \text{Idea}$$

Ideas for Hegel are not abstract and numinous, because the Hegelian Idea consists of chunks of solid, concrete reality interpreted, worked over, and otherwise transformed in the light of concepts. Or, conversely formulated, the Hegelian Idea consists of concepts that have been concretely realized, whether by deploying concepts merely to interpret reality or as blueprints for transforming it. The Hegelian Idea is identical to the human world, and the human world is the world of concrete natural objects interpreted and transformed by human beings.

Hegel's use of "Spirit" is similar to his use of idea. Again, in ordinary usage, "Spirit" has an abstract and numinous connotation, but for Hegel, Spirit can be as solid and concrete as a rock, so long as the rock has been transformed in light of human concepts. So the aforementioned rock/paperweight is a chunk of Spirit, a chunk of Idea. History proper is not, however, the history of mundane concepts, mundane Ideas, and humble chunks of Spirit like a paperweight. History is the history of fundamental concepts, fundamental Ideas: fundamental interpretations of human existence, both as abstractly articulated and as concretely embodied.

To sum up:

The Human World = Idea = Concepts + Concretes

## HISTORY AS DIALECTIC

Hegel claims that all fundamental interpretations of human existence that fall within history are partial and inadequate interpretations, which are relative to time, place, and culture. This is the position known as "historicism"; it is the source of the commonplace assertion that a person or a cultural production belongs to a particular time and culture.

Since there is a plurality of different times, places, and cultures, there is also a plurality of different fundamental interpretations of human existence. The existence of a plurality of different interpretations of human existence on the finite surface of a globe means that eventually these different interpretations and the cultures that concretize them will come into contact — and, inevitably, into conflict — with one another.

History is the record of these confrontations and conflicts between different worldviews. It follows, then, that the logical structure of history is identical with the logical structure of the conflict of different worldviews. The logical structure of the conflict of different worldviews is called "dialectic." History, therefore, has a dialectical structure.

Dialectic is the logic of conversation. It is the process whereby partial and inadequate perspectives work for mutual communication and intelligibility, thereby creating a broader, more encompassing and adequate perspective.

Dialectic is the process whereby different individual or cultural perspectives, with all of their idiosyncrasies, work their way toward a more encompassing common perspective.

Dialectic is the process wherein largely tacit cultural horizons—myth, religion, language, institutions, traditions, customs, prejudices—are progressively articulated and criticized, casting aside the irrational, idiosyncratic, parochial, and adventitious in favor of the universal, rational, and fully self-conscious.

What drives the process forward is the search for an interpretation of human existence that is *adequate* to our nature. It is the search for a *true* understanding of human existence. And this presupposes that human beings have a fundamental need for a correct understanding of themselves and their world, a need that drives the dialectic forward.

Now, since fundamental interpretations of human existence take the form not merely of abstract theories, but concrete institutions, practices, cultures, and ways of life, the dialectic between these worldviews is not carried on merely in seminars, symposia, and coffee houses. It is carried on in the concrete realm as well in the form of the struggles between different political parties, interest groups, institutions, social classes, generations, cultures, forms of government, and ways of life, insofar as these embody different conceptions of human existence. The struggle is carried on in the form of peaceful rivalries and social evolution—and in the form of bloody wars and revolutions—and in the form of the conquest and annihilation or assimilation of one culture by another.

## ABSOLUTE TRUTH & THE END OF HISTORY

If all fundamental interpretations of human existence in history are partial, inadequate, and relative to particular times and cultures, this implies that if and when we arrive at an interpretation of human existence that is comprehensive and true, then we have somehow stepped outside of history. If history is the history of fundamental ideological struggle, then history ends when all fundamental issues have been decided.

In the abstract realm, the realm of concepts, the end of history comes about when a final, true, and all-encompassing interpretation of human existence is articulated. This interpretation, unlike all the others that came before it, is not partial or relative but Absolute Truth, the Absolute Concept. It is important to note that the Absolute Truth, unlike all previous partial and relative truths, does achieve a wholly articulated form; it is not a merely tacit and unarticulated cultural horizon; it is fully articulated, all-encompassing system of ideas.

However, just because the Absolute Truth is wholly articulated in abstract terms, it is not complete if it remains abstract. For Hegel, the Absolute Truth about man is that *all men are free*. But this truth is merely abstract unless all men are *actually* free. When the Concept of Freedom is concretely realized in terms of social institutions, we have arrived at the Idea of Freedom, which is the goal and end of history.

For Hegel, the Idea of Freedom allows distinct nations and states. Kojève, however, speaks of a "universal homogeneous state," which sounds like global government. Whether distinct nations remain or not, however, in all important things — that is, in all issues relating to the correct interpretation of human nature, namely that all men are free — uniformity reigns.

Hegel does not hold that Absolute Truth is merely possible, merely the speculations of an agile and perhaps fevered mind. He holds that it is already actual. The Absolute Truth is to be found — where else? — in Hegel's writings. Specifically, it is to be found in his *Encyclopedia of the Philosophical Sciences*. The *Phenomenology of Spirit* is only a ladder leading up to Absolute Truth, proving that it exists and what it must be like, but giving no specifics. And, as we have seen, Hegel holds that ideological history comes to an end with the ideals of the French Revolution: the universal rights of man; liberty, equality, and fraternity; secularism and scientific and technological progress.

The Idea of Freedom encompasses the modern scientific and technological mastery of nature. A particular chunk of Idea is a chunk of nature, of given reality, transformed by human discourse and/or human work. The Idea of Freedom, therefore, is the totality of nature transformed by human discourse and work, which includes science and technology.

Now, this doesn't imply that Freedom comes into being only after the entire universe has been scientifically understood and technologically appropriated and transformed, for this is an infinite task. But one still gives meaning to the whole simply by seeing it as the kind of place where these infinite tasks can unfold.

This is what Heidegger called the "essence of technology": seeing the world as, in principle, infinitely knowable by science and, in principle, infinitely malleable by technology. All limitations encountered in the unfolding of this infinite task are encountered as merely temporary impediments that can always, in principle, be overcome by better science and better technology.

The end of history does not mean the end of history in the more mundane sense. The newspaper will still come in the morning, but it will look more like the *Atlanta Journal* than the *New York Times*: a global village tattler, chronicling untold billions of treed cats, weddings, funerals, garage sales, and church outings, bulging with untold billions of pizza coupons. Remember: The end of history means the end of ideological history. It means that no ideological and political innovations are possible, that there are no causes worth killing or dying for anymore, that we fully understand ourselves.

The end of history is a technocrat's dream: Now that the basic intellectual and political parameters of human existence have been fixed once and for all, we can get on with the business of living: the infinite task of the mastery and possession of nature; the infinite play made possible by an endless stream of new toys.

**THE QUESTION OF HISTORICISM**

It is often said that Hegel holds that human nature itself is relative to particular times, places, and cultures, and that as history changes, so does human nature. This strikes me as false. It is man's nature to be historical, but this fact is not itself a historical fact. It is a natural fact that makes history possible. It is natural in the sense that it is a fixed and permanent necessity of our natures, which founds and bounds the realm of human action, history, and culture. Different interpretations of human nature are relative to different times, places, and cultures; different worldviews change and succeed one another in time.

Absolute Truth = a true self-interpretation of man = a final account of human nature. If such an account is not possible, because a fixed human nature does not exist, then Hegel could never hold that history comes to an end. There would merely be an endless series of historically relative self-interpretations, none of which could claim any greater adequacy than any other, because of course there would be no objective standard of truth. For Hegel, man gains knowledge of his nature through history. But he does not gain his nature itself through history.

## Kojève

Will the end of history—self-knowledge and universal human equality—make us happy?

This brings us to Aleksandr Vladimirovič Koževnikov (1902–1968), known simply as "Kojève." Kojève was the 20th century's greatest, and most influential, interpreter and advocate of Hegel's philosophy of history. Kojève's *Introduction to the Reading of Hegel* has its errors; it has its obscurities, eccentricities, and ticks. But it is still the most profound, accessible, and exciting introduction to Hegel in existence.

Ironically, though, by stating what he took to be Hegel's views clearly and radically, Kojève pushed Hegel to the breaking point, forcing us to confront the question: Is Hegel's end of history really the end of history? And if it is, can it really claim to be fully satisfying to man?

Kojève was born in Moscow in 1902 to a wealthy bourgeois family, which, when the Communists took over in 1917, was subjected to the indignities one would expect. Kojève was reduced to selling black market soap. He was arrested and narrowly escaped being shot. In a paradox that has called his sanity into question in the minds of many, he left prison a convinced Communist. In 1919, he left Russia with the family jewels, which he cashed in for a small fortune in Berlin. (He might be called a limousine Communist.)

He studied philosophy in Heidelberg with Karl Jaspers and wrote a doctoral dissertation on Vladimir Solovieff, a Russian philosopher and mystic. In the late 1920s, he moved to Paris. His fortune was wiped out by the Great Depression, and he was reduced to severely straightened circumstances. Fortunately, during the 1920s, Kojève had met and befriended Alexandre Koyré, a historian of philosophy and a fellow Russian émigré, who arranged for Kojève to take over his seminar on Hegel's *Phenomenology of Spirit* at the École pratique des hautes études.

Kojève taught this seminar from 1933 to 1939. Although the seminar was very small, it had a tremendous influence on French intellectual life, for its students included such eminent philosophers and scholars as Jacques Lacan, Maurice Merleau-Ponty, Georges Bataille, Raymond Queneau, Raymond Aron, Gaston Fessard, and Henri Corbin. Through his students, Kojève influenced Sartre, as well as subsequent generations of leading French thinkers, who are known as "postmodernists," including Foucault, Deleuze, Lyotard, and Derrida—all of whom felt it necessary to define their positions in accordance with or in opposition to Hegel as portrayed by Kojève.

I am convinced that it is impossible to understand the peculiar vehemence with which many French postmodernists abuse such concepts as "modernity" and "metaphysics" until one sees that these refer ultimately to Kojève's reading of Hegel. And this brings us to another reason for reading Hegel and Kojève: It is an ideal way to understand French postmodernism, a tremendously influential school of thought. Indeed, it seem that on some academic presses now, every third book contains "postmodern" or one of its cognates in its title.

Kojève's seminar came to an end in 1939, when World War II broke out. During the German occupation, Kojève joined the French resistance. Or so he said. After the war it was hard to find someone who didn't claim to have joined the resistance.

After the war, Kojève did not return to academia. Instead, one of his students from the 1930s, Robert Marjolin, got him a job in the French Ministry of Economic Affairs, where he worked until his death in 1968. Through his position at the ministry, Kojève exercised almost as great an influence as De

Gaulle on the creation of the post-war European economic order. He was the architect of GATT and was instrumental in setting up the European Economic Community. He was also quite prescient in predicting a number of political, economic, and cultural trends. For instance, in the 1950s he was already confident that the West would win the Cold War. He also offers profound diagnoses of the logic of contemporary culture's obsession with senseless violence and cruelty. Finally, in the late 1950s he glimpsed the logic of Japan's rising power. Up until his death in 1968, Kojève was a trusted advisor to a number of French politicians, mostly on the Right, all the while puzzling his friends by maintaining that he was still an ardent Stalinist. He even bought a house on the Boulevard de Stalingrad in Vanves, near Paris.

Kojève was fully convinced that history had come to an end in 1806 with the battle of Jena. Accordingly, he held that nothing of any fundamental historical importance had happened since then: not the First World War, not the Second World War, not the Russian and Chinese revolutions. All of these were, in Kojève's eyes, simply petty squabbles about the implementation of the principles of the French Revolution. Even the Nazis were regarded by Kojève as simply history's way of bringing democracy to Germany.

Kojève was not, however, convinced that the end of history would mean the complete satisfaction of man. Indeed, he thought that it would spell the abolition of mankind. This does not mean that Kojève thought that human beings would become extinct. He simply thought that what makes us humans, as opposed to contented animals, would be abolished at the end of history.

Kojève held that it was the capacity to engage in struggle over fundamental interpretations of human existence—the struggle for self-understanding—that set us apart from the beasts. Once these struggles are ended, that which sets us apart from the beasts disappears. The end of history would satisfy our animal natures, our desires, but it would offer nothing to satisfy our particularly human desires.

Kojève does not, however, argue that everyone is reduced to

a beast at the end of history. Traditionally, human beings have regarded themselves as occupying the space between beasts and gods on the totem pole. When one loses one's humanity, one can do so either by becoming a beast or by becoming a god.

Kojève held that most human beings at the end of history would be reduced to beasts. But some would become gods. How? By becoming *wise*. At the end of history, the correct and final interpretation of human existence, the Absolute Truth, has been articulated as a system of science by Hegel himself. This system is the wisdom that philosophy has pursued for more than 2,000 years.

Philosophy is the pursuit of wisdom, not the possession of wisdom. Hegel, by possessing wisdom, is no longer a philosopher; Hegel is a wise man. In putting the period on history, Hegel brings philosophy to an end as well.

A post-historical god takes up a critical distance from the end of history. He does not live post-historical life. He tries to understand it: how we got here, what is happening, and where we are going—all things we can learn from Hegel and Kojève. If dehumanization is our destiny, at least we can try to become gods, which is reason enough to read Hegel.

*Counter-Currents*, February 19, 2015

# A Hole in Being:
## Notes on Negativity*

G. W. F. Hegel and his able interpreter Alexandre Kojève claim that the essence of consciousness is "negativity," that man lives "outside himself," that man "negates" or "nihilates" nature, that man is a "nothingness" or a "hole in being," that man is "time that negates space." What does this all mean?

First, let's consider the claim that man contains a negativity or absence within him. Imagine you are holding a rock in your hand. A rock is a paradigmatic natural object. It is an inert lump of matter. A rock is complete and self-contained. To say that the rock is self-contained is to say that it does not need anything from outside of itself in order to go on being a rock. A plant, by contrast, is not self-contained; it needs things outside of itself—water, nutrients, sunlight—in order to go on being a plant. Without these things, it is reduced to a mass of inert matter, like the rock.

To say that the plant is not self-contained and self-sufficient is to say that it has an absence or lack within it; its need is a hole in it that must be filled by something from outside it. The rock, because it has no needs, is wholly self-sufficient and self-contained; it has no absences within it.

Another way of understanding this is to say that what makes the plant whole lies *outside* of its skin, outside of the *space* that it inhabits and occupies; what makes the plant whole is literally outside it; the plant is outside of itself, displaced from the physical space that it occupies; another way of putting this is to say that the plant is "ecstatic," for the word "ecstatic" literally means "out-standing," being outside of or beside oneself.

The rock, by contrast, is not ecstatic; because it needs nothing from outside itself to make it complete, all that it is lies within the physical space it occupies. To understand a plant as a whole, one cannot simply look at the plant, for what the plant is, is not

---

*From an adult education class on "The End of History" given in Atlanta in the mid-1990s.

wholly within its skin; the things that make the plant a whole are found outside it, in the needs that are fulfilled from the environment in which it dwells.

When Hegel/Kojève claims that man contains negativity and absence in him, they mean, first of all, that man has needs and desires, that man is not wholly self-sufficient and self-contained. Human beings lie outside of themselves, outside of their skins, for it is only outside of ourselves that we find those things that fulfill our needs and make us complete.

Next, let's consider the ideas of "negating" and "nihilating" nature. When a plant or an animal finds something from the external world that fulfills its needs, it must remove that thing from the outside world and transform and incorporate it into itself. Hegel and Kojève refer to this activity as "negating," i.e., saying "no."

A plant transforms sunlight, nutrients, and water into something that they are *not*; it in effect says "no" to them as they are given and transforms them into something it can use; it says "no" to their objective, external being and makes them part of itself.

When a cow eats the plant, it says "no" to the plant as an objective, external being and incorporates it into itself.

When a human being takes a rock and transforms it into a paperweight or an example, we say "no" to its objective, external being and incorporate it into the network of human meanings and purposes.

Now what does it mean to say that man is "time" that negates "space"? To understand this, we must appreciate an essential difference between human beings and other kinds of beings. All living things, save for human beings, have needs that are given by nature and that are satisfied within the natural world. Animals may say "no" to given nature, but it is only to satisfy their natural needs, so the process of negation is situated within and bounded by the order or economy of nature.

This is not the case with human beings. Human beings have needs that are not given by nature and that cannot be satisfied by given nature. Human beings, unlike all other living things, can say "no" to their own *naturally given* needs—to their animal natures—and to the entire economy of the natural world. Human beings say "no" to the real in the name of the unreal or the unrealized, of the ideal or the idealized.

Human beings have the power of language, reason, speech, abstraction, invention, creativity, *logos*—what Hegel calls the realm of the Concept (*Begriff*)—which allows them to create needs, ideals, and plans that are not based on nature and cannot be satisfied by it. They can be satisfied only by the transformation of the natural world through *work*. It is here that the dimension of time enters in.

Hegel claims that:

Man = Negativity = Time = Concept

To say that the Concept = time is to say that the Concept is a plan, a blueprint for a process of transforming what is given in the present into what is desired in the future. To say that man = time is to say that man's unique mode of being, man's unique mode of negativity, is the transformation of the natural world through our projects. Man, therefore, is time that negates.

But what does it mean to say that man is time that negates space? By space, Hegel/Kojève mean nature, given being, inert reality, which is to be changed in light of our Concepts and plans. Hegel/Kojève use "space" to designate *given being*, because given beings, unlike living beings, are wholly self-contained and self-sufficient; because they need nothing outside of themselves to be complete, all that they are is found within their given spatial location.

To say that man is time that negates space, is, therefore, to say that man is time that negates given being in the light of his Concepts and plans. We say "no" to what is *given now* in the name of the *not yet*, what is conceived in the mind and realized through the transformation of given nature.

There is a phrase from Jean-Paul Sartre that is often quoted by people who want to argue that French philosophy is all a bunch of gobbledygook:

Man is what he is not and is not what he is.

On the surface this does sound like nonsense, but it actually makes a great deal of Kojèvian sense.

To say that man is what he is not, is to say that human beings are not just lumps of inert given being; human beings have physical-material-animal bodies, but the body is simply the site at which a potential infinity of plans and projects burst out in all directions, toward myriad possible futures.

Human beings are what they are not because they live in their plans and projects, encountering their given reality as incomplete in light of all the things they want to achieve.

Human beings are not what they are—i.e., the given matter within our skins—because what we are is radically incomplete, and can be completed only by completing our plans and projects, and since we always have uncompleted plans and projects, which are cut off only by death, man is always incomplete, a hole in being that will never be fully filled.

*Counter-Currents*, December 15, 2012

# NOTES ON NIHILISM*

It is often said that nihilism is one of the leading characteristics of the modern age, but what is nihilism? Nihilism literally means "nothingism." Its meaning encompasses the "death" of God, the denial of objective meaning and value, the erasure of moral distinctions and hierarchies, the dissolution of a common world into individual perspectives, and the dissolution of a common culture into subjective "given preferences."

Nietzsche defines nihilism as the devaluation of the highest values, the core values, of a civilization. On that account, to understand nihilism we must, therefore, grasp: (1) the nature of values, (2) the role of values in life, (3) the nature of the claim that values make upon us, and (4) how it is possible for values to lose their claim upon us. I propose that we answer these questions through an examination of four thinkers: Giambattista Vico, Søren Kierkegaard, Friedrich Nietzsche, and Ernst Jünger.

### NIETZSCHE ON LIFE & VALUES

Nietzsche called the ultimate stuff of the world Will to Power. This is a highly anthropomorphized name for something that is neither a will (for there is no agent behind it that wills) nor is it "to power" (for it is not directed toward the goal of power, or any other goal). Will to Power is Nietzsche's name for chaos, which he conceived of as a virtual infinity of points of force charging and discharging entirely without pattern or purpose.

Chaos somehow gives rise to life, life to consciousness, and consciousness to self-consciousness. Self-consciousness, however, presents a problem for life, because self-conscious beings demand reasons for continuing to live; they demand meaning and purpose in life. And this is a demand that chaos cannot meet. In a world of chaos, all options are equal. Nothing is any better or any worse than anything else. No option is preferable to any other. Choosing is not preferable to not choosing. Action,

---

* From an adult education class on "Heidegger, Metaphysics, & Nihilism" given in Atlanta in the mid-1990s.

therefore, is fundamentally irrational. There is no reason to get out of bed in the morning. There is no reason to prefer continued existence to non-existence. Nothing matters. Nothing makes a difference. This is a condition so terrifying to self-conscious beings that they are annihilated when they encounter it directly.

Life, however, goes on. It preserves itself behind the back of consciousness by manufacturing values. These manufactured values are fictions that consciousness mistakenly thinks it discovers as objective facts. Fictional though they may be, values change everything. Once values are created, some things show up as better than others; some actions show up as better than others; some things show up as goals to be pursued; others show up as evils to be avoided. Life takes on meaning, purpose, and structure. Things begin to make a difference. One suddenly has a reason to get out of bed in the morning. Life can go on. The truth of chaos is a truth that kills. But the lie of values is a lie that we can live with. It is a necessary lie, a noble lie.

For Nietzsche, nihilism results when the core values of a culture cease being believed. There are two types of nihilism: passive and active. The passive nihilist deeply identifies with the core values of his civilization. Thus he experiences their loss as demoralizing and devitalizing. The active nihilist primarily experienced the reigning values as impediments to the freedom of his desires and imagination. Therefore, he experiences their downfall as liberating. For Nietzsche, the age of nihilism will be terminated by a particular kind of active nihilism: setting up and imposing new core values for a new civilization.

## VICO & CASSIRER

At this point, I wish to add an aside on the accounts of the origins of language, myth, and culture offered by Giambattista Vico and Ernst Cassirer, for I think that these naturalistic accounts are broadly compatible with Nietzsche's account of the origins of values and they supplement it nicely by describing the concrete embodiment of values in language, myth, and culture. Vico and Cassirer give essentially the same account of the origin of language and myth, for both hold that the first words were proper names of gods, and around these names grew up the myths and languages that formed the cores of cultures.

Vico offers a wonderful myth to illustrate the origins of language and myth. After the biblical flood, when the Earth was drying out and slowly re-populating, the sons and grandsons of Noah went back to nature, becoming very much like the Natural Man described in Rousseau's *Discourse on the Origins of Inequality*. They lost all arts and sciences, organized families and communities, myth and religion, and even the use of language. And, because they also lost personal cleanliness and wallowed in their own urine and feces, Vico claimed—in accordance with an old wives' tale then current in his hometown of Naples—they grew to a gigantic stature. Thus Vico offers us a picture of giants, devoid of language and culture, without families or cities, wandering alone in a vast forest that covered the drying Earth, occasionally bumping into one another and fornicating and then going their separate ways.

Eventually, though, evaporation from the drying Earth brewed up huge thunderstorms—thunderstorms greater than any seen before or since, thunderstorms that blanketed the entire Earth, and from the storm came a flash of lightning that lighted up the entire world and a mighty clap of thunder that shook it to its foundations, and the giants cried out in their terror a single word: "Jove."

Jove was the first word. It is a proper name. And what it names is a terrifying force of nature. But when this force is named Jove and personified, something remarkable happens. The storm is no longer such a terrifying mystery. Rather, it is the product of a deity who has his reasons for sending it. The storm suddenly becomes intelligible. Furthermore, if we can discover the reasons behind the storm, then perhaps we can avoid riling Jove up again. Or, if we can find his price, we can bribe him. Either way, we gain some control over our world. Myth and language, then, are man's first attempts to master and understand an otherwise chaotic, inscrutable, and terrifying world.

But note that the origins of language and myth are pre-rational or irrational. They are not deliberately constructed, but spontaneous and automatic reactions to environmental stimuli. Nobody sat down and created languages and myths as conventions. Rather, the existence of conventions already presupposes the existence of a common language and a common community that can discuss and agree upon the adoption of certain conventions.

But if language and myth, culture and values are pre-rational fictions, then what kind of claim can they make upon us? What would motivate us to believe and follow them? What is the source of their authority and allure? For an answer to these questions, we turn to Kierkegaard.

## KIERKEGAARD ON THE CLAIM OF VALUES

Søren Kierkegaard was the first self-proclaimed "existentialist." Kierkegaard, like many skeptics and fideists, reverses the traditional philosophical valorization of theory over practice. Kierkegaard holds that it is practical, engaged activity, not disengaged theoretical reflection, that gives us access to the true and the good. We learn what is true and what is good through being socialized into a community and culture, and the process of socialization is primarily a practical matter.

We learn by doing—by doing as others do around us, by imitating authoritative persons and following their commands. We learn what is true and what is good by apprenticeship in the concrete institutions and practices of a society, and the true and the good are accessible to us only so long as we participate in these concrete institutions and practices and recognize their authority.

In short, the primary locus of values is culture. The primary means of disseminating values is enculturation. And the authority of values derives from our pre-reflective, pre-rational identification with our culture and way of life.

Because values are disclosed through practice, not theory, their claim upon us is pre-rational. Therefore, the attempt to use reason to reflect upon, criticize, and perhaps give a foundation for our values, serves instead only to alienate us from them by weakening our pre-rational commitments to them.

In his 1846 work, *The Present Age*, Kierkegaard described how reason and reflection had undermined all authoritative institutions and practices of Western culture, thereby undermining commitment to its core values, leading to the collapse of moral distinctions, the flattening out of moral hierarchies, and the subjectivization of values. He prophesied the coming of age of nihilism.

Kierkegaard's question was how to regain a meaningful existence, how to save values from withering away from a sickly and effeminate rationalism, how to claw our way out of the quicksand of passive nihilism. Kierkegaard's answer was simple: Each individual must make a conscious and absolute commitment to some form of life and its constitutive values. Once we make such a commitment, the world is no longer a matter of indifference to us; things again show up as good or bad, right or wrong—so long as we maintain our commitment unwaveringly. In short, for Kierkegaard the cure for passive nihilism is active nihilism—and the fact that Kierkegaard's own commitment was to Christianity makes that commitment no less nihilistic.

## JÜNGER ON TECHNOLOGY & THE DEATH OF VALUES

Ernst Jünger is in essential agreement with Nietzsche on the origin and nature of values and with Kierkegaard on the nature and cure for nihilism, but he adds a significant new dimension to our understanding of the means by which nihilism comes to reign. It is an account that profoundly influenced Heidegger, and with which Heidegger was in essential agreement.

The central concept of Jünger's account of nihilism is technology. If values are fictions posited by life to sustain itself, and if values are encoded in and transmitted through concrete cultural institutions and practices, then one can see culture as a protective wall that we erect against the enervating terrors of a chaotic reality. For Jünger, modern technology is the Trojan Horse that leads us to open the gates of culture to the overwhelming forces of chaos.

Modern technological civilization is a form of culture. But it is a form of culture that undermines all other forms of culture—and also undermines itself as a culture—for the modern technological worldview is premised on the use of reason, science, and technology to progressively liberate mankind from all external and irrational impediments to the satisfaction of his desires.

While the ancients experienced nature as a fixed and eternal order founding and bounding the realm of human action, moderns experience nature as simply a pile of resources that are, in principle, infinitely transparent to human knowledge and infinitely malleable to human ends. From the technological point of view, there are no fixed boundaries to human action; there are only temporary impediments that will eventually yield, in time, to better science and better technology.

Unfortunately, however, the technological mentality regards values and their concrete cultural and institutional embodiments in religion, myth, and practice as such impediments. Values, after all, arise out of pre-rational or irrational sources. They are by necessity falsifications of reality. And they impose limitations on the technological satisfaction of our desires.

How many of us sigh and shake our heads bitterly when we hear of people refusing their children blood transfusions and vaccinations "merely" on religious grounds, merely in the name of something sacred? Technological civilization must, therefore, set itself at war with myth, religion, tradition, custom, values, and the kind of pre-rational attachments that, for instance, make us want to help our own children even though other people's children might need our help more.

However, as we progressively bargain away more and more of the sacred and the moral for the benefits of technological culture, we also bargain away the sanctity and dignity of our own humanity; we find ourselves slowly transformed from sovereign subjects employing technology to satisfy our desires, into passive objects of technology.

For instance, we find that more and more of our desires are supplied by the imperatives of the very technological system that was designed to satisfy them. Once our activities are determined not by ideals and values, but by bodily desires—by our pre-cultural, naturalistic selves—the body, not the soul, becomes the subject, the driving agent, of the technological system.

But the body's agency is illusory, for the body is—and always has been—primarily the object, not the subject, of technological manipulation. From makeup and fashion to piercing and tattooing, from diet and exercise regimens to plastic surgery to genetic engineering, the body is the object of technological manipulation, largely in response to imperatives generated by the technological system itself.

In our pursuit of freedom through the mastery of our environment, we soon discover that each one of us is an object in somebody else's environment, and that the other side of mastery is domination. But it is a form of domination in which everybody is an object and nobody is a subject, i.e., it is domination without a dominator, domination by an impersonal technological machine that grew as an unintended consequence of individual actions, that was not consciously designed by anyone, and that cannot be consciously controlled by anyone.

Domination without a dominator is another way of speaking of will without a willer; it is another way of speaking of the Will to Power. The Will to Power is the very chaos that culture was supposed to protect us from. But technological culture, by undermining the pre-rational origins, necessary falsehoods, and constitutive values of culture, has brought the Will to Power into the heart of the human world and installed it as our master.

The most chilling image of the triumph of the technological Will to Power are the "Borg" in *Star Trek—The Next Generation*. The Borg are humanoid creatures whose lives became so intertwined with technology—including technological implants in their own bodies—that they lost all individual consciousness and became almost literally mere cogs in their own machines They became objects, not subjects, of an autonomous technological system. And although this system had attained a collective consciousness of its own, which drowned out the individual consciousnesses of its humanoid components, the Borg collective mind is driven by a single imperative: to assimilate all other technologies and all other living beings into its technological system. Why? There is no ultimate end beyond the simple continuation of the process itself. The Borg assimilate only in order to continue to assimilate. The Will to Power wills only one thing: the continuation of its willing.

What is Jünger's solution to technological nihilism? Jünger believed that the technological Will to Power is unstoppable, that it will subjugate the entire Earth and the entire universe, that nothing can stand in its way. Jünger's experiences in the trenches of the First World War led him to believe that the war was an autonomous technological system, a human creation that quickly escaped the control of its creators and subjected them to the technological imperatives of its own continued existence. All moral and political motivations, all policy objectives, all means-ends rationality became moot, but the war went on; it carried itself on, simply for the sake of carrying on. Jünger became convinced that the only way to understand the phenomenon of total and autonomous war is to view it as an expression of the Will to Power, as its unstoppable volcanic eruption into the human world.

And, if you can't beat it, join it. Jünger was convinced that the only way to salvage some meaning from the unfolding of technological nihilism was to submit oneself to it, to will the inevitable, and thus to internalize it and make it one's own. In *Battle as Inner Experience*, he writes:

> All goals are past, only movement is eternal, and it brings forth unceasingly magnificent and merciless spectacles. To sink into their lofty goallessness as into an artwork or as into the starry sky, that is granted only to the few. But he who experiences in this war only negation, only inherent suffering and not affirmation, [not] a higher movement, experiences it like a slave. He has no inner, but only an external experience.

Like Kierkegaard, Jünger holds that the solution to passive nihilism is active nihilism, which still leaves us within the realm of nihilism.

## HEIDEGGER

Is there a fundamental alternative to nihilism? Is there an alternative to strong wills positing or negating values? Is there an alternative to weak wills receiving or losing the values imposed or negated by others? Is there an alternative to all this willing? For the root of nihilism is the will—specifically, the inflation of the will to the point that it becomes the defining trait of Being itself. Martin Heidegger's philosophical project can be understood as an attempt to overcome nihilism at its root, the inflation of the will into the meaning of Being.

Heidegger's account of nihilism agrees with Nietzsche's account of the origins and the nature of values, with Kierkegaard's account of the cultural embodiment and transmission of values, with Kierkegaard's account of the role of reason in the undermining of commitment, and with Jünger's account of technology as the Trojan Horse that allows the Will to Power to invade and conquer the human world. But Heidegger does not agree with their solutions, which all boil down to replacing passive nihilism with active nihilism. For active nihilism is still nihilism.

Overcoming nihilism, however, is no simple task. For Heidegger traces the metaphysics of the will back to the origins of Western metaphysics. Thus to overcome nihilism, we must overcome metaphysics. But Heidegger does not see the metaphysical tradition as merely a record of human errors, but as the product of Being's *self-concealment*. Thus trying to overcome nihilism, or trying to overcome metaphysics — as if they are merely human errors that can be corrected by human means — is itself essentially nihilistic. We may only be done with nihilism when we accept the possibility that nihilism may not yet be done with us.

*Counter-Currents*, October 23, 2010

# Yeats' Pagan Second Coming*

William Butler Yeats penned his most famous poem, "The Second Coming," in 1919, in the days after the Great War and the Bolshevik Revolution, when things truly were "falling apart," European civilization chief among them. The title refers, of course, to the Second Coming of Christ. But as I read it, the poem rejects the idea that the literal Second Coming of Christ is at hand. Instead, it affirms two non-Christian senses of Second Coming. First, there is the metaphorical sense of the end of the present world and the revelation of something radically new. Second, there is the sense of the Second Coming not of Christ, but of the paganism displaced by Christianity. Yeats heralds a pagan Second Coming.

The poem reads:

Turning and turning in the widening gyre,
The falcon cannot hear the falconer;
Things fall apart; the center cannot hold;
Mere anarchy is loosed upon the world,
The blood-dimmed tide is loosed, and everywhere
The ceremony of innocence is drowned;
The best lack all conviction, while the worst
are full of passionate intensity.

Surely some revelation is at hand;
Surely the Second Coming is at hand.
The Second Coming! Hardly are those words out
When a vast image out of *Spiritus Mundi*
Troubles my sight: somewhere in the sands of the desert
A shape with lion body and the head of a man,
A gaze blank and pitiless as the sun,
Is moving its slow thighs, while all about it
Reel shadows of the indignant desert birds.

---

\* From an adult education class on "Heidegger, Metaphysics, & Nihilism" given in Atlanta in the mid-1990s.

A darkness drops again; but now I know
That twenty centuries of stony sleep
Were vexed to nightmare by a rocking cradle
And what rough beast, its hour come round at last,
Slouches towards Bethlehem to be born?

If one reads this poem as an allegory of modern nihilism, quite a lot falls into place. "Turning and turning in the widening gyre." Picture here a falcon flying in an ever-widening spiral trajectory. At the center of the gyre is the falconer, the falcon's master. As the gyre widens, there comes a point at which "the falcon cannot hear the falconer."

Presumably, what the falcon cannot hear is the falconer calling the bird back to his arm. No longer able to hear the falconer's voice, the falcon continues to push outwards.

But without the pull toward the center, the falcon's flight path will lose its spiral structure, which is constituted by the connection between the falcon and the falconer, and the falcon will have to determine his flight path on his own, a path that will no doubt zig and zag with the currents of the air and the falcon's passing desires, but will not display any intelligible structure—except, maybe, some decayed echoes of its original spiral.

The falcon is modern man. The motive force of the falcon's flight is human desire, pride, spiritedness, and Faustian striving. The spiral structure of the flight is the intelligible measure—the moderation and moralization of human desire and action—imposed by the moral center of our civilization, represented by the falconer, the falcon's master, our master, which I interpret in Nietzschean terms as the highest values of our culture. The tether that holds us to the center and allows it to impose measure on our flight is the "voice of God," i.e., the claim of the values of our civilization upon us; the ability of our civilization's values to move us.

We, the falcon, have, however, spiraled out too far to hear our master's voice calling us back to the center, so we spiral onward, our motion growing progressively more eccentric (un-centered), our desires and actions progressively less measured ...

Thus, "Things fall apart. The center cannot hold." When the

moral center of civilization no longer has a hold, things fall apart. This falling apart has at least two senses. It refers to disintegration but also to things falling away from one another because they are also falling away from their common center. It refers to the breakdown of community and civilization, the breakdown of the government of human desire by morality and law, hence ...

"Mere anarchy is loosed upon the world." Anarchy, meaning the lack of *arche*: the Greek for origin, principle, and cause; metaphorically, the lack of center. But what is "mere" about anarchy? Anarchy is not "mere" because it is innocuous and unthreatening. In this context, "mere anarchy" means anarchy in an unqualified sense, anarchy plain and simple. Thus:

The blood-dimmed tide is loosed, and everywhere
The ceremony of innocence is drowned;
The best lack all conviction, while the worst
Are full of passionate intensity.

Why would nihilism make the best lack all conviction and fill the worst with passionate intensity? I think that here Yeats is offering us his version of Nietzsche's distinction between active and passive nihilism. The passive nihilist—because he identifies on some level with the core values of his culture—experiences the devaluation of these values as an enervating loss of meaning, as the defeat of life, as the loss of all convictions. By contrast, the active nihilist—because he experiences the core values of his culture as constraints and impediments to the free play of his imagination and desires—experiences the devaluation of these values as liberating, as the freedom to posit values of his own, thus nihilism fills him with a passionate creative—or destructive—intensity.

This characterization of active and passive nihilism captures the struggle between conservatives and the Left. Conservatives are the "best" who lack all conviction. They are the best, because they are attached to the core values of the West. They lack all conviction, because they no longer *believe* in them. Thus they lose every time when faced by the passionate intensity of the

Left, who experience nihilism as invigorating.

The second stanza of Yeats's poem indicates precisely which core values have been devalued. The apocalyptic anxiety of the first stanza leads one to think that perhaps the Apocalypse, the Second Coming, is at hand:

> Surely some revelation is at hand;
> Surely the Second Coming is at hand.

But this is followed by the exclamation, "The Second Coming!" which I interpret as equivalent to "The Second Coming? Ha! Quite the opposite." And the opposite is then revealed, not by the Christian God, but by the pagan *Spiritus Mundi* (world spirit):

> Hardly are those words out
> When a vast image out of *Spiritus Mundi*
> Troubles my sight: somewhere in the sands of the desert
> A shape with lion body and the head of a man,
> A gaze blank and pitiless as the sun,
> Is moving its slow thighs, while all about it
> Reel shadows of the indignant desert birds.
> A darkness drops again; but now I know
> That twenty centuries of stony sleep
> Were vexed to nightmare by a rocking cradle
> And what rough beast, it hour come round at last,
> Slouches towards Bethlehem to be born?

Two images are conjoined here. First, the shape with the body of a lion, the head of a man, and a blank, pitiless stare is an Egyptian sphinx—perhaps the Great Sphinx at Giza, perhaps one of the many small sphinxes scattered over Egypt. Second, there is the nativity, the birth of Christ in Bethlehem. The connection between Bethlehem and Egypt is the so-called "flight into Egypt." After the birth of Jesus, the holy family fled to Egypt to escape King Herod's massacre of newborn boys.

Yeats is not the first artist to conjoin the images of the sphinx and the nativity. For instance, there is a painting by a 19th-century French artist, Luc Olivier Merson, entitled "Rest on the Flight into Egypt," which portrays a night "twenty centuries" ago in which Mary and the infant Jesus are asleep, cradled between the paws of a small sphinx.

This painting was so popular in its time that the artist made three versions of it, and one of them, in the Museum of Fine Arts, Boston is so popular that reproductions of it as framed prints, jigsaw puzzles, and Christmas cards can be purchased today.

I do not know if Yeats was thinking about this specific painting. But he was thinking about the flight into Egypt. And the poem seems to indicate a reversal of that flight, and a reversal of the birth of Christ. Could Mary, resting on the flight into Egypt, rocking Jesus cradled between the paws of a sphinx, have vexed the stony beast to nightmare? Could it have finally stirred from its troubled sleep, its womb heavy with the prophet of a new age, and begun the search for an appropriate place to give birth? "And what rough beast, its hour come round at last, slouches towards Bethlehem to be born?" And what better place than Bethlehem, not to repeat but to reverse the birth of Christ and inaugurate a post-Christian age.

One can ask, however, if the poem ends on a note of horror or of hope. As I read it, there are three distinct stages to Yeats' narrative. The first is the age when Christian values were the unchallenged core of Western civilization. This was a vital, flourishing civilization, but now it is over. The second stage is nihilism, both active and passive, occasioned by the loss of these core values. This is the present-day for Yeats and ourselves.

The third stage, which is yet to come, will follow the birth of the "rough beast." Just as the birth of Jesus inaugurated Christian civilization, the rough beast will inaugurate a new pagan civilization. Its core values will be different from Christian values, which, of course, horrifies Christians, who hope to revive their religion. But the new pagan values, unlike Christian ones, will actually be *believed*, bringing the reign of nihilism to its end and creating a new, vital civilization. For pagans, this is a message of hope.

*Counter-Currents*, February 16, 2015

# A LEVELING WIND:
## READING CAMUS' *THE STRANGER*

Albert Camus' *The Stranger* had a powerful effect on me when I first read it at the age of 18. Recently I had cause to pick it up again when I re-read Bill Hopkins' *The Leap!* (a.k.a. *The Divine and the Decay*). Hopkins' manner of constructing a plot out of seemingly trivial, tedious, and disconnected events that suddenly come together in an emotionally shattering climax—a climax that seems utterly surprising yet in hindsight utterly inevitable—brought to mind *The Stranger*.

*The Stranger* is a literary presentation of atheistic existentialism as incarnated by Camus' anti-hero Patrice Meursault, a Frenchman in Algiers who, through a chain of absurd contingencies, impulsively kills an Arab, yet is successfully portrayed as a depraved, cold-blooded killer who must be sentenced to death for the protection of society.

Yet the real danger Meursault poses is not to the lives of his fellow citizens, but to their worldview. He is an outsider (another translation of the French title *L'Etranger*). Meursault does not think and feel as other people do. He is an intelligent man denied higher education by poverty. He bases his beliefs on his own experiences, not on what other people believe. He does not believe in God or providence or progress.

Meursault sees life as a series of contingencies without an overall meaning or purpose, whereas his fellow men insist on seeing patterns of significance that simply do not exist, whether they be divine providence, premeditated criminality, or the expressions of a depraved character. Thus, after a darkly comic trial, he is sentenced to die for what is essentially an act of manslaughter simply because he does not believe in God and did not cry at his mother's funeral, which signify depravity to judge and jury alike.

There really is something unsettling about Meursault. Is he a sociopath, as the prosecutor claims? The answer is no. He does not lack feeling for his mother, for his elderly neighbor and his mangy dog, or for his mistress Marie. But he is emotionally distant and undemonstrative. I imagine him as a taciturn Nordic — a strong, silent type — who does not easily show or speak about his feelings. Indeed, he is not sure what certain words like "love" even mean. This does not mean he is incapable of love, but merely that he is loath to use words loosely.

Meursault's characteristic idleness, benign indifference, and lack of ambition strike one as depressive. He turns down a promotion and a transfer to Paris because he is content where he is. On weekends, he lounges around smoking until noon, then whiles away the afternoon and evening watching the street. When he is in jail, he sleeps 16 hours a day.

But Meursault is not an unhappy man. He is never bored. The secret to his happiness lies in his ability to live in the present. Since he does not employ concepts he does not understand, he experiences the world directly, with a minimum of social mediation. He is intelligent, but not over-burdened with reflectiveness. When in jail, he occupies himself by recalling vivid, fine-grained experiences of ordinary things. He is complacent simply because he is easily contented. He is a particular kind of outsider: a naïf, a savage — and to all appearances, not a particularly noble one.

Meursault's naïve immersion in the present may be his happiness, but it is also his undoing. He is rendered almost senseless by the oppressive Algerian sun — another reason to picture him as a Nordic rather than a Mediterranean type — particularly on the day of his mother's funeral and on the day he shot the Arab. In both cases, he reflexively reacts to his environment, because his sunbaked brain is simply not capable of reflective action, of premeditated agency, of raising him out of sensuous immersion in the present. But others interpret his acts as springing from a lack of feeling rather than an excess — from premeditation rather than blind reflex.

Meursault is a kind of existentialist Christ who is martyred because of the threat that his naïve authenticity poses to those who live second-hand, conventional lives. But Camus thinks that Meursault's life is not exemplary until the very end of the book, when he overcomes his naïveté and comes to reflectively understand and affirm the life he had previously lived only thoughtlessly.

After Meursault is condemned to die, he files an appeal then awaits either reprieve or execution. In his cell, he falls into a kind of hell built on the hope and desire to escape or master his fate. He lies awake all night because he knows that the executioner comes at dawn, and he does not want to be caught sleeping. Only when he knows that he has another 24 hours, does he allow himself to rest. During his waking hours, he runs through all the possible outcomes, trying to construct consoling arguments even in the face of the worst-case scenario.

It is only when Meursault has to endure an exacerbating visit from a priest offering supernatural solace that he comes to his senses. In a burst of anger, he rejects the false hopes offered by the priest—and his own apparatus of false hopes as well. He realizes that all men erect such rationalizations as barriers to evade the certitude of death. We picture death as out there in the future somewhere, at a safe distance. Or we picture ourselves as somehow surviving it.

But Meursault realizes that "From the dark horizon of my future a sort of slow, persistent wind had been blowing toward me, my whole life long, from the years that were to come. And in its path, that wind had leveled out all the ideas that people tried to foist on me in the equally unreal years that I was living through." This wind, of course, is death, and it comes to us all. Or, to be more precise, it is a possibility that we carry around inside ourselves at all times. It is a possibility we must face.

Part of Pascal's wager is that if we believe in Christianity and turn out to be wrong, we will have lost nothing. Camus disagrees: If we believe in any system of false consolation in the face of death, we will still die, but we will have lost everything—everything real—for we will never have truly lived in the world around us. Hope for an unreal world deprives us of the real one. So perhaps we should at least try to live without supernatural consolation.

But to do that, we must embrace the leveling wind, allowing it to carry away false hopes. We must squarely confront the terrifying contingency and finitude of life. We must let go of our fear of death in order to truly live. For if we cease to fear death, we should be free of all lesser fears as well, which will give us the freedom to make the most of life. But this does not merely allow us to accept our mortality, but perhaps also to love it for adding poignancy to life.

This realization brings Meursault peace. He understood why his mother, as she neared her death in an old folks' home, took on a fiancé: "With death so near, mother must have felt like someone on the brink of freedom, ready to start life all over again. No one, no more in the world, had any right to weep for her." And Meursault did not weep, although at the time he did not know the reason why.

Now that Meursault had faced his mortality, he too "felt ready to start life all over again. It was as if that great rush of anger had washed me clean, emptied me of hope . . ." It is the absence of false hope that allows him to face death and to experience freedom. The priest mentions that he is certain that Meursault's appeal will be granted, but at this point, it does not matter, because whether his death comes sooner or later, Meursault has embraced his death as a potentiality he carries at all times.

He continues: ". . . gazing up at the dark sky spangled with its signs and stars, for the first time, the first, I laid my heart open to the benign indifference of the universe. To feel it so like myself, indeed, so brotherly, made me realize I'd been happy, and that I was happy still." Meursault had always lived his life as if the universe were benignly indifferent, i.e., there is no cosmic plan, divine or secular, but merely a play of contingencies. To "lay his heart open" to such a universe means that Meursault is for the first time coming to reflective awareness of the previously unstated presuppositions of his life. And he realizes that his life is good. That he was happy, and that he is happy still.

*The Stranger* ends with defiant, enigmatic words: "For all to be accomplished, for me to be less lonely, all that remained to hope was that on the day of my execution there should be a huge crowd of spectators and that they should greet me with howls of execration." Why would Meursault be more lonely if his fellow men did not hate him? Because he has embraced his mortality and recognized his kinship with a Godless, aimless universe. He is no longer a stranger to the real world. Thus his estrangement from the unfree, inauthentic human world that condemned him is complete.

*The Stranger* is not really a political novel, but it belongs on the "Red Pill" curriculum. When I first read *The Stranger*, it harmonized nicely with my adolescent individualism and alienation. Today, I have outgrown the individualism, but the alienation is still with me, backed up with a slew of sound reasons. You cannot overthrow a society you are invested in. You can't be a citizen of a better world until you are a stranger to this one. So Meursault's proud pariahdom should be an example to us all.

**Note**: There are several translations of *The Stranger*. On purely literary grounds, I prefer Stuart Gilbert's 1946 Knopf translation — which I have quoted above with some modifications — over more recent efforts.

*Counter-Currents*, June 3, 2014

# ALEXANDRE KOJÈVE & THE END OF HISTORY*

We live in a time when there's a lot of talk about the ends of ages. Last year, at the end of 1999, the vast majority of people celebrating the New Year were celebrating the millennium a year early. But still, there's a sense that when we reach a round number something important is going to happen. There's a lot of talk about the "end of modernity" in academia today. So-called postmodernist philosophers and literary critics are quite popular, and certain religious thinkers and writers are of course concerned that time itself may end very soon.

A friend of mine who is an Orthodox monk in Bulgaria emailed me just before the New Year saying not only did some people in Bulgaria think that all the computers were going to fail, they thought the end of time was at hand. I wrote back saying, "Well, if I don't hear from you again, it's been nice knowing you."

I want to talk about one of the most stunning claims that history is over, namely the claim popularized by Alexandre Kojève, who is probably the single most influential philosopher in the 20th century, although at the same time he's one of the least known. He's influential not only in the world of ideas but also in the world of politics. In fact, he's had an enormous influence on the post-Second World War global economic and political order that we live in today. People sometimes call it the "New World Order." It's very much influenced by Kojève's thought and actions.

Kojève claimed that history is not about to end, but that it had *already* ended, and that it ended in 1806. So, all of the expectant people who are waiting for the millennium have already missed it. History is already over. It's been over for nearly two centuries, and it came to an end in 1806 when Georg Wilhelm Friedrich

---

* This is transcript by V.S. of a talk that I gave to The Atlanta Philosophical Society sometime in 2000. I have eliminated some wordy constructions and some back-and-forth with the audience.

Hegel was sitting in his study in Jena writing his book *Phenomenology of Spirit* and nearby Napoleon was defeating his enemies at the great Battle of Jena, which turned the tide of resistance in Europe toward the ideas of the French Revolution.

According to Kojève, history ended with the triumph of the ideals of liberty, equality, and fraternity *and* Hegel's understanding of the significance of these events. Everything that's happened since then, he said, including the two World Wars, is just post-historical "mopping up." It's of no real historical significance. It's just a matter of carrying the ideals of the French Revolution to the farthest corners of the globe.

Last night I saw a trailer for a film called *The Cup*, which is set in Bhutan in the Himalayas. This is a movie about the mopping-up process. It's about some intrepid young Buddhist monks who fall in love with soccer and decide to bring satellite television to Bhutan. According to Kojève, this is just the kind of mopping-up process you'd expect as the world becomes completely integrated and its culture becomes entirely homogenized. Of course, this is presented as a heart-warming tale of intrepid youth.

Now, who was Alexandre Kojève? Aleksandr Vladimirovič Koževnikov was born in 1902 in Moscow into a very wealthy family. After the Russian Revolution, the family fell on hard times, and Kojève was eventually reduced to selling black-market soap on the street. He was arrested for this and narrowly escaped execution. His experiences with the GPU led to a rather unusual outcome. He converted to Marxism and maintained that he was an ardent Stalinist to the very end of his life.

In 1920, ardent Marxist-Stalinist that he was, Kojève still saw fit to flee the Soviet Union to Germany. He enrolled at the University of Heidelberg, studying philosophy with the great German existentialist thinker Karl Jaspers, and wrote a dissertation on Vladimir Soloviev, a Russian mystical philosopher of some interest, although he is little known in the West.

Apparently, the Koževnikovs had money abroad, so while he was in Germany Kojève was actually something of a *bon vivant*. He lived the high life. He was a sort of limousine Stalinist. But he invested his family money poorly, and in 1929 he was pretty much wiped out by the great stock market crash.

In that year, Kojève moved to France and started trying to find work. He had many friends, Russian émigrés, who helped him out. One of them was Alexandre Koyré, a historian of philosophy and science who in 1933 went off to Egypt as a visiting professor and got Kojève the job of substituting for him in a seminar on Hegel's *Phenomenology of Spirit*.

Kojève did such a spectacular job that he gave the seminar every year until 1939, when the Germans moved in and French intellectual life changed somewhat. Kojève spent the war in the south of France, writing, and some of the works that he wrote during the war were published posthumously. He probably sat out the war because he believed it was of no historical significance.

In 1945, he returned from his exile and was immediately given a position in the French Ministry of Economic Affairs, the head of which had been a student in his Hegel seminar during the 1930s.

From 1945 to 1968, Kojève held the same position, a kind of undersecretary position, yet while he did not have any official leadership role, he was—as one person who knew him put it— the Mycroft Holmes of the French government. He was the guy who knew everything and everybody, and kept everybody abreast of everything else. He was a nerve center or brain center for the French government for a period of more than 20 years.

Kojève claimed, in his typically hyperbolic style, that De Gaulle took care of foreign affairs, and "I, Kojève," as he put it, "took care of everything else." And apparently Raymond Aron, who was another of his students and an extremely sober fellow, actually said that this was pretty much true, that Kojève was probably second only to De Gaulle in importance in the French government in the 22 years that he occupied his position.

And what did Kojève do? Well, he was one of the architects of what's now called the European Economic Community. He was also one of the architects of what is known as the General Agreement on Trades and Tariffs, or GATT.

Right after the Second World War, Kojève gave a speech to a bunch of technocrats in West Germany, in which he laid out the model for what was then called pejoratively "neo-colonialism."

In his terms, colonialism after the Second World War and the end of the old colonial empires would now take the form not of taking, but of giving, namely of investing in and developing the underdeveloped countries, the former colonies, and integrating them into the world economic system. His model was more or less carried out to a "T." Organizations like the World Bank basically follow to this day the Kojèvian model of neo-colonialism.

Kojève was also the first person to announce what is sometimes called the convergence thesis. Zbigniew Brzezinski, National Security Adviser to Jimmy Carter, is often credited with this view. The convergence thesis is basically the claim that as the Cold War wore on, the pressures of fighting it would cause both sides to gradually converge and become indistinguishable from one another.

Kojève was instrumental in creating—through the economic and political integration of the Western, non-Communist nations—one of the most important factors in helping them win the Cold War. But the French intelligence service also believed that Kojève was passing information to the KGB the whole time. So he was playing both sides in a very dangerous game. I want to give some suggestions about what Kojève's dangerous game actually was.

Before I do that, though, I want to talk about his influence in the world of ideas. I've talked about his political activity. Really, of all the philosophers in the 20th century, Kojève had the most impressive record of actually changing the world instead of just theorizing about it. Much of the world that we know today and think of as normal was influenced by this strange Russian. So, we need to understand the ideas behind his actions.

Kojève's students at his Hegel seminar in the 1930s included the following people: Raymond Aron, who was probably the most brilliant conservative political theorist in France in the 20th century; Maurice Merleau-Ponty, who was something of a Marxist-Stalinist at one time and one of the most significant phenomenological philosophers in 20th-century France; Jacques Lacan, the great interpreter of Freud, who fused Freud with Kojève's Hegel and is probably the leading Freudian thinker after Freud; Henry Corbin, who made the first (partial) French translation of

Heidegger's *Being and Time* but is far more famous for the work that he did in medieval Arabic philosophy and mysticism; Robert Marjolin, the leader of the French Ministry of Economic Affairs who gave Kojève a job; Gaston Fessard, who was little-known outside France but was an extraordinary scholar and a Jesuit priest as well; André Breton, who was one of the founders of French Surrealism; Georges Bataille, famous for writing really rather gross and untitillating pornography, as well as many books and essays on the philosophy of culture—a rather profound although difficult and quite perverted thinker; and Raymond Queneau, a novelist whose most famous novels are translated as *The Sunday of Life* and *Zazie in the Metro*. These are "end of history" novels and were very much influenced by Kojève's vision of life at the end of history.

And, of course, these members of the seminar in turn had their own students and readers. Among them are some of the most important 20th-century French thinkers of the next generation: Jacques Derrida, Michel Foucault, Gilles Deleuze, Jean-François Lyotard, and the like. None of them were students of Kojève himself, but I would maintain that nobody can really understand these French postmodernists—especially their use of certain words like "metaphysics," "modernity," "difference," and "negativity"—without understanding how all of these derive from Kojève's interpretation of Hegel. The peculiar vehemence with which terms like "metanarrative," "history," "being," "absolute knowledge," and so forth are spoken by these writers has everything to do with Kojève's specific interpretation of the meaning of these terms in Hegel's *Phenomenology of Spirit*. One can't read French postmodernism and understand it without understanding that most of these thinkers are reacting to Kojève. They would not call themselves Kojèvians. They're all anti-Kojèvians. But insofar as they're opposing themselves to him and to his very peculiar takes on things, they're very much influenced by him. They bear the trace of Kojève.

Another contemporary thinker who's really quite trendy today is the Slovene writer Slavoj Žižek. I hope there are no Slovenians in the audience who will knock my pronunciation. Žižek has written quite a number of books with titles like *Everything*

*You Always Wanted to Know About Lacan . . . But Were Afraid to Ask Hitchcock,* and he's enormously influenced by Kojève's view of Hegel, and also Lacan's reading of Kojève's Hegel.

Kojève attracted students even after he stopped teaching. Two of them were Allan Bloom, the author of *The Closing of the American Mind,* and Stanley Rosen, who is a very well-known commentator on Greek philosophy, as well as on Hegel and Heidegger. Their teacher, Leo Strauss, sent them to study with Kojève in the early 1960s. Bloom and Rosen would go to his office at the Ministry. He would close the door, and they would talk philosophy.

More recently, Francis Fukuyama, who was a student of Allan Bloom, became famous for his book *The End of History and the Last Man,* which is really a popularization of Kojèvian ideas. Just as the Communist regimes in Eastern Europe were coming down, Fukuyama raised the question: What if Kojève were wrong and history hadn't ended in 1806, as Hegel wrote the *Phenomenology of Spirit?* What if history ended in 1989, as Communism fell and Fukuyama was in the process of interpreting it as the global triumph of Western liberal democracy? That started a huge debate.

Of course, people on the Right in America were particularly delighted to hear that their perseverance in the Cold War had brought about not just the end of Communism but the end of history itself, and everything would be smooth sailing from then on. Little things like the Gulf War were just mopping-up.

Some of Kojève's peers—people he corresponded and interacted with and who influenced him—include Leo Strauss, who is one of the most important 20th-century philosophers. He was a German-Jewish philosopher who met Kojève in the 1920s. They met again in Paris in the 1930s, where they spent a lot of time together, and they corresponded throughout the rest of their lives. Strauss, of course, was a conservative thinker, a thinker of the Right, and yet he derived both pleasure and knowledge from his friendship with Kojève, the ardent Stalinist.

Carl Schmitt was the notorious German jurist and political philosopher who wrote the brief showing how Hitler's seizure of power in 1933 was perfectly legal according to the Weimar constitution—which was indeed a brief anybody could have written because, strictly speaking, it *was* legal. Schmitt, of course, had been tarred with the Nazi association until he died at a very old age. Schmitt was a friend of Kojève's, and they corresponded over a period of many decades. Another improbable intellectual friendship.

Georges Bataille was not just a student of Kojève, but really a peer. I think Bataille dramatically influenced Kojève's intellectual development. Bataille is certainly a thinker of the far Left.

So, we have a strange phenomenon: Kojève had close intellectual relationships with, and a powerful influence on, thinkers on the Right and on the Left, but what all these thinkers have in common is a vehement rejection of modernity, precisely the modernity that Kojève himself is so eager to proclaim as inevitable. All of Kojève's students and most passionate admirers ended by rejecting, vehemently, his vision of the end of history. That's an interesting thing to puzzle through.

If Hegel and Kojève believe that history came to an end in 1806, then they obviously mean something very different by "history" than the rest of us do. If history can come to an end, it has to be something different from what is reported every day in the newspapers. Hegel and Kojève didn't claim that human events would cease. There are post-historical human events, just as there were pre-historical human events. So, history isn't just the record of human events. It is a very specific thing.

For Hegel, history is the human quest for self-knowledge and self-actualization. There was a time when human beings were not actively pursuing those aims. This was characteristic of pre-historical forms of life, when men were brutish and dumb. And there will be a time when human beings will no longer actively pursue self-knowledge and self-actualization, because we will have already achieved them. That will be post-historical life.

History is the human quest for self-knowledge and self-actualization. When that quest comes to an end, when we know ourselves and become ourselves, then there will be no more history. That's how history will stop.

Hegel posits that human beings have a fundamental need for self-knowledge. In fact, in the last analysis, for him self-actualization *just is* self-knowledge. So, human beings are fulfilled by knowing themselves. That's what it's all about. That's what we're all striving for. That's what the whole record of history has been pointing to: self-knowledge.

How is the pursuit of self-knowledge connected with history? Isn't self-knowledge just something we have through introspection? Can't we just have self-knowledge on a desert island or lying in bed in the morning? Why do we need to do things like build civilizations or cathedrals and fight wars? Why do we need history in order to pursue self-knowledge?

Hegel would agree that we do have a kind of immediate self-awareness, which Rousseau would call the "sentiment of existence." But that feeling is shared with all the animals, too. Therefore, insofar as we have an immediate feeling of self, that really doesn't constitute knowledge of ourselves as distinctly human creatures. Second, knowledge as such requires more than just immediate feeling. It has to be more articulated, reflective, and, as Hegel puts it, "mediated" rather than immediate. It has to be on the level of thought rather than the level of feeling. In order to arrive at self-knowledge of our distinctly human characteristics, and to know them in a distinctly human way through reason, through thought, we have to go beyond mere feeling. We have to do things.

Now, to know ourselves as physical beings we can look in a mirror. Although we have to *recognize* the being that we see in the mirror *as* ourselves. Animals don't seem to be able to recognize their own reflections. But when human beings reach a certain point in our development, we realize, "Aha! That's us!" And there's something extraordinary about recognizing ourselves as reflected in something other, something external.

Hegel believes that self-knowledge of our soul, if you will, requires a similar process. We need to find a mirror in which our soul can be reflected, and in which we can recognize our reflection, thereby coming to know ourselves as spiritual beings.

Now, what is the appropriate mirror of the soul? Well, the first and most obvious answer would be another soul, another human being. The way that we come to know ourselves as human beings is by recognizing ourselves in others. The best form of recognition would be to recognize ourselves in the eyes of somebody who is very similar to us, who can really show us who we are. The kind of relationship where that happens is friendship or love. We can know ourselves through people who antagonize us, but the best kind of self-awareness is through love and friendship. The most complete sort of self-awareness is through love and friendship.

But that's not enough. Love is not enough for Hegel. Friendship is not enough to explain history. If we could know ourselves adequately, if we could satisfy our need for self-knowledge simply through interpersonal relationships, we never would have embarked on this long quest towards civilization, because we could have satisfied that need in the prehistorical family, in little villages, in thatched huts, in hunter-gatherer bands. We don't need buildings and technologies and civilizations that extend thousands of miles. We don't need cathedrals and skyscrapers or any of that just to have interpersonal relationships.

So, the quest for self-knowledge has to be understood more precisely here. We need to know ourselves. To know ourselves as individuals does not require history, so what kind of self-knowledge requires history? Hegel seems to believe that history is required if we are to know ourselves *universally*, to know ourselves in an abstract sense, and not just as particular individuals—in other words, to know what is man *in general*. Ultimately, this is the aim of philosophy.

Your best friend or your spouse is not going to be adequate to give you this kind of universal self-knowledge. Another human being isn't an adequate mirror for that. Only philosophy can show that to you, and so Hegel believes that we have to understand history as arising out of the need for universal self-knowledge.

But of course philosophy wasn't there at the beginning of history. So, how do we try to *begin* to satisfy that need for universal self-knowledge?

Hegel's argument is simple: We have to make a mirror for ourselves. We have this material called nature—rocks and rivers and trees—and we need to remake it. We need to go out there and transform the world, to put the stamp of humanity upon it, to humanize the world, to remake the world in our own image—and to recognize ourselves, to recognize the truth about mankind in general, in our work.

Every culture is basically an ensemble of practices, artifacts, and institutions in which, and by which, human beings embody a particular attempt to understand themselves. Culture is the mirror in which human beings know themselves in a universal way. The record of cultures and their transformation is what we call history. Therefore, history is necessitated as our first step towards universal self-understanding.

There are many cultures and thus many interpretations of our nature. But there is only one truth. Therefore, all cultures can't be rated equally. Some are truer to man and his nature than others. So it's possible to rank cultures in a hierarchy in terms of how well or how poorly they reflect the true nature of man. But Hegel is also clear that ultimately, culture as such is an inadequate medium for coming to universal self-understanding. Thus what happens at a certain point in at least some cultures—three, to be exact—is the emergence of philosophy. The Greeks, the Indians, and the Chinese all spontaneously evolved philosophical traditions.

Hegel's view is that we finally come to universal self-understanding through philosophy—ultimately through Hegel's philosophy, as it turns out. History is the pursuit of wisdom. Hegel has become wise. He knows the truth about man, and therefore the philosophical quest and the historical quest both came to an end in 1806, when Hegel wrote his book *Phenomenology of Spirit*.

Now, this might sound grandiose to you, but really every philosopher worth his salt is grandiose, because they're searching for the Truth with a capital "T." Hegel is just one of the more immodest philosophers, because he claims that not only is he searching for it, he's actually found it, and therefore he's not really a philosopher anymore. He's a wise man. He's a sage.

What is this big Truth that has brought history to an end? According to Kojève, the truth about man is that *we're all free and equal*. That might sound banal, but he says that that's what human beings have been fighting for and struggling for—sculpting and painting, composing music and writing books for, over thousands of years—in order to discover that we're all free and equal. Once this discovery has been announced, and once the world has been remade in the image of freedom and equality, history has come to an end.

Kojève claims that history comes to an end with what he calls the universal and homogeneous state. When we recognize that all men are free and all men are equal, the only thing left is to create a form of society that recognizes this freedom and equality. That form of society has to be universal. It can't be attached to any particular culture, because culture is over, too. History is just a record of cultures, and when history ends, culture is over, too. Culture becomes, in some sense, unnecessary, because it's really not the best medium for coming to self-understanding. Kojève glimpses a tendency towards the complete homogenization of the world within this universal state. So he calls the end of history the universal homogeneous state, and he thinks this is great. This is wonderful.

We're rapidly seeing this all around us. In Bhutan, they're getting TV today. Tomorrow, they're going to be wearing little baseball caps—backwards, of course—listening to rap music, and wearing t-shirts with American brand names on them. Eventually it will be more practical to just learn one language: English. As one friend puts it, "language *par excellence*." And we'll all be English speakers; we'll all be buying the same things; we'll all be watching the same TV shows. We'll be one big, happy, peaceful world, and mankind will be entirely satisfied, because we'll all be free, and we'll all be equal. But we won't all be philosophers. Only the very smart ones will become philosophers. Because we're not going to all be equal in that respect. We'll be *politically* equal.

That's the Kojèveian story, in a very crude overview. It's crude, but it's completely correct and accurate. It's completely correct and accurate to Kojève's view, if not to Hegel, or to reality; let's put it that way.

This is Kojève's description of the end of history: "In the final state, there are naturally no more human beings." Why? Because man is a historical being, too, and when history comes to an end, what is distinctively human disappears. "The healthy automata are satisfied. They have sports, art, eroticism, and so forth, and the sick ones get locked up." Or they get Prozac. Or other mood-altering drugs to make them happier. "The philosophers become gods. The tyrant becomes an administrator, a cog in the machine fashioned by automata for automata."

This is his view of the end of things. Now, if somebody were to step forward and declare, "I have a dream of a world of healthy, well-fed automata, de-humanized robots ruled over by technocrats that think they are gods," would you be at all inclined to be inspired by that vision of things? It is a very strange way of speaking about something that Kojève at least officially regards as utopia, the form of society that totally satisfies all of mankind.

Here we arrive at an odd problem, because as Kojève becomes more and more enthusiastic about the end of history—at least putatively enthusiastic, apparently enthusiastic—he begins phrasing it in ways that are more and more chilling, unappetizing, and unappealing.

The notes for Kojève's Hegel seminar were edited and published in 1947 by Raymond Queneau as *Introduction to the Reading of Hegel*. After it was published, it was reprinted in a number of different editions. As the new editions came out, Kojève would add notes to them. About half of the French volume has been translated into English. The good stuff. There's a famous note in here. Kojève adds a note to the second edition and then adds a note to that note in the third edition. As the notes pile up, the vision of the end of history becomes more and more disturbing and unappealing.

What's going on here? Surely, Kojève, who was a master of rhetoric, knew the likely effects of his rhetoric. So, why was he praising something in terms designed to produce discomfort and disgust? It's a very interesting question.

His second thoughts about the end of history were expressed in his later writings as a thesis that man is coming to an end. The end of history is the end of man. Man, properly understood, is being erased. The masses of people at the end of history, he said, will become beasts. And another term for them, he said, is slaves without masters.

He said: Bourgeois man is a slave without a master. He is a slave spiritually, because there is nothing for which he is willing to die.

The worst possible thing for the bourgeoisie, he says, is a violent death. They'll do anything to avoid that. The greatest possible thing is comfortable living. They'll betray virtually anything for that. "Do it to Julia!" He says that the end of history is a society where the vast majority of human beings are slaves without masters. They're officially free, but spiritually speaking, they are slavish. They have no ideals. There's nothing they're willing to die for. Nothing is more important than just being comfortable and secure.

The small minority who will rule everything will at least understand everything. They are the philosophers. And they too are dehumanized. Not by becoming beasts, but by becoming gods.

What's left out are just men, and by "man" Kojève means people who have what Plato called spiritedness. And what is spiritedness? Well, part of spiritedness for Plato is the capacity to respond passionately to ideals. In the most primitive sense, spiritedness is just a kind of touchiness about points of honor. A desire to be treated with respect. But the same kind of attachments to one's ideal vision of one's self that used to lead us to fight duels to the death over matters of honor can also be attached to higher things like countries and causes, and so forth. It can even be attached to a love of the good itself.

Kojève thinks that the end of history will mark the elimination of the spirited part of man's soul. Once we know the truth about mankind — that we are all free and equal — there will be nothing to fight over and no propensity to fight, anyway. The capacity to get angry over points of honor or ideology will simply disappear. This is what he means by the end of man.

Again, it's not a very appealing picture. Yet it's a picture that's increasingly true.

The philosophers, as I said, are increasingly dehumanized as well. They become gods, which means that they are de-spirited creatures as well—effete, cosmopolitan, rootless, and so forth. They jet from one end of the globe to another. They interpret things. They give little papers at conferences. They graze at the buffets and crowd around the open bars. And they experience nothing greater than themselves. They look down on the cultures of the past with detachment, but they buy their artifacts and playfully display them in an eclectic jumble on their mantlepieces.

At the very time Kojève was painting this bleak picture of the end of man, he maintained it was his dream—indeed, that it's all of our dreams. This is what history is aiming towards, and we'll all be completely satisfied by it. You'll love it! Believe me! You're already loving it! But why in the world did he say things that undermine his overall thesis?

The interpretation I want to give is this: Kojève became very much influenced by Nietzsche, and Nietzsche is really the great 19th-century antipode of Hegel. If you want to find two thinkers who are most fundamentally opposed in philosophy of history and culture, Nietzsche and Hegel are the most opposite you can find. The influence of Nietzsche, I think, was primarily mediated through the influence of Georges Bataille, Kojève's student, peer, and friend. Bataille was something of a Nietzschean, and I think that as their friendship progressed and as Kojève thought more about things, he came to think that Bataille was fundamentally correct that there was something true about Nietzsche's view of history.

So, what is Nietzsche's view of history? Hegel has a linear view of history. History proceeds in a straight line from a beginning to an end. The progress of history arises from a single fundamental need, which is the human need for self-knowledge. Once we achieve that goal, history ends, and that's it. It's paradise.

Nietzsche, by contrast, has a cyclical view of history, and he believes that there are two fundamental principles that make the historical world go around. One is the need for self-knowledge, but the other is what I would like to call "the need for vitality," the need to feel alive and express that feeling.

In Nietzsche's view, history begins with a kind of vital upsurge, which is leading towards self-knowledge. History begins with a kind of barbarous vitality. As culture progresses, however, and become more refined, our reflectiveness and refinement come to interfere and undermine the sources of cultural vitality.

Culture, at the beginning, is necessary for us to be healthy, but as it progresses and becomes more refined, it becomes a source of sickness, decline, and decay. At this point we have a decadent culture in which people are very reflective, dispassionate, corrupt, and lacking in virtue. And what eventually happens when decadence grows widespread? Everything collapses, everything falls apart. You can't have a functioning society full of rotten people. The few survivors who are left return to barbarism. All the cobwebs of fine-spun theories are swept away, human vitality returns, and history begins again.

Now, in the portrait that Kojève paints of the end of history, you really can see this Nietzschean perspective at work. The "last man," which was Nietzsche's term for decadent and dehumanized men, is the true outcome of Hegel's drive for universal freedom and equality. But the last man can't sustain civilization, so history must start all over again. The last man, in Nietzsche's terms, is precisely what Kojève is describing as slaves without masters and masters without slaves, the dehumanized beasts and gods that exist at the end of history. Both beasts and gods lack a distinctively human vitality to give rise to culture and values.

I want to argue that Kojève's ambivalence about the end of history really arises out of the fact that he simultaneously affirms two completely contradictory theories of history. One is Hegel's and the other is Nietzsche's. Kojève was not an idiot. In fact, people whom I respect enormously said that he was the smartest man they ever knew. He was extraordinarily intelligent. The best-functioning and best-stocked brain of the century, according to one person who knew him. Thus he was not so stupid as to overlook the fact that he was affirming two diametrically opposed views. So why was he doing this?

I'll answer this question, but I want to raise another one first. Why did Kojève play both sides of the Cold War? Clearly he had to see that there was something a little immoral, or there was at least an appearance of impropriety, in passing secrets to the KGB. Why did he do this? Why was he affirming opposed theories of history, and why was he playing both sides against each other in the Cold War? I think that the answers to both questions are related.

Let me answer the first question this way. I follow Plato, and Plato recommends that in order to understand a philosopher's teachings, you don't just look at his words, you also look at his deeds, and then you put the words and the deeds together and look at the total effect. The total effect of a philosopher's teaching is what he is really getting at. Not necessarily what he says or what he does, but the total effect of the two together on the actions of the people who read it, understand it, and follow it. These guys are smart. They know the likely effect of their writings. So, if you want to understand the meaning of a philosopher's teachings, look at the effect, not what he says in isolation, not what he does in isolation, but the effect of what he says and what he does taken together.

What's the effect of Kojève's teaching about modernity? The fact is that every single person who took Kojève seriously as a teacher—Left or Right, far Left or far Right—ended up rejecting the end of history, the vision of modernity that Kojève was loudly trumpeting as his dream—and everybody's dream—come true. He was not so stupid as to be caught unaware by this. I refuse to believe that.

I think that the meaning of Kojève's teachings is precisely this: Kojève presented Hegel's view of history in such dire and dystopian terms to induce people to revolt against it. He was presenting the end of history in a way that was designed to make people want to get history started all over again. If history can start all over again, that means that, fundamentally, we affirm the Nietzschean cyclical view rather than the Hegelian linear view. So, I think that ultimately Kojève was a kind of Nietzschean who was deeply disturbed by modernity and wanted to bring it to an end.

How is this connected with his political actions? Well, some people may say, "Look, the reason why he was on both sides of the Cold War is because he believed in the convergence thesis and didn't think there was any difference between the two."

But that really doesn't explain it, for this reason: If he didn't believe that either side was fundamentally different from the other, then why wouldn't he have worked as hard as possible on one side to ensure its ultimate triumph? It would be a matter of indifference as to which side he supported. But why was he helping both sides? That can't be explained from a Hegelian point of view, because by helping both sides in the Cold War, he was actually helping to *perpetuate* the Cold War rather than bring it to an end. Why would he want us to keep fighting?

But this makes sense if Kojève is fundamentally a Nietzschean who wanted to *forestall* as long as possible the end of history that Fukuyama—his somewhat unsubtle and popularizing student—was so happy about.

I think that perhaps Kojève's very dangerous political game had an aim similar to that of his philosophical game, namely not to bring history to an end but to keep it going, to keep the conflict going. Why? Because as a Nietzschean, he believed that, ultimately, conflict about values is the thing that makes us most human. The capacity to aspire to and ultimately die for ideals, is the most glorious and distinctly human characteristic we have. And the Cold War was one long conflict over fundamental ideas, and it would be perfectly consistent with the Nietzschean view to want to keep that conflict going, especially if he foresaw that the outcome of one side winning would be McWorld. If that was the case, then it makes perfect sense that he would be playing both sides. He didn't want either one to win. The longer Kojève could forestall the end of history, the better. The better for all of us.

And now that history has ended, we need to go to Plan B, which is to start history all over again. And we don't need to wait for the barbarians. They are already here.

*Counter-Currents*, September 19, 2018

# POSTMODERNISM, HEDONISM, & DEATH*

"Postmodernism" is one of those academically fashionable weasel words like "paradigm" that have now seeped into middlebrow and even lowbrow discourse. Those of us who have fundamental and principled critiques of modernity quickly learned that postmodernism is not nearly postmodern enough. Indeed, in most ways, it is just an intensification of the worst features of modernity.

I wish to argue two philosophical theses: (1) there is an inner identity between postmodern culture and hedonism, and (2) hedonism, taken to an extreme, can lead to its self-overcoming by arranging an encounter with death—an encounter that, if survived, can expand one's awareness of one's self and the world to embrace non-hedonistic motives and actions.

For my purposes, postmodernity is an attitude toward culture characterized by (1) eclecticism or *bricolage*, meaning the mixing of different cultures and traditions, i.e., multiculturalism, and (2) irony, detachment, and playfulness toward culture, which is what allows us to mix and manipulate cultures in the first place. The opposite of multiculturalism is cultural integrity and exclusivity. The opposite of irony is earnestness. The opposite of detachment is identification. The opposite of playfulness is seriousness.

The core of a genuine culture is a worldview, an interpretation of existence and our place in it, as well as of our nature and the best form of life for us. These are *serious* matters. Because of the fundamental seriousness of a living culture, each one is characterized by a unity of style, the other side of which is an exclu-

---

* This article and the two that follow it were adapted from my long essay on Quentin Tarantino's *Pulp Fiction*, written under the pen name Trevor Lynch and reprinted in *Trevor Lynch's White Nationalist Guide to the Movies*, ed. Greg Johnson (San Francisco: Counter-Currents, 2012).

sion of foreign cultural forms. After all, if one takes one's own worldview seriously, one cannot take incompatible worldviews with equal seriousness. (Yes, cultures do borrow from one another, but a serious culture only borrows what it can assimilate to its own worldview and use for its greater glory.)

The core of a living culture is not primarily a set of ideas, but of *ideals*. Ideals are ideas that make *normative* claims upon us. They don't just tell us what *is*, but what *ought* to be. Like Rilke's "Archaic Torso of Apollo," ideals demand that we change our lives. The core of a living culture is a pantheon of ideals that is experienced as *numinous* and *enthralling*. An individual formed by a living culture has a fundamental sense of identification with and participation in his culture. He cannot separate himself from it, and since it is the source of his ideas of his nature, the good life, the cosmos, and his place in it, his attitude toward culture is fundamentally earnest and serious, even pious. In a very deep sense, he does not own his culture, he is owned by it.

In terms of their relationship to culture, human beings fall into two basic categories: healthy and unhealthy. Healthy human beings experience the ideals that define a culture as a challenge, as a tonic. The gap between the ideal and the real is bridged by a longing of the soul for perfection. This longing is a tension, like the tension of the bowstring or the lyre, that makes human greatness possible. Culture forms human beings not merely by evoking idealistic longings, but also by suppressing, shaping, stylizing, and sublimating our natural desires. Culture has an element of mortification. But healthy organisms embrace this ascetic dimension as a pathway to ennoblement through self-transcendence.

Unhealthy organisms experience culture in a radically different way. Ideals are not experienced as a challenge to quicken and mobilize the life force. Instead, they are experienced as a threat, an insult, an external imposition, a gnawing thorn in the flesh. The unhealthy organism wishes to free itself from the tension created by ideals—which it experiences as nothing more than unreasonable expectations (unreasonable by the standards of an immanentized reason, a mere hedonistic calculus). The unhealthy organism does not wish to suppress and sublimate his natural desires. He wishes to validate them as good enough and then express them. He wants to give them free reign, not pull back on the bit.

Unfortunately, the decadent have Will to Power too. Thus they have been able to free themselves and their desires from the tyranny of normative culture and institute a decadent counter-culture in its place. This is the true meaning of "postmodernism." Postmodernism replaces participation with detachment, earnestness with irony, seriousness with playfulness, enthrallment with emancipation. Such attitudes demythologize and profane the pantheon of numinous ideals that is the beating heart of a living culture.

Culture henceforth becomes merely a wax museum: a realm of dead, decontextualized artifacts and ideas. When a culture is eviscerated of its defining worldview, all integrity, all unity of style is lost. Cultural integrity gives way to multiculturalism, which is merely a pretentious way of describing a shopping mall where artifacts are bought and sold, mixed and matched to satisfy emancipated consumer desires: a wax museum jumping to the pulse of commerce.

Yet, even when desire becomes emancipated and sovereign, it has a tendency to dialectically overcome itself, for the reckless pursuit of pleasure often leads to brushes with death, which can cause a fundamental re-evaluation of one's life and priorities. As William Blake said, "The fool who persists in his folly will become wise."

Furthermore, as much as hedonists wish to become mere happy animals, they remain botched human beings. The human soul still contains longings for something more than mere satiation of natural desires. These longings, moreover, are closely intertwined with these desires. For instance, merely natural desires are few and easily satisfied. But the human imagination can multiply desires to infinity. Most of these artificial desires, moreover, are for objects that satisfy a need for honor, recognition, status, not mere natural creature comforts. Hedonism is not an animal existence, but merely a perverted and profaned human existence.

Thus there will always be a "surplus" of humanity over and

above what can be satisfied by natural desires. This surplus demands satisfaction too, causing a deep dissatisfaction and restlessness in every hedonist. This restlessness can also lead, ultimately, to a transformative encounter with death.

If *animal* life is all about contentment, plenitude, fullness — the fulfillment of our natural desires — then a distinctly *human* mode of existence emerges when hominids mortify the flesh in the name of something higher. It could be that the perforation of the flesh was the first expression of human spirit in animal existence. This throws an interesting light on the popularity of body piercing and tattooing in the context of postmodern culture, which is the subject of the essay after next.

For Hegel, however, the truly anthropogenic encounter with death is not the "little death" of self-mortification, but rather *an intentionally undertaken battle to the death over honor*, which is the subject of the next essay.

*Counter-Currents*, October 23, 2010

# The Beginning & the End of History

The duel to the death over honor is a remarkable phenomenon. Animals duel over dominance, which ensures their access to mates. But these duels result in death only by accident, because the whole process is governed by their survival instincts, and their "egos" do not prevent them from surrendering when the fight is hopeless. The duel to the death over honor is a distinctly human thing.

Indeed, on Alexandre Kojève's reading of Hegel's *Phenomenology of Spirit*, the duel to the death over honor is the beginning of history—and the beginning of a distinctly human form of existence and self-consciousness.

Prehistoric man is dominated by nature: the natural world around him and the natural world within him, namely his desires. History, for Hegel, is something different. It is the process of (1) our discovery of those parts of our nature that *transcend* mere animal desire, and (2) our creation of a society in accord with our true nature.

When we fully know ourselves as more than merely natural beings and finally live accordingly, then history will be over. (History can end, because it is a process of discovery and construction, which is the kind of thing that can end.) Hegel claimed that history ended with the discovery that all men are free and the creation of a society that reflects that truth.

When two men duel to the death over honor, the external struggle between them conceals an internal struggle within each of them as they confront the possibility of being ruled by two different parts of their souls: *desire*, which includes the desire for self-preservation, and *honor*, which demands recognition of our worth by others.

When our sense of honor is offended, we become angry and seek to compel the offending party to respect us. If the other party is equally offended and intransigent, the struggle can escalate to the point where life is at stake.

At this point, two kinds of human beings distinguish themselves. Those who are ruled by their honor will sacrifice their lives to preserve it. Their motto is: "Death before dishonor." Those who are ruled by their desires are more concerned to preserve their lives than their honor. They will sacrifice their honor to preserve their lives. Their motto is: "Dishonor before death."

Suppose two honorable men fight to the death. One will live, one will die, but both will preserve their honor. But what if the vanquished party begs to be spared at the last moment at the price of his honor? What if his desire to survive is stronger than his sense of honor? In that case, he will become the slave of the victor.

The man who prefers death to dishonor is a natural master. The man who prefers dishonor to death — life at any price — is a natural slave. The natural master defines himself in terms of a distinctly human self-consciousness, an awareness of his transcendence over animal desire, the survival "instinct," the whole realm of biological necessity. The natural slave, by contrast, is ruled by his animal nature and experiences his sense of honor as a danger to survival. The master uses the slave's fear of death to compel him to work.

History thus begins with the emergence of a warrior aristocracy, a two-tiered society structured in terms of the oppositions between work and leisure, necessity and luxury, nature and culture. Slaves work so that the masters can enjoy leisure. Slaves secure the necessities of life so the masters can enjoy luxuries. Slaves conquer nature so masters can create culture. In a sense the whole realm of culture is a "luxury," since none of it is necessitated by our animal desires. But in a higher sense, it is a necessity: a necessity of our distinctly human nature to understand itself and put its stamp upon the world.

### THE END OF HISTORY

Hegel had the fanciful notion that there is a necessary "dialectic" between master and slave that will lead eventually to universal freedom; that at the end of history, the distinction between master and slave can be abolished; that all men are potential masters.

Now, to his credit, Hegel was a race realist. He was also quite realistic about the tendency of bourgeois capitalism to turn all men into spiritual slaves. Thus his view of the ideal state, which regulates economic life and reinforces the institutions that elevate human character against the corrupting influences of modernity, differs little from fascism. So in the end, Hegel's highflown talk about universal freedom seems unworthy of him, rather like Jefferson's rhetorical gaffe that "all men are created equal."

The true heirs to Hegel's universalism are Marx and his followers, who really believed that the dialectic would lead to universal freedom. Alexandre Kojève, Hegel's greatest 20th-century Marxist interpreter, came to believe that both Communism and bourgeois capitalism/liberal democracy were paths to Hegel's vision of universal freedom. After the collapse of communism, Kojève's pupil Francis Fukuyama declared that bourgeois capitalism and liberal democracy would create what Kojève called the "universal homogeneous state," the global political and economic order in which all men would be free.

But both capitalism and communism are essentially materialistic systems. Yes, they made appeals to idealism, but primarily to motivate their subjects to fight for them. But if one system triumphed over the other, that necessity would no longer exist, and desire would be fully sovereign. Materialism would triumph. (And so it would have, were it not for the rise of another global enemy that is spiritual and warlike rather than materialistic: Islam.)

Thus Kojève came to believe that the universal homogeneous state would not be a society in which all men are masters, i.e., a society in which honor rules over desire. Rather, it would be a world in which all men are slaves, a society in which desire rules over honor.

This is the world of Nietzsche's "Last Man," the world of C. S. Lewis's "Men without Chests" (honor is traditionally associated with the chest, just as reason is associated with the head and desire with the belly and points below). This is the postmodern world, where emancipated desire and corrosive individualism and irony have reduced all normative cultures to commodities that can be bought and sold, used and discarded.

This is the end of the path blazed by the first wave of modern philosophers: Thomas Hobbes, John Locke, David Hume, etc., all of whom envisioned a liberal order founded on the sovereignty of desire, in which reason is reduced to a technical-instrumental faculty and honor is checked or sublimated into economic competitiveness and the quest for material status symbols.

From this point of view, there is no significant difference between classical liberalism and Left-liberalism. Both are based on the sovereignty of desire. Although Left liberalism is more idealistic because it is dedicated to the impossible dream of overcoming natural inequality, whereas classical liberalism, always more vulgar, unimaginative, and morally complacent, is content with mere "bourgeois" legal equality.

In Quentin Tarantino's *Pulp Fiction*, a black gangster named Marsellus Wallace bribes a boxer named Butch Coolidge to throw a fight. Butch is a small-timer near the end of his career. If he was going to make it, he would have made it already. So he is looking to scrape up some retirement money by throwing a fight. Marsellus Wallace offers him a large sum of cash to lose in the fifth round. Wallace plans to bet on Butch's opponent and clean up.

Butch accepts the deal, then Wallace dispenses a bit of advice: "Now, the night of the fight, you may feel a slight sting. That's pride fuckin' wit ya. Fuck pride! Pride only hurts, it never helps. Fight through that shit. 'Cause a year from now, when you're kickin' it in the Caribbean, you're gonna say, 'Marsellus Wallace was right.'" Butch replies, "I've got no problem with that, Mr. Wallace."

The great theorists of liberalism offered mankind the same deal that Marsellus Wallace offered Butch: "Fuck pride. Think of the money." And our ancestors took the deal. As Marsellus hands Butch the cash, he pauses to ask, "Are you my nigger?" "It certainly appears so," Butch answers, then takes the money.

In modernity, every man is the "nigger," the spiritual slave, of any man with more money than him—to the precise extent that any contrary motives, such as pride or religious/intellectual enthusiasm, have been suppressed. (Marsellus, a black man, calls all of his hirelings "niggers," but surely it gives him special pleasure to deem the white ones so.)

But history can never really end as long as it is possible for men to choose to place honor above money or even life itself. And that is always possible, given that we really do seem to have the ability to choose which part of our soul is sovereign.

*Counter-Currents*, October 23, 2010

# A LITTLE DEATH:
## HEGELIAN THOUGHTS ON PIERCING & TATTOOS

It is safe to say that urban youth culture in the contemporary West is pretty much saturated with hedonism. Yet in the midst of all this hedonism, tattooing and body piercing are huge industries, and they *hurt*.

It is, moreover, *shared pain*, broadcast to and imposed upon all who see it. It is natural for human beings to feel sympathy for people in pain, or who show visible signs of having suffered pain. Perhaps this is a sign of morbid oversensitivity, but I believe I am not the only person who feels sympathy pains when I see tattoos and piercings, especially extensive ones. Sometimes I actually shudder and look away.

Sexual sadism and masochism fit into a larger hedonistic context, since the are merely intensifications or exaggerations of features of normal heterosexual relations. But what is the place of the non-sexual masochism of body piercing and tattooing in a larger hedonistic society?

This question first occurred to me when I saw Quentin Tarantino's *Pulp Fiction*, in which Jody, the wife of the drug dealer Lance, launches into a discourse about piercing. Jody, it is safe to say, is about as complete a hedonist as has ever existed. Yet Jody has had her body pierced sixteen times, including her left nipple, her clitoris, and her tongue. And in each instance, she used a needle rather than a relatively quick and painless piercing gun. As she says, "That gun goes against the whole idea behind piercing."

Well then, I had to ask, "What *is* the whole idea behind piercing?" Yes, piercing is fashionable. Yes, it is involved with sexual fetishism. (But fetishism is not mere desire either.) Yes, it is now big business. But the phenomenon cannot merely be reduced to hedonistic self-indulgence. It is irreversible. And it *hurts*. And apparently, if it doesn't hurt, that contradicts the "whole idea."

For Hegel, history begins when a distinctly human form of

self-consciousness emerges. Prehistoric man is merely a clever animal who is ruled by his desires, by the pursuit of pleasure and the avoidance of pain, including the desire for self-preservation. When we enjoy creature comforts, however, we are aware of ourselves as mere creatures.

But human beings are more than clever animals. Slumbering within prehistoric man is a need for self-consciousness. To see our bodies, we need a mirror. To see our self also requires an appropriate "mirror." For Hegel, the first mirror is the consciousness of others. We see ourselves as we are seen by others. When the reactions of others coincide with our sense of self, we feel pride. When we are treated in ways that contradict our sense of self, we feel anger. Sometimes this anger leads to conflict, and sometimes this conflict threatens our very lives.

For Hegel, the duel to the death for honor reveals the existence of two different and conflicting parts of the soul: *desire*, including the desire for self-preservation, and *honor*, which is willing to risk death to find satisfaction. For Hegel, the man who is willing to risk death to preserve his honor is a natural master. The man who is willing to suffer dishonor to preserve his life is a natural slave. For the master, honor rules over desire. For the slave, desire rules over honor. Hegel sees the struggle to the death over honor as the beginning of history, history being understood as a process by which human beings come to self-understanding.

Of course not every road to self-understanding involves an encounter with death. But the primary means by which we understand ourselves is participation in a culture, and civilized life entails countless repressions of our physical desires, countless little pains and little deaths.

According to Hegel, if history is a process of self-discovery, then history can end when we learn the truth about ourselves and live accordingly. And the truth is that all men are free. Hegel's follower Francis Fukuyama became famous for arguing that the fall of communism and the globalization of liberal democracy was the end of history. But he also followed Alexandre Kojève, Hegel's greatest 20th-century interpreter, who argued that the end of history would not bring a society of universal freedom, but a society of universal slavery: slavery in the spiritual sense of the rule of desire over honor. And that is a perfect description of modern, hedonistic, bourgeois society.

But there is more to the soul than desire. Thus man cannot be fully satisfied by mere hedonism. The restless drive for self-consciousness that gave rise to history in the first place will stir again. In a world of casual and meaningless self-indulgence, piercing and its first cousin tattooing are thus deeply significant; they are tests; they are limit experiences; they are encounters with something—something in ourselves and in the world—that transcends the economy of desire. To "mortify" the flesh literally means to kill it. Each little hole is a little death, which derives its meaning from a big death, a whole death, death itself. Thus one can see the contemporary craze with body modification as the re-enactment of the primal humanizing encounter with death within the context of a decadent and dehumanizing society. History is beginning again.

*Counter-Currents*, October 23, 2010

# Postmodernism vs. Identity*

What is postmodernism, and how is it inconsistent with a robust politics of identity? There are two senses of postmodernism. The first is postmodern philosophy. When people talk about postmodern philosophy, they mean things like the critique of Cartesianism, atomistic individualism, and other ideas that came out of modern Western philosophy. I have no quarrel with the postmodern attempt to get beyond modern Western philosophy. In fact, I agree with 90% of it.

The other kind of postmodernism comes out of literary and cultural studies and refers to an attitude toward culture, which is characterized in two ways: by *eclecticism* and by *irony*.

I would like to argue that eclecticism and irony are profoundly subversive of identity. Since White Nationalism is all about defending racial and cultural identity, we need to have a sense of what's wrong with postmodernism. What's wrong with cultural eclecticism and irony?

What does it mean to be eclectic? Eclecticism today basically means multiculturalism. To be eclectic is to lack a unity of taste and style. Instead, one's tastes are diverse and all-encompassing. Now what's wrong with that? Isn't it possible to like a little bit of everything?

Yes and no.

One can arrive at broad and eclectic tastes through authentic or inauthentic paths.

The inauthentic ones are far more common. First, if one has no real tastes at all, eclecticism is the default position in an increasingly multicultural society, in which we are bombarded with opportunities to buy decontextualized artifacts from other cultures, and some of them are bound to stick. Second, eclecticism can follow simply from an ideological commitment to multiculturalism and inclusion. Third, eclecticism can be adopted

---

* The following text is the basis of a talk that I gave to The Scandza Forum in Oslo on July 1, 2017. I also gave an earlier, stand-alone version of the section on irony as a talk in Budapest on June 21, 2017.

simply as a currency of social signaling to gain status.

You might decorate your apartment with little kilim pillows from somewhere in the Middle East. You might have a little Buddha figure on a shelf and some "World Music" sampler CDs you bought at a chain coffee shop, and you'd feel like you're a better person because of all that. You'd preen and congratulate yourself on your openness to different cultures by visiting certain boutiques, or flipping through catalogues, and buying things that are produced by other cultures. You might gush over the mawkish folk art of South American Indians, but you would never surround yourself with folkish décor from your own society. In fact, you'd look down on it as "kitsch," which is a tasteless counterfeit of beauty.

What unites the inauthentic forms of eclecticism is that they really have nothing to do with taste and everything to do with social conditioning, social signaling, political ideology, and market forces.

The authentic path to developing broad and eclectic tastes is actually developing taste in the first place. And taste, by its very nature, forbids most forms of eclecticism.

What is taste? Taste is, first and foremost, a faculty of discrimination, of seeing differences, and not just any old differences, but differences of quality and rank. Thus, by its very nature, taste overthrows the multiculturalist commandment to be undiscriminating and eclectic. To like everything indiscriminately is not to have eclectic tastes. It is to have no taste at all.

Taste is often said to be subjective, but this is false. Taste is a faculty of perceiving real distinctions in the world. Judgments of taste are often thought to be subjective because it is not possible to fully articulate exactly how one perceives these distinctions. Thus it is not possible to codify principles of taste and write them down. But taste is not subjective simply because you can't learn it from a textbook. One can learn taste only through direct comparative experience, and the best way to do so is under the guidance of someone with more refined tastes who can draw your attention to objective differences that you might otherwise have overlooked but which, once seen, cannot be unseen.

Thus the development of taste presupposes a tradition, a set of practices developed and refined in the crucible of experience and passed on by apprenticeship to new generations. An education in taste is just one aspect of enculturation, that is to say, the propagation of a culture through time.

A culture is ultimately an outlook on the world, a worldview that exists not just in the form of abstract ideas but also concrete social practices and artifacts. As a worldview, every culture gives us access to the same common world, but from a distinct perspective shared by a group of people. To have a culture is to share something in common with other people. To have a culture is to see the world in the same way as others. A culture is a unity. And, as Nietzsche points out, cultures express their inner unity by a unity of style.

This was illustrated to me most strikingly by Chinese dog breeds. Chinese guardian lion figures are ferocious and highly stylized. But through selective breeding, the Chinese have imposed that style even on their dogs. From large Chow dogs to small Shih Tzus and Pekinese, they have the same short muzzles, deep chests, regal bearing, and mane-like hair. Indeed, Shih Tzu just means "lion dog."

Culture, moreover, is a core component of our identity. Biology provides the hardware, but our native culture and mother tongue are the basic operating system, the framework in terms of which we experience the world.

If having taste presupposes enculturation, and cultures are characterized by a unity of style, and our culture is at the core of our identity, what should one's attitude be toward eclecticism? If one has a healthy identification with one's own culture and well-developed tastes, one will quite naturally find foreign cultures distasteful, ranging from mild discomfort with slightly different cultures to strong distaste for radically different ones.

Now this claim will sound shocking to educated Westerners, but these very people are quite comfortable expressing distaste for the lower classes of their own societies even as they gush over the crude handicrafts of Third World peasants. But this sort of eclecticism is actually a manifestation of cultural decadence. Eclecticism presupposes a lack of taste, based on a lack of enculturation. A lack of enculturation means lack of identity with one's own culture, an alienation from it that permits the loosening of its unity of style and the infiltration of foreign elements.

But isn't it possible to have a genuine and healthy appreciation for the creations of other cultures? And isn't this a very white thing to do? Indeed, arguably this is part of the process of enculturation, for the bulk of European high culture is foreign to any particular European folk culture. But it is an even greater stretch to genuinely appreciate non-European cultures, and to be authentic, such an appreciation must be solidly grounded in one's own culture and taste. Such an achievement is about as rare as being fluent in a foreign language. In other words, it is an achievement of elites and can never be a characteristic of a mass society.

The eclecticism of the masses, by contrast, is simply what one would expect from barbarians and philistines reared in multicultural consumer societies. Does such multiculturalism give you a genuine taste and appreciation for other cultures? Of course not. It simply makes one a consumer of dead and decontextualized cultural artifacts, which function simply as tools of social signaling.

As with all other forms of multiculturalism, eclecticism is not really promoted because it enriches us, but because it impoverishes us. By embracing eclecticism and multiculturalism, you don't really gain the exotic; you simply lose the familiar. You don't gain the whole world; you simply lose your sense of home. You don't really encounter foreign cultures; you just alienate yourself from your own.

Eventually, though, if that process is continued to the nth degree — and nobody is opposing that today except reactionaries like us — there will be a new unity of style. Namely, everything is going to be turned into a homogeneous gray consumer goo. As cultures mingle and jostle and rub together, all their differences will be erased, and the new universal style that emerges will not be the product of any particular people and its genius, but a least-common-denominator precipitate of all the peoples in the world who have had their unique cultural identities erased.

So, when people extol cultural eclecticism — embracing and fetishizing cultural differences — I want you to hear it as a threat to your cultural identity. When I hear people talking about eclecticism, I reach for my revolver. That's the attitude that you should have as well.

The second postmodernist trope is irony. Ironism, like eclecticism, is a form of cultural decadence. But it is even more dangerous, because while most identitarians have the good sense to reject eclecticism, our movement actually embraces and revels in irony.

What is irony? By "irony," I do not mean the trope whereby one intends something different from, or opposed to, what one literally says. Nor do I mean situations in which what actually happens is very different from, or sometimes opposed to, what one expected. For instance, when Oedipus vows to find the cause of the plague, not knowing that it is he himself. Nor do I mean Socratic irony, which is a kind of dissimulation and condescension in speech.

Instead, by "irony" I mean a refusal to take serious things seriously, an attitude of detachment and condescension toward things that one should regard with respect or adoration. Detachment from small and silly things is healthy. But ironic detachment from great and serious things is a sign of decadence, because we need ideals. Ideals are what raise human beings above animals. Men without ideals are just clever animals, whose reason is subservient to the satisfaction of their natural desires.

When irony becomes an ethos, I call it "ironism." Ironism in the postmodern sense means relating to culture, ideas, and especially ideals without committing to them, without owning them, without making them a part of you, and especially without opening yourself to their power to transform you. In his book *Postscript to The Name of the Rose*, Umberto Eco describes this postmodern ironism brilliantly:

> I think of the postmodern attitude as that of a man who loves a very cultivated woman and knows that he cannot say to her "I love you madly," because he knows that she knows (and that she knows he knows) that these words have already been written by Barbara Cartland. Still there

is a solution. He can say "As Barbara Cartland would put it, I love you madly." At this point, having avoided false innocence, having said clearly it is no longer possible to talk innocently, he will nevertheless say what he wanted to say to the woman: that he loves her in an age of lost innocence. If the woman goes along with this, she will have received a declaration of love all the same. Neither of the two speakers will feel innocent, both will have accepted the challenge of the past, of the already said, which cannot be eliminated; both will consciously and with pleasure play the game of irony.... But both will have succeeded, one again, in speaking of love.[1]

What Eco means here by "innocence" is sincerity, earnestness, and commitment. Barbara Cartland wrote lots of torrid romance novels, which, whatever their flaws, were brimming with sincere professions of passion. But the couple in question would feel silly speaking of love in such a naïve and straightforward way. They can't own or commit to such emotions. Yet they must speak of love. But they also feel the need to communicate that they think themselves above it. So they speak of love ironically and condescendingly. They put "love" in scare quotes. They put love in the mouth of a ladies' romance novelist.

Eco says this is a solution to the problem of speaking of love while still being hyper self-conscious. Unfortunately, I don't think that's a solution at all, because to be hyper self-conscious is unhealthy, and it is especially unhealthy in relation to things that we should take seriously, like moral and political ideals and our racial and cultural identity.

How is self-consciousness subversive of identity? First, we will deal with identity, then with self-consciousness.

Some things are us, and some things are not us. Your identity is what you are. The rest of the world is what you are not.

Some things that are not us can become us. I am going to use a neologism for this process that is so ugly that even Heidegger scholars have rejected it: "enowning." Enowning means making

---

[1] Umberto Eco, *Postscript to The Name of the Rose*, trans. William Weaver (San Diego: Harcourt Brace Jovanovich, 1984), 67–68.

something part of you. Enowning is more than just ownership, since the things we own really aren't part of us, although we can more or less invest ourselves in them.

Conversely, some things that are us can become no longer us. I call this process "disowning."

When we eat and drink, we are enowning—literally incorporating—things that are not us. When we learn a language or a skill, we are enowning something that is not us. We are becoming the vehicle through which a tradition of practices stretching back into unrecorded history lives and perpetuates itself. When we adopt ideas, really believe them, and live accordingly, we are enowning them. When we cut our hair or trim our nails, we are disowning parts of ourselves. When we decide that certain ideas are no longer true and values no longer good, we disown and disavow them.

There are, however, some things that you can enown but cannot disown, chief among them your mother tongue and the culture instilled along with it. If your brain is your hardware, your mother tongue and culture are your operating system. If our genes constitute our first nature, our language and culture constitute our second nature, which provide the context and framework for all subsequent experience. No matter how many other languages you learn, no matter how widely you might travel, no matter how rootless and cosmopolitan you might aspire to be, these new acquisitions do not erase your mother language and culture. They are simply added on top of them. You can never fully uproot yourself from your mother tongue and culture. You cannot get rid of them. It's like trying to run away from your own shadow. It always follows you. It's always there, whether you own up to it or not.

Self-consciousness is a form of consciousness. Consciousness involves a distinction between the *act* of consciousness and the *object* of consciousness—between seeing the painting, and the painting that we see, between hearing the melody and the melody that we hear. As conscious beings, we are first and foremost conscious of things *other* than ourselves. We are like the sun, with rays of consciousness streaming out in all directions revealing all manner of objects. We are agents not objects of awareness who are involved with the world, not with ourselves. But if there is a difference between consciousness and its objects, how can be become self-conscious? Self-consciousness is a turning inwards, which is possible because we can first *disengage our consciousness from the world*, then *introduce a split in ourselves* between agent of consciousness and object of consciousness, then contemplate this objectified fragment of ourselves.

If self-consciousness presupposes *disengagement from the world* and *self-objectification*, one has to ask: Is self-consciousness healthy? Yes, within limits. Life can be viewed as a constant process of enowning and disowning, both things in the world and aspects of ourselves. For conscious beings, self-consciousness is healthy as a tool of self-criticism and self-improvement. Self-consciousness allows us disengage, objectify, and then either improve and enown or simply disown beliefs and patterns of feeling and behavior that might otherwise harm us.

But there are limits to self-consciousness.

First, there are limits to its utility. One can be too self-conscious—too disengaged from the world, too self-objectified, too much of a navel-gazer—to lead a good life. Life can be improved by self-consciousness, but self-consciousness is not life itself, and being hyper-self-conscious is self-defeating. For instance, you might be a highly practiced speaker or musician or warrior.

The acquisition of these skills requires self-consciousness as a means of self-criticism and self-improvement. This is, for example, why gyms, dance schools, and martial arts academies are filled with mirrors. This is why we have teachers, trainers, and friends: to see ourselves through their eyes, in the hope of improving ourselves.

But when the time comes to actually perform, we have to thrust self-consciousness aside and simply engage with our task. And if, at that point, self-consciousness creeps back in—"Am I saying this right? Am I pronouncing this right? Am I communicating this right? Does this finger go here?"—you are disengaging from your task, objectifying your performance, and thinking about yourself rather than the matter at hand. You are second-guessing yourself. You are withdrawing energy and focus from the task. And you will start slipping up. You will start getting tongue-tied and stammering. You will start hitting the wrong keys. Your defense and attack will slacken. You will lose your edge. Because you're no longer fully present, no longer in the moment, no longer performing these acts anymore. You're reflecting on them. Even the most accomplished master can trip himself up simply by starting to reflect on what he's doing, because then he's no longer really, fully, committedly doing it. The performer must be engaged, not disengaged. His self must be one, not split. He must be fully into the task, not half in it, half out of it. He must be fully an actor, not in part a spectator viewing himself from the stands.

Second, there are metaphysical limits to self-consciousness. J. G. Fichte once enjoined his students, "Gentlemen, think the wall." Then he said, "Gentlemen, think he-who-thinks the wall." In other words, disengage from the wall, objectify yourself, and think about yourself instead. But who is performing that act? Obviously, the thinker is another part of you. And by asking that question, I have now objectified him as well. Now we are thinking he-who-thinks he-who-thinks the wall. But who did that? Yet another part of you. Obviously, this process can go on forever, mincing up the self into tinier and tinier pieces.

But the self can never be fully objectified, because there always remains a distinction between the *act* and the *object* of consciousness. Thus complete self-consciousness is not possible, for every act of self-consciousness presupposes splitting the self into subject and object, and as long as the subject is a subject, it is never an object. Consciousness only *works* when it is not an object of consciousness. Consciousness only works when the drive for self-consciousness stops and *simply lets consciousness happen*.

When I was a child, I would freak myself out with morbid, obsessive thoughts that would recur when I was trying to fall asleep. One of my hippy cousins told me that it would help me relax and fall asleep if I focused simply on my breathing and my heartbeat. So I would shadow each of these automatic processes with self-consciousness. But then the absurd idea would steal through my head that maybe these processes would stop if I no longer reflected on them, which would induce a feeling of panic that would stave off sleep even more. This morbid fixation was quickly banished by induction. For I would eventually fall asleep, and yet I have woken up every morning since. Our consciousness, like our heart and lungs, is at root an automatic biological process that does not require the shadow of self-consciousness to operate. This makes sense, for man is part of the animal kingdom, and consciousness exists in animal species that show no sign of self-consciousness at all.

How is the hyper-self-consciousness of ironism subversive of cultural identity? Irony as a cultural form is all about stepping back from your culture, severing your commitment to it, severing the seriousness that is at the root of that commitment, and objectifying it — even discarding it.

There is a sense, though, in which one's deep identity is actually immune to ironism. Your mother tongue and native culture are acquired before you are self-conscious. They exist on a deeper level of your mind than self-consciousness. They are one of the conditions that make self-consciousness possible in the first place. Self-consciousness can spiral in on itself and try to uproot itself from its origins, but the effort is futile.

Such efforts are not, however, without consequence, for although they cannot change your deep identity, they can alienate you from who you really are and lead to a shallow and inauthentic existence. You have no choice about your deep identity, but you do have a choice to embrace it or flee from it, to own up to it or disown it, to be authentic or inauthentic, to be real or a fake.

In "The Second Coming," W. B. Yeats brilliantly describes a decadent culture on the brink of collapse. Two lines are especially resonant:

The best lack all conviction, while the worst
Are full of passionate intensity.

The best are the defenders of civilization. The worst are the rabble that would tear it down if given the chance. What happens when the best no longer feel a passionate attachment to civilization? What happens when they are detached and ironic toward their identity, willing to enact it only in "scare quotes"? More to the point, what happens when such men face off with a rabble animated by passionate intensity? Obviously, other things being equal, the rabble will triumph, and civilization will fall.

One of the reasons why ironism is rife today is because our culture is dominated by Jews, who are outsiders. Jews do not feel an identity with our civilization. They are all too happy to appropriate the best of its products, but they spend far more time mocking and degrading the rest of it. Jewish ironism makes perfect sense, because this is not their culture. Unfortunately, they have the power to mainline their ironism into the rest of us. But it makes no sense for us to accept it, since this really is our culture. Moreover, while Jews teach us to lack all conviction toward our culture and interests, they cultivate a passionate intensity toward their own, which is how whites have lost and Jews have gained control over our society.

It is important to understand the dangers of ironism, because the Right today is rank with it—the whole "LOL dude, it's just a meme," "I'm only being ironic" culture.

There's a place and a role for irony. People are not overly eager to commit to new things, especially if they are radical and marginal. This is why we have changing rooms at clothing stores, so you can try clothes on and see if they look good on you before you buy them. This is why we let people test drive a car before they commit to buying it. This is why merchants have 30-day money back guarantees. If you don't have to fully commit upfront, then you're more likely to try something, and if you try it, then you are more likely to buy it.

Ironic spaces where people can encounter White Nationalist ideas and memes perform an important function for our movement. They allow people to try on radical ideas for size before committing to them. Irony gives them deniability if mom looks over their shoulder. They can just jump back and say, "Whoa! I'm just playing around here! Don't take this seriously! I'm not committed to this. I disavow! I was just being ironic!" If more people feel safe trying on our ideas without committing to them, more people will ultimately come on board.

But we must never lose sight of the fact that, in the end, we have to close the deal. The salesman who lets you take a test drive can't let you remain non-committal. The shop girl who lets you try on a shirt can't let you remain non-committal. When people are exploring our ideas, we can't let them remain non-committal either. This is not a game. We are not just playing with ideas. We are fighting for the survival of our race against cunning and ruthless enemies who are out to exterminate us. If you are detached and bemused about that, you haven't gotten the message. This is war, and there is no room for ironists in foxholes.

The ironists also need to recognize that ideas inspire actions. So we must ask ourselves: What is more likely to inspire a movement that actually changes the world for the better: a worldview that is based on objective reality and calibrated for practical success—or a grab bag of edgy memes, drunken pranks, and audio clips from TV shows? People are going to take ideas seriously regardless, so we need to provide them with serious ideas.

Irony is useful as a tool, but ironism as an ethos is decadent. Thus the great problem of our movement is to move people from an ethos of ironism to an ethos of commitment. We must move from play to seriousness, bemused detachment to passionate intensity, self-indulgence to self-sacrifice—from being children to being grownups. It is time to put away froggy things and act like men. For, in the end, the people who are going to save our race must be 100% committed to the struggle because it is a matter of identity, of who they really are, not something they can just jump back from and pretend is just a game.

*Counter-Currents*, August 11, 2017

# WHY WE MEET AS WE DO:
## THOUGHTS ON LIBERAL EDUCATION*

Why do we meet as we do? Obviously I can't answer this question on behalf of all of us, but nevertheless I suspect that in answering it, I speak for more than just myself.

We here are dedicated to liberal education, with an almost exclusive focus on the most liberal of the liberal arts: philosophy. But what is liberal education? And why does it draw us here again and again? Ask a college student today, and the likely answer is that liberal education is education by liberals. But liberal education is not liberal in that sense. Indeed, although philosophy has always been a part of a liberal education, every great philosopher before Marx, including those deemed classical liberals, would have to be considered politically conservative by today's standards.

Liberal education is not liberal as opposed to conservative. Liberal education is liberal as opposed to servile. Liberal education is liberated and liberating education: it is liberated, and it liberates, from the bondage of necessity, specifically the necessities, the promptings, or drives of our physical nature. Most of our lives are devoted to satisfying such drives and desires. The activity of satisfying these desires is work, and the arts we deploy to satisfy them are servile or utilitarian arts.

If the servile arts belong to the world of work, the liberal arts belong to the world of leisure, of play. If the servile arts produce the necessities of life, the liberal arts produce luxuries; indeed, they are luxuries. If the servile arts are part of the economy of nature, the liberal arts are part of the economy of culture. The servile arts embody what can be called technical-instrumental

---

* This is the text of a talk that I gave on August 15, 1996 to The Invisible College in Atlanta. I recall that the actual lecture was much longer and involved discussions of Rousseau, Kant, Schiller, and Hegel. If a tape comes to light, I will have it transcribed and make it available.

rationality, whereas the liberal arts are enjoyed as ends in themselves.

The servile arts are governed by the logic of investment, of spending money to make money; they measure their usefulness by how much they save and how much they make; a successful expenditure not only circulates back to its source, it returns increased, pulling more and more reality into the economy of necessity—each tiny fish returns home to spawn; because of this, investment is characterized by a horizontal movement of recirculation within the material domain.

The liberal arts are governed by what Georges Bataille calls the logic of expenditure, of investing material wealth not for material gains but for spiritual ones; expenditure cashes in material wealth for spiritual wealth; because of this, expenditure is characterized by a vertical movement of transcendence, the movement from the material to the spiritual. From the point of view of expenditure, this movement of transcendence is a gain, for it rates the spiritual above the material in a hierarchy of value.[1]

From the point of view of investment, however, expenditure is not the transcendence of the material for the spiritual, but a hemorrhage of the material for . . . nothing; it is seen simply as loss and waste. Bataille characterizes non-material values to which material values are subordinated as the sacred; the subordinate material values are the profane.[2]

The liberal arts, therefore, are part of the non-material economy of the sacred; the servile arts are part of the material economy of the profane. The sacred does, however, satisfy some dimension of the human being; it is in some sense necessary. This means that we have to make distinctions within the human soul, and at this point I shall recur to the Platonic distinction between

---

[1] In this context, it makes sense to speak in terms of a movement from the material to the spiritual; for Bataille, it is more accurately deemed a movement from the profane to the sacred, and the profane can just as well be spiritual as the sacred can be material.

[2] Bataille leaves open the possibility that sacred non-material values can become routinized and therefore profane, allowing their material negations to assume the role of the sacred. This could serve as a good beginning for a definition of cultural decadence.

reason, spirit, and desire, reason being the part that responds to the true, spirit being the part that responds to the beautiful and the good, and desire being the part that responds to the necessities of life; whereas the profane satisfies the desiring soul, we might say that the sacred serves the needs of the rational and spirited dimensions of the soul.

Putting these elements together, we can offer a preliminary definition of liberal education: Liberal education is liberated and liberating education—as opposed to servile and utilitarian education; it belongs to the world of leisure and play—as opposed to the world of work; liberal education belongs to the world of culture—as opposed to the world of nature; it is ruled by the economics of expenditure—as opposed to the economics of investment; liberal education is one of the luxuries—as opposed to the necessities—of life; it belongs to the realm of the sacred—as opposed to the profane; and because it belongs to the realm of the sacred, it satisfies the needs of the spirit and the intellect.

By now, I hope that liberal education seems desirable. But now we can raise another question: Is it good? And if it is good for the individual, is it good for society? To answer these questions, I wish to give a loosely "Marxist" analysis of the origins of liberal education. The idea of liberal education arises in ancient Greece. The distinction between liberal and servile arts is based on the distinction between the liberal and servile classes of Greek society. The liberal class was the warrior aristocracy. The servile class consisted of slaves, farmers, and artisans. To understand the origins of the distinction between liberal and servile education, we have to understand the origins of the distinction between liberal and servile classes. To do this, we must go back to the primal scene, the original social order, and the original struggle, from which the distinction between master and slave emerged. Let us take Plato and Hegel as our guides here.

In *Republic*, Book II, Plato offers us an image of an egalitarian society ruled by the principle of necessity, i.e., the provision of food, clothing, and shelter; the society is characterized by communal property and the division of labor and craft specialization; it has a money economy and external trade; it has some wage earners, but most people are independent artisans; there is no government and no class structure, nor is there a professional army; culturally, it is somewhat primitive, with a religion that can be characterized as magical, devoted to the procurement of favorable economic conditions, their festivals and feasts being determined by the seasons and the harvest. There are no real arts, but many crafts. They seem to be vegetarians.

Once Socrates finishes setting out this picture of a city ruled by necessity, the spirited Glaucon objects, "You seem to make these men have their feasts without relishes" and calls it "the city of pigs." To this, Socrates responds that Glaucon wishes "a luxurious city," which Socrates then proceeds to describe in such a way that it is unmistakably a warrior aristocracy.

The luxurious city is a city whose needs are beyond the necessary. It is an economy centered on the pursuit of honor and glory, not the satisfaction of desire. To satisfy its lust for honor, it is a warlike city, with a distinct caste of professional warriors. When these warriors are not fighting for honor, they struggle to win it by other means: by the lavish expenditure of looted wealth for private luxuries and public monuments; by hunting wild animals, the more dangerous the better; by athletic contests, like the Olympic games; by collecting beautiful and useless things; and by the cultivation of exquisite arts, manners, and conventions, the more liberated from nature, the better, such as the art of courtly love, which measured its sublimity by its remoteness from physical consummation, or the Japanese tea ceremony, or the peculiar code of the English gentleman.

The luxurious city is one where men eat from tables, recline on couches, and sleep in comfortable beds; it is a city requiring such professions as perfume makers and pastry chefs, painters and embroiderers, beauticians and barbers, wet nurses and governesses, grooms and huntsmen, gardeners and courtesans, swineherds and butchers, doctors and dieticians, etc. These servile arts, unlike those of the early city, exist only to produce luxuries for the rich, not the necessities needed by all. To expand the servile class, we need more servile men. Thus the luxurious city adds slaves to the ranks of free craftsmen.

It is Hegel—and the American founding fathers—who help us to understand the creation of the slave class. Cynics never tire of pointing out the irony that the Declaration of Independence, which speaks so eloquently about liberty and equality, was penned and signed by slave owners. Suffice it to say that the slave owners saw no such irony. But why not? Were they simply blinded by their self-interest? A clue can be found in the Declaration itself, where the signatories pledge their lives, fortunes, and sacred honor to the fight for freedom. By pledging their lives and fortunes, they were signaling their willingness to give them up for the cause of freedom. But they were not willing to give up their sacred honor; indeed, because they held their honor sacred, they were not willing to give it up—even to save their lives; and because they preferred death to dishonor, they thought themselves worthy of being free men.

As for men who were willing to sacrifice their honor to save their lives and property: These men were slavish; they were unworthy of freedom. In short, the aristocratic mind thinks that it is legitimate for there to be free and servile classes, because there are free and servile men. Free men prefer death before dishonor. Servile men prefer dishonor to death.

But how do we determine which men are free and which men are servile? Hegel's famous struggle between master and slave in the *Phenomenology of Spirit* describes the process. The process is a duel to the death for honor. Such duels are fraught with contingency, but if the contingencies follow a certain pattern, the outcome is an aristocratic-slave society. First, there has to be a clear winner and a clear loser in the battle. Second, the defeated party must survive his defeat. This means that the victor must chose to spare him by making him a slave. It also means that the vanquished must choose not to kill himself. The choice of the vanquished to preserve his life at the cost of his honor legitimated his servitude in the mind of the master, and frequently enough in his own mind as well. Furthermore, in the master's mind, it was his own certainty of his preference of death to dishonor that made him feel worthy of elevating himself while reducing the vanquished to a mere tool for better enjoying his freedom.

It is Hegel's claim that it is the slave, working for the glorification of the master, who creates the cultural and historical world, the human city as opposed to the city of pigs; the master, by seeking his own glorification, contributes unintentionally to the glorification of all mankind. Indeed, history shows that every advanced culture practiced slavery, that every high art was created by servile men under aristocratic patronage, and that philosophy thought of itself as the noblest of professions because it was the idlest and most useless of them all.

Given that the idea of liberal versus servile education is founded on the social distinction between free and servile men, how can liberal education be legitimate in an egalitarian, democratic society that denies the legitimacy of such a social hierarchy? The answer of most liberal educators today is, unfortunately: It can't. Liberal education cannot be legitimated in an egalitarian society. The distinction between high culture and low culture, high arts and low arts, freedom and necessity, culture and nature, sacred and profane, must be collapsed.

What does it collapse into? Vocational, scientific, and technological education flourish, and humanities departments, having been subjected to the egalitarian purge of all elitist culture, seem to be dividing themselves into departments of pop culture studies and departments of permanent revolution: gender studies, ethnic studies, queer theory, etc., *kvetch* tanks dedicated to permanent political campaigning—and dumping grounds for the otherwise unemployable affirmative action tokens. Liberal education becomes, in short, education by liberals—racially, ethnically, and sexually diverse, to be sure—as long as they are liberals. Its content becomes a progressively thinner gruel after repeated straining through the uniform mesh that forms the *a priori* categories of the liberal mind.

The result? To appreciate the danger of an education increasingly accommodated to popular culture, we have to make a distinction between institutions oriented toward the consumer and what we might call ethical or character-building institutions.

Consumer institutions cater to the given preferences—in Heideggerian terms, the *Geworfenheit* and *Befindlichkeit*—of the individual, no matter how foolish, immature, vain, or vulgar he may be. According to the consumer ethic, the individual finds himself with a certain set of interests and preferences, and then goes out into the world to satisfy them. If he walks into a store and finds his given preferences satisfied, he will buy; if not, he looks elsewhere.

Ethical institutions are different in that they do not cater to the given preferences of the individual; they do not accommodate themselves to the individual, they accommodate the individual to the institution. Why would anyone put up with this? Because individuals have both the capacity and the need to grow, to mature and deepen their preferences and characters, and character-building institutions offer the opportunity and incentives to learn from those who are older and wiser, those who have been in our shoes, who have grown out of them, who know how to help us along, and who have the authority needed to pull and prod us through the tough spots, when, left to consult our given preferences, we would just as soon give up.

According to Hegel, such institutions as marriage, family life, productive work, education, military service, and other forms of civil service are paradigmatic ethical institutions. The problem that education shares with marriage, the family, the workplace, and the military in today's society are the egalitarian and individualist demands to transform them from ethical institutions shaping preferences to consumer institutions catering to preferences, no matter how immature and ignoble those preferences may be.

The emphasis on popular culture is symptomatic of this trend. Popular culture, unlike high culture, requires no taste and cultivation to enjoy. It caters to our preferences. We do not have to work to enjoy it. Indeed, popular culture is better called consumer culture, for it is created primarily for mass consumption, and bears all the marks of mass production, such as cheesiness and planned obsolescence. Consumer education thus serves not to liberate the mind from desire, from nature and necessity, from the vulgar and workaday; consumer education serves to further ensnare us, by attacking the institutions and conventions that sublimate desire toward something higher.

If what is distinctly human about us is our capacity to create and participate in the culture of reason and spirit, then we have to say that modern education, by tending toward the abolition of high culture in favor of the popular culture of desire, tends toward the abolition of the distinctly human. Thus the question: "Is liberal education a good thing?" really boils down to the question: "Is being human a good thing—or can we be content with merely being clever animals?" The whole tendency of modern education, and of modern life in general, is geared toward reducing us to clever, slavish, appetitive, security-loving, risk-averse, unheroic animals. All too many are content with that lot. But you are not. That is why we meet as we do.

*Counter-Currents*, October 23, 2010

# INDEX

Numbers in bold refer to a whole chapter or section devoted to a particular topic.

**A**
Achilles, 5–6
actualization, of a Concept, 101–104
affirmative action, 198
Alfarabi, 22–23
Alfonso X of Castile, 83, 84
Almirante, Giorgio, 82
America, 48–49n5, 66–67, 196
anarchy, 79; in Yeats, 144
Anubis, 36–37n3
Apocalypse, 145
Arcadia, 89
"Archaic Torso of Apollo," 170
aristocracy, in Aristotle, 49–51, 55, 60–62; warrior, 174, 195–98
Aristophanes, 29
Aristotle, iii, 7, 13–14, 29–30n2, **42–67**, 95
Aron, Raymond, 126, 154, 155
arts, liberal, 23, 193–94; cf. servile arts; see also logic of expenditure
arts, servile, 193–95; cf. liberal arts; see also logic of investment
Atlantis myth, 37n

**B**
Balla, Giacomo, 113
Bataille, Georges, 126, 156, 158, 165, 194

*Battle as Inner Experience*, 140
The Beatles, 4
*Befindlichkeit*, 198
*Being & Time*, 26, 97, **108–12**, 156
being, 129–32; Heidegger's Being (*Sein*), 109–11, 118, 141
beings, given, 131–32
Bethlehem, 145–46
Bhutan, 153, 162
Bible, 1, 74, 76
Blake, William, 171
Bloom, Allan, 83n1, 85n4, 93, 97n1, 157
Bolshevik Revolution, 142
Borg, 139
bourgeoisie, 164, 175–76, 180
Bowden, Jonathan, 68
Breton, André, 156
bricolage, 169
Brzezinski, Zbigniew, 155
Buchanan, Patrick J., 66
Bulgaria, 152

**C**
Caesarism, 80
Calhoun, John C., 57n10
Camus, Albert, iii, iv, **147–51**
Care (in myth), 26–27
care of the soul, 34–38, 45
Carter, Jimmy, 155
Cartland, Barbara, 185–86

Cartesianism, 181
Cassirer, Ernst, 77, 84n3, **134–36**
Castro, Fidel, 116
cave (Plato's parable), 10, 72
Cephalus, 97–98
chaos, in Nietzsche, **133–34**
Charondas, 64
checks & balances, in Aristotle, **51–53**, 66
Christ, 118, 142–46, 148
Cicero, 29n2
city of pigs, in Plato, 42, 195–96, 198; cf. luxurious city
civilization, 1, 25, 66, 74, 82, 91, 95–96, 103, 123, 133–34, 141, 159–60, 166, 179, 190–91; in Rousseau, 82, **83–96**; European, 142–46; pagan, 146; technological, 137–40; Western, 1, 103, 146
classes, social, 49–50, 52, 122, 195
Clinton, Bill, 8
*The Closing of the American Mind*, 157
*Clouds* (Aristophanes), 29
Cold War, Kojève's role in, 127, 155, 157, 166–68
communism & communists, 4n1, 16, 21, 47, 70, 116, 125–26, 155, 157, 175, 179
Concept (*Begriff*), in Hegel, 101–108, 120–21, 131
consciousness, 109, 129, 133–34, 139, 187–90; see also self-consciousness
conservatism, 73, 96, 144, 155, 157, 193
consumer ethic, 198

conventions, 136, 196, 199; in Vico, 71–72, 76–78
Corbin, Henri, 126, 156
corruption, **59–60, 60–61**
counter-Enlightenment, 75; see also Enlightenment
Cowling, Maurice, 68
*Critias*, 1n, 25n
cultural integrity, 169, 171; cf. multiculturalism
culture, 1, 11, 16, 19–20, 25, 28, 41, 68, 71, 73–74, 76, 77, 82, 108, 116, 118–22, 124–25, 127, 133–39, 142–43, 153, 156, 161–62, 165–66, 169–72, 174–75, 178–87, 190–91, 193, 195, 198–200
culture, high, 184, 198–200; cf. pop or popular culture
culture, living, 169–71; cf. postmodern culture
culture, pop or popular, 19, 198–200; cf. high culture
culture, postmodern, 169, 172; cf. living culture
*The Cup* (film), 153
cycles, historical, 70
Cyclops, 45

D
Dante, 1, 4, 36
Darwin, Charles, 80
Darwinism, Social, 80
*Dasein*, 109–10
death, 25, 38, 132, 133, 147–50, 164, 169–72, 178–80, 197
Declaration of Independence, US, 78, 197
De Gaulle, Charles, 127, 154
Deleuze, Gilles, 126, 156

democracy (liberal), 70, 157, 175, 179
democracy or democratic regime, 3, 10, 79, 127, 157, 175; in Aristotle, 49–51, 56, 60–61, 65, 70
Derrida, Jacques, 126
desire, 12–13, 17, 18, 19, 22, 53, 63, 72, 90, 91, 92, 105, 127, 130, 131, 134, 137, 138, 143–44, 149, 164, 170, 171, 172, 173–80, 185, 193, 195–96, 199–200
dialectic, iii, iv, v, **97–115**, 171, 175; Hegelian, **101–108**, **121–22**; Platonic, **97–101**; Heideggerian, **108–12**; Husserlian, **112–15**
dialogue, Platonic, 16–17, 25, 29–30, 33, 41, **97–101**
*Did the Greeks Believe Their Myths?*, 27
*Discourse on the Origins of Inequality* (Second Discourse), 85, 135
*Discourse on the Sciences and the Arts* (First Discourse), 85
*The Divine and the Decay*, 197
*Divine Comedy*, 36
*Dr. Zhivago*, 4n1
duel to the death over honor, 172, 173, 179, 197
*Dvapara Yuga*, 76

E
eclecticism, 165, 169, 181–85
Eco, Umberto, 185–86
economic man, 106
ecstasy, 129

education, liberal, iii, 22–23, **193–200**; public, in Aristotle, **45–48**
Egypt, 36n3, 145, 146, 154
*Emile*, 83–93
Enlightenment, 68–82, 85, 90; see also counter-Enlightenment
enowning & disowning, 186–88
Epicurus & Epicureanism, in Vico, 70–73, 77; in Rousseau, 85, 91–96
"erotics," iv, 35
*Essay on Man* (Pope), 84
*Essay on the Origin of Language*, 92–93
ethnic studies, 198
ethology, 70
*eudaimonia*, 43; see also happiness; well-being
eugenics, 2, 16, 40
European Economic Community, 127, 154
*Euthyphro*, 97
*Everything You Always Wanted to Know About Lacan . . . But Were Afraid to Ask Hitchcock*, 156–57
evil, problem of, 84; see also theodicy
Evola, Julius, 71, 82
evolutionary psychology, 70, 73
expert knowledge, **59**; cf. technology, *techne*, technique
explication, in Heidegger, 109, 111; in Hegel, 103

**F**
faith, 39–40; see also risk
family, in Aristotle, 43; in
 Plato, 2, 16, 18; in Hegel,
 108, 160, 199; in Vico, 69,
 76–79
Fessard, Gaston, 126, 156
fetishism (sexual), 178
*Finnegans Wake*, 75–76
first philosophy, iv
flight into Egypt, 145
Foucault, Michel, 126, 156
free will, 12, 85–86, 88–91,
 104–108, 144
freedom, 12, 39, 43, 44, **47–48**,
 51, 52, 54, **58–59**, 60, 63,
 64–66, 70, 79, 86, 88, 89, 90,
 91, **101–108**, 123–24, 134,
 139, 144, 150–51, 161–62,
 164, 166, 173–75, 179–80,
 197–98; in Hegel, 102–107;
 in Rousseau, 85–91
French Revolution, 118, 123,
 127, 153
Freud, Sigmund, 155
Fukuyama, Francis, 70, 157,
 168, 175, 179

**G**
Gadamer, Hans-Georg,
 58n11, 83n1
Galileo (Galileo Galilei), 69
gender studies, 198
General Agreement on
 Trades and Tariffs
 (GATT), 127, 154
General Will, 87
genetics, 71, 139
Geneva, 89, 90
*Geworfenheit*, 198

Glaucon, 6–7, 11, 13–15, 21–
 22, 196
globalism & globalization, 1,
 66–67, 123, 152, 157, 175,
 179
God (Christian or Biblical), iv,
 74, 83–84, 86, 94, 133, 143,
 145, 147
gods, Egyptian, 31, 36–37n3;
 generic, 98, 128; see also
 God
Golden Age, 70–73
good citizen, in Aristotle, 51,
 **53–54**; cf. good man
good life, 26, 27, 32, 48, 58,
 170
good man, in Aristotle, **53–54**;
 cf. good citizen
Good, 4, 20, 21, 41, 85, 164,
 195; see also values
*Gorgias*, 36, 38
government, popular, 79; in
 Aristotle, 46, 53–67
Great Sphinx at Giza, 145
Great War, 142
guardians, 1, 2, 13, 40, 52

**H**
Habermas, Jürgen, 58n11
Hades, 35
happiness, 38, 43, 47–48, 49,
 53–54, 64–65, 73, 148; see
 also *eudaimonia*; well-being
Hayek, Friedrich A., 57–58n11
heaven, 36
hedonism & hedonists, 19–20,
 169–72, 178, 180
Hegel, G. W. F., iii, iv, 70, 97,
 **101–108**, 109, 111, **116–28**,
 **129–32**, 155–65, **169–72**,

173–77, **178–80**, 195–97, 199
Heidegger, Martin, 26, 68, 97, **108–12**, 118, 124, 133, 137, **140–41**, 156, 157, 186, 198
Heine, Heinrich, 117
hell, 36
hermeneutic, method or circle, 97, **108–12**
Herod, 145
Hesiod, 71, 76
Himalayas, 153
Hinduism & Hindus, 70, 72, 76
Hippodamus of Miletus, 47
historicism, 121, 124–25
history, cyclical theory of, in Nietzsche, 165, 167; in Vico, 69–82
history, end of, 117, 118–19, **121–22**, **122–24**, 125–27, **152–68**, **173–77**, 179–80; see also history in Hegel; worldviews
history, in Hegel, **116–28**; see also end of history; worldviews
Hitler, Adolf, 157
Hobbes, Thomas, 88, 176
Hoffer, Eric, 72
Hölderlin, Friedrich, 116
Holy Spirit, 118
Homer, 5, 29n2, 71, 79
honor, 3, 5–6, 12, 17, 28, 48, 58, 63, 164, 171–72, 173–77, 179–80, 196–97
Hopkins, Bill, 147
Horus, 37n3
Hume, David, 176
Husserl, Edmund, 97, **112–15**

**I**
Idea (*Idee*), in Hegel, 101–108; 120–21
Idea, Absolute, 122–24
ideals, 17–18, 19–20, 131, 138, 164, 168, 170–71, 185–86
identity, **181–92**
imagination, 70, 73–76, 82, 107–108, 134, 171
individualism, 81, 82, 151, 175, 181
*Individualism and Economic Order*, 57n11
*Inferno*, 1
inquiry, 110–11
institutions, consumer, 198–99; cf. ethical institutions
institutions, ethical, 199; cf. consumer institutions
institutions, primal, 75–77
internet, 81
*Introduction to the Reading of Hegel*, 125, 163
irony, 169, 171, 175, 181, 185–86, 190–92, 197
Isles of the Blessed, 36
Italian Social Movement, 82

**J**
James, William, 40–41
Jaspers, Karl, 126, 153
Jeffers, Robinson, 68
Jena, Battle of, 117, 127, 153
Jews, 191
Jove, 76, 135; see also Jupiter
Joyce, James, 75–77
Jünger, 133, **137–40**, 141
Jupiter (god), 26; see also Jove
juries, in Aristotle, 57–58, 66
jurisprudence, 103

justice, 1, 5, 7–10, 36, 49, 54, 82, 84, 87–88, **97–101**

**K**
*Kali Yuga*, 70, 76, 79
Kant, Immanuel, 40–41, 83–86, 91, 94, 107, 117, 193
KGB, 155, 167
Kierkegaard, Søren, 133, **136–37**, 140, 141
kingship, in Aristotle, 49–50, 60–61; in Plato, 23
*kitsch*, 182
knowledge, tacit, 108, 111, 119, 122–23
Kojève, Alexandre (Aleksandr Vladimirovič Koževnikov), iii, iv, v, 70, 118, **125–28**, 129–31, **152–68**, 175, 179
Koyré, Alexandre, 126, 154

**L**
Lacan, Jacques, 126, 155, 157
Lampert, Jay, 112n9
*Language and Myth*, 77
*Laws* (Platonic dialogue), 11
laws, human, 45, 47, 49, 52–53, 54, 56, 59–60, 80; in Rousseau, 85, 90–96
*The Leap*, 147
Left (political), 69, 70, 144, 158, 176
Leibniz, Gottfried Wilhelm, 84, 86
leisure, 48, 174, 193, 195; see also play
Lenin, Vladimir, 116
*Letters Written from the Mountain*, 93

Lewinsky, Monica, 8
liberalism, iv, 43–44, 66, 69, 157, 175, 176, 179, 193
libertarianism, 43, 47
liberty, 46, 48, 59, 67, 79–80, 118, 123, 153, 197; negative, 47–48; positive, 47
life, 4–5, 11, 133–34
Locke, John, 176
logic, of expenditure, 194; cf. logic of investment; see also servile arts
logic, of investment, 194; cf. logic of expenditure; see also liberal arts
*Logical Investigations*, 97, **112–15**
logos, divine, 118
love: in Aristotle, 44, 54, 63; in Camus, 148–50; in Hegel, 160, 164; in Plato, 12, 20, 97; in postmodernism, 185–86; see also self-love
Lucretius, 92–93
luxury, 63, 73, 80, 174, 193–96; luxurious city in Plato, 195–96; cf. city of pigs
Lycurgus, 64
Lynch, Trevor, iii, 169n
Lyotard, Jean-François, 156

**M**
Machan, Tibor R., 42n
Madison, G. B., 58n11
Mani, 83, 84
Manicheanism, 84
many, in Aristotle, 44, 50–59
Mao Zedong, 116
Marcuse, Herbert, 82

Marjolin, Robert, 126, 156
Marx, Karl, 69, 82, 91, 116, 175, 193
Marxism, 116, 153, 175, 195
masochism, 178
master, natural, 174, 179; cf. natural slave; see also slavery
Masters, Robert D., 85n5, 85n6, 93
master-slave relationship, in Aristotle, 43, 47, 63
materialism, in the New Right, 70; in Rousseau, 91–93; in Vico, 71–74
memes, 191–92
*Memorabilia* (Xenophon), 6
men, free, 197; cf. servile men; see also natural master
men, servile, 196–98; cf. free men; see also natural slave
Merleau-Ponty, Maurice, 126, 156
Merson, Luc Olivier, 145f.
metaphysics, iv, 26, 96, 126, 156; Heidegger's overcoming of, 141
middle-class regime, in Aristotle, 49, 52, **61–64**, 65
mixed regime, **48–51**, 52, 53, 56, 58, 62
Miller, Geoffrey, 73
modernity, 69, 124, 126, 152, 156, 158, 167, 169, 176
moments (vs. pieces), 105, 108, 113–15
moral philosophy, 34
moral sentiments theory, 18, 21
multiculturalism, 66–67, 169, 171, 181–82, 184; cf. cultural integrity
Museum of Fine Arts, Boston, 146
Myth of Er, 11
myth, 4, 11, **25–41**, 69, 70, 75–77, 119, 122, 132–36, 138
mythology, Egyptian, 36n3; Greek, 30–31, 35
*muthos*, 25, 30, 39

**N**

Napoleon, 117–18, 153
nature, state of, in Rousseau, 86–95; in Vico, 72, 74
needs, material, 43, 73–74, 129–30, 195; of the soul, 11–12, 19–20, 22, 42, 195
negating, in Hegel, 130
negativity, **129–32**, 156
neo-colonialism, 155
Neo-Platonism, 71
New Right, 68–82,
*New Science*, 68–82
New Testament, 39
New World Order, 152
*The New Yorker*, 78
Newton, Sir Isaac, 69, 83–84
Nichols, James H., 92
*Nicomachean Ethics*, 7, 13–14, 42, 45, 47, 49, 62
Nietzsche, Friedrich, iv, 40, 119, **133–34**, 137, 141, 144, 165, 166, 168, 175, 183
nihilating, in Hegel, 129, 130
nihilism, iii, iv, 18–19, 78, **133–41**, 143–44, 146
Noah, 135
nuptial number, 2–3, 10

## O

*Odyssey* (Homer), 5, 29n2
*Of the Social Contract*, 86–90
oligarchy, 3, 10–11; in
    Aristotle, 49–51, 60–61, 64
Osiris, 37n3

## P

Paris, 89, 126, 127, 148, 157
Pascal, Blaise, 40, 149
Pascal's Wager, 149
passion, 45, 47, 59, 74, 89–90,
    142, 144, 164, 166, 186,
    190–91
Pasternak, Boris, 4n1
*Phaedo*, 38–39
*Phaedrus*, 11, 30–31
Phaedrus, 30–31
*Phenomenology of Spirit*, **117–
18**, 123, 126, 154, 156–57,
173, 197
phenomenology, Hegel's, 102;
    see also *Phenomenology of
Spirit*
phenomenology, Heidegger
    & Husserl, 112
philosopher-kings, 2, 10, 12–
13, 23
philosophers, 2, 3, 4, 5, 7, 10,
12–13, 15, 16, 22–24, 29, 31,
34–35, 39, 40, 70, 72, 97,
124, 126, 152, 155, 157,
161–64, 167, 176, 193; cf.
Wise Man
*Philosophy of Right*, 97, **101–
108**
philosophy, 23, 128, 198;
    academic, 29, 33; French,
131; German, 116; Greek,
14, 26, 31, 34, 157; Italian,
68; moral, 34; natural, 31–
32, 34–35, 39; of history,
11, 68, 118, 125, 165;
Platonic, 16–17, 22, 97;
political, 1, 11, 157;
postmodern, 181; vs.
myth, 25–41; Western, 68,
181; see also dialectic;
individual philosophers
and schools
piercing (body), 139, 172, **178–
80**
Plato, iii, iv, v, **1–24**, **25–41**,
71–72, 83n1, **97–101**, 107,
109, 111–12, 164, 167, 194,
195
play, 124, 192, 193–95; see also
leisure
"Poems on the Lisbon
Disaster," 86
poetic language, 33–34, 41
poetry, 3–4, 11, 33–34, 41, 119
Pol Pot, 116
Polemachus, 97–99
political rule, in Aristotle, **51–
53**, 54
*Politics* (Aristotle), **42–67**
polity, in Aristotle, 49, **51–53**,
61, 64
Polus, 38
Pope, Alexander, 83, 84, 86
Popper, Karl, 58n11
postmodernism, **169–72**, **181–
92**
postmodernists, French, 126,
152, 156
pragmatism, iv, 27–28, 37–38,
40–41
preferences, given, 106, 133,
198–99

*The Present Age*, 137
privacy, 4n1, 47
profane, 194–95
*Profession of Faith of a Savoyard Vicar*, 87, 93
progress, of civilization & culture, 1, 85; of history, 69–70, 118, 147, 165; of technology, 123
property, private, 2, 10, 43, 47
providence, iv, 40, 74, 79–81, **83–96**, 147
prudence, in Aristotle, 45, 54–55
psychagogy, 11–12, 13, 15
*Pulp Fiction*, iii, 169n, 176, 178
purgatory, 36

**Q**
queer theory, 198
Queneau, Raymond, 126, 156, 163

**R**
reason, 12–14, 17–23, 31, 34–35, 41, 45, 63–64, 69, 106, 119, 131, 136–38, 141, 159, 170, 175–76, 185, 195, 199
*Republic*, **1–24**, 38, 40, 47, 67, 83, **97–101**, 195
*Rest on the Flight into Egypt*, 146
*Reveries of a Solitary Walker*, 93
righteousness, 7
Rilke, Rainer Maria (René Karl Wilhelm Johann Josef Maria), 170
risk, 39–41, 179, 200
Rosen, Stanley, 157
Rousseau, Jean-Jacques, iii, iv, 40, 47, **83–96**, 107, 135, 159, 193n
rule of law, in Aristotle, **51–53**
rulership, in Aristotle, 50
Rushton, J. Phillipe, 71

**S**
sacred, 27, 77, 138, 194–95, 197
sadism, 178
Sartre, Jean-Paul, 126, 131
*Satya Yuga*, 76
Schelling, Friedrich Wilhelm Joseph, 116
Schmitt, Carl, 157–58
Second Amendment, 47
Second Coming, Christian or pagan, 142–46
"The Second Coming," (Yeats), **142–46**, 190
Second World War, 127, 152, 154, 155
self-actualization, 41, 47, 74, 82, 90, 95, 158–59
self-consciousness, 20, 31, 133, 173–74, 179–80, 186–90; see also consciousness
self-indulgence, 178, 180, 192
self-knowledge, 32, 34–35, 109, 158–60, 165–66
self-love, 85, 91; see also love
sentiment, sentimentality, 18, 21, 88, 90, 91, 159
Set, 37n3
*Seventh Letter* (Plato), 15
Shakur, Tupac, 4
Simpson, Peter L. Phillips, 42n1
sin, original, 86
slavery, in Aristotle, 43, 63; in Hegel, 105–107, 174, 176–

77, 179–80; in Jünger, 140; in Kojève, 164–66; in Rousseau, 86; in Vico, 80; in warrior aristocracy, 195–98; see also master-slave relationship
Smith, Adam, 18
social contract, theory of, in Rousseau, 85–87; in Vico, 77–78
sociobiology, 70, 73
Socrates, 1, 3, 5–13, 15, 21, 24, 29–32, 34–39, 41, 97, 98–100, 105, 196
Sokolowski, Robert, 112n9
Solon, 58, 64
Solovieff, Vladimir, 126, 153
sophistry & sophists, 5, 31, 39, 44, 62
Sorel, Georges, 75
soul, iv, 7, 12–24, 26, 32, 34–40, 42, 45, 48, 87, 90, 96, 100, 138, 159, 164, 170–71, 173, 177, 179–80, 194–95
Sparta, 45–46, 58, 89
Spengler, Oswald, 75, 80
sphinx, 145–46
spirit (in Hegel), 118, 121
spirit (in Plato), 12–13, 195; see also spiritedness; *thumos*
spiritedness, 12, 14–15, 17–18, 21–22, 53, 143, 164, 195; see also spirit (in Plato); *thumos*
*Spiritus Mundi*, 145; see also World Spirit; cf. God
Spock, 14–15, 19
*Star Trek*, 14–15, 19, 79
*Star Trek: The Next Generation*, 139
Starr, Ken, 8
*The Stranger*, **147–51**
Strauss, Leo, iv, 22–23, 91, 93, 157
subway, New York, 81
Sulla, 29n2
*The Sunday of Life*, 156
Surrealism, French, 156

T
Tarantino, Quentin, 169n, 176, 178
Tartarus, 36
taste, 57, 181–86, 199; in Rousseau, 89–90
tattoos, 139, 172, **178–80**
technology, *techne*, technique, 100n4, 123–24, **137–40**, 141, 176, 193, 198
teleology, 85, 92–93
*Theodicy* (Leibniz), 84
theodicy, **83–96**; see also providence
Theognis, 44
Thrasymachus, 5, 97, 100
*thumos*, 22; see also spirit (in Plato); spiritedness
*Timaeus*, 1n, 22, 25n, 29n2
*timarchy* or *timocracy*, 3, 10, 11
time, 129–31
Tocqueville, Alexis de, 48–49n5
totalization, in dialectic, 98, 101, 107
tradition, 28, 34, 69, 138, 169, 182, 187
Traditionalists, 70–72
*Treta Yuga*, 76
Trevor Lynch's White

*Nationalist Guide to the Movies*, 169n
Tripp, Linda, 8
Truth, Absolute, in Hegel, **122–24**, 128
truth, correspondence theory of, 28, 37; pragmatic model of, 38, 40
Typhon, 31–32
tyranny, 3, 10, 79, 171; in Aristotle, 49, 50, 51, 60–61, 63

**U**
United States, 9, 48–49n5, 66–67

**V**
values, 4n1, 17–22, 106–107, 119, **133–41, 142–46**, 166, 168, 187, 194; see also the Good
vanity, in Rousseau, 87, 92, 96
Vernes, Jacob, 93
Veyne, Paul, 27
vice, 9, 13–14, 43, 44, 52, 54, 56, 59, 62–63, 80
Vico, Giovanni Battista (Giambattista), iii, iv, v, **68–82**, 133, 133–35
virtue, 7, 9, 12, 13–14, 21, 42–48, 51–56, 60–64, 66, 88–90, 96, 166
vitality, 73–74, 82, 119, 133–34, 146, 165–66
Voegelin, Eric, 83n1
Voltaire (François-Marie Arouet), 85–86, 93

**W**
well-being, 43; see also *eudaimonia*; happiness
White Nationalism & nationalists, 181, 191
will to power, 133, 139–41, 171
will, in Hegel, 104–108; free, 12, 85–86, 88–91, 104–108, 144
Wise Man, 128, 162; cf. philosopher
World Bank, 155
World Spirit, 118, 145; see also *Spiritus Mundi*; cf. God
world, human, in Jünger, **139–41**; in Hegel, 119–21; in Rousseau, **84–96**
worldviews, 71, 169–70, 183; in Hegel, 118–25; see also history, in Hegel; end of history

**X**
Xenophon, 6
*The X-Files*, 19

**Y**
Yeats, W. B., iii, **142–46**, 190

**Z**
*Zazie in the Metro* (novel), 156
Žižek, Slavoj, 156–57

# ABOUT THE AUTHOR

Greg Johnson, Ph.D., is Editor-in-Chief of Counter-Currents Publishing Ltd. and Editor of *North American New Right*, its webzine (http://www.counter-currents.com/) and occasional print journal.

He is the author of eleven books, including *Confessions of a Reluctant Hater* (San Francisco: Counter-Currents, 2010; second, expanded ed., 2016); *New Right vs. Old Right* (Counter-Currents, 2013); *Truth, Justice, & a Nice White Country* (Counter-Currents, 2015); *In Defense of Prejudice* (Counter-Currents, 2017); *You Asked for It: Selected Interviews*, vol. 1 (Counter-Currents, 2017); *The White Nationalist Manifesto* (Counter-Currents, 2018); and *Toward a New Nationalism* (Counter-Currents, 2019).

Under the pen name Trevor Lynch, he has published *Trevor Lynch's White Nationalist Guide to the Movies* (Counter-Currents, 2012), *Son of Trevor Lynch's White Nationalist Guide to the Movies* (Counter-Currents, 2015), and *Return of the Son of Trevor Lynch's CENSORED Guide to the Movies* (Counter-Currents, 2019).

He has also edited many books, including *North American New Right*, vol. 1 (Counter-Currents, 2012); *North American New Right*, vol. 2 (Counter-Currents, 2018); *Dark Right: Batman Viewed from the Right* (with Gregory Hood) (Counter-Currents, 2018); and *The Alternative Right* (Counter-Currents, 2018).

His writings have been translated into Czech, Danish, Dutch, Estonian, French, German, Greek, Hungarian, Norwegian, Polish, Portuguese, Russian, Slovak, Spanish, Swedish, and Ukrainian.

www.ingramcontent.com/pod-product-compliance
Lightning Source LLC
Chambersburg PA
CBHW030342131224
18858CB00004B/134